Wharton B Marriott

Testimony of the Catacombs

And of Other Monuments of Christian Art

Wharton B Marriott

Testimony of the Catacombs
And of Other Monuments of Christian Art

ISBN/EAN: 9783337162580

Printed in Europe, USA, Canada, Australia, Japan

Cover: Foto ©ninafisch / pixelio.de

More available books at **www.hansebooks.com**

THE TESTIMONY OF THE CATACOMBS

AND OF OTHER

MONUMENTS OF CHRISTIAN ART,

FROM THE SECOND TO THE EIGHTEENTH CENTURY,

CONCERNING QUESTIONS OF DOCTRINE NOW DISPUTED IN THE CHURCH.

BY THE

REV. WHARTON B. MARRIOTT, B.D. F.S.A.

SOMETIME FELLOW OF EXETER COLLEGE, OXFORD, AND ASSISTANT
MASTER AT ETON ; SELECT PREACHER, ETC.

LONDON:
HATCHARDS, 187 PICCADILLY.
MDCCCLXX.

LONDON:
STRANGEWAYS AND WALDEN, Printers,
Castle St. Leicester Sq.

CONTENTS.

PART I.

MONUMENTS OF CHRISTIAN ART, FROM THE SECOND TO THE EIGHTEENTH CENTURY, ILLUSTRATING THE GRADUAL DE- VELOPMENT OF THE CULTUS OF THE VIRGIN MARY . . Pp. 1–63

PART II.

MONUMENTS OF CHRISTIAN ART HAVING REFERENCE TO THE SUPREMACY CLAIMED FOR THE SEE OF ROME .   65–111

PART III.

THE AUTUN INSCRIPTION, HAVING REFERENCE TO THE SACRA- MENTS OF BAPTISM AND OF HOLY COMMUNION, AND TO THE STATE OF THE FAITHFUL AFTER DEATH .   113–188

APPENDIX   189–223

LIST OF ILLUSTRATIONS.

P. 13. [Woodcut.] Figure of an Orante (male). From the Cemetery of SS. Marcellinus and Petrus. (Aringhi R. S. tom. ii. p. 111.)

P. 14. [Woodcut.] Ornamented Glass, with Male and Female Oranti.

P. 22. [Woodcut.] The Adoration of our Lord by the Magi. From the Cemetery of SS. Marcellinus and Petrus. (Aringhi R. S. t. ii. p. 117.

P. 24. [Woodcut.] The Holy Family. [For another interpretation of the Picture see p. 25.] From the Cemetery of S. Priscilla.

P. 37. The Adoration of the Magi. From a Mosaic in the Church of S. Maria Maggiore at Rome, in its original state, *circ.* 438 A.D. From a Drawing in a Collection formed for Pope Clement XI, hitherto unpublished.

Plate I. The Ascension. From a Syriac MS. of the Gospels written A.D. 586. (See 'Vestiarium Christianum,' p. 238.)

Plate II. The Assumption of the Virgin Mary. From the Church of St. Clement at Rome, *circ.* 850 A.D.

Plate III. The Virgin Mary as Queen of Heaven: Popes Calixtus II. and Anastasius IV. kneeling at her feet. (12th century.)

P. 63. [Woodcut.] The ancient Mosaic of Xystus III. in the Church of S. Maria Maggiore at Rome, as altered in the 18th century to suit modern Roman ideas.

Plate IV. The Diptych of St. Paul. [The more important of the two leaves of this Diptych is more perfectly reproduced, as a photograph, in the frontispiece to 'Vestiarium Christianum.'

LIST OF ILLUSTRATIONS.

The Book of the Gospels in the hands of the Bishop (supposed to be such) is there clearly seen. In the photolithograph of this volume it has been accidentally obscured.]

Plate V. Fresco representing St. Cornelius Papa and St. Cyprian.

Plate VI. The Frescoes of the Triclinium Lateranum.

P. 96. [Woodcut.] St. Peter bestowing the Pallium on Leo III. and the Vexillum of the Empire upon Charlemagne. From the Collection of Pope Clement XI.

Plate VII. The Donation of Constantine, and his (supposed) Baptism by Sylvester, Bishop of Rome.

Plates VII. and VIII. The Coronation of the Emperor Sigismund. The Council of Florence. From the Alti Relievi on the Gates of St. Peter's at Rome, executed by command of Pope Eugenius IV.

Plate IX. The Autun Inscription.

P. 123. [Woodcut.] The Episcopal Ring of St. Arnulph, Bishop of Metz. (6th century.) The basket (containing a fish) there represented closely resembles some still used by labourers in central France.

P. 143. [Woodcut.] Capital of a Column in the Baptistery of the Church of St. Germain des Prés at Paris. The original church dated from the 6th century. The present church, the oldest in Paris, is mainly of the 12th century; but many of the capitals and shafts belonging to the earlier church have been used in the construction.

P. 144. [Woodcut.] The Fish-God. From an ancient Gem.

P. 147. [Woodcut.] Phœnician and Cyzicene Coins, presenting the type from which the Ichthyography of Autun, and of St. Germain des Prés, appears to have been derived.

P. 149. [Woodcut.] Small Figure (11th century) of (? a Priest or Bishop) one holding in his hands a Chalice, on which rests a Fish. Found at Autun.

PART I.

THE

CULTUS OF THE VIRGIN MARY,

Its Rise and Progress:

AS EXHIBITED

IN MONUMENTS OF ART FROM THE SECOND TO THE
EIGHTEENTH CENTURY.

THE
CULTUS OF THE VIRGIN MARY,

&c. &c.

FROM various causes, upon which we need not now dwell, a great impulse has been given of late years to the study of primitive Christian Art. Early monuments are still in existence, many but recently discovered, not a few of them either all but unknown or known only in disguise, which are of the highest importance for their bearing upon disputed questions of doctrine or of discipline. And of all the fields for such research open to the student, none is more rich in hidden treasure than 'Subterranean Rome;' no records of Primitive Christendom more suggestive than the rude frescoes depicted on the walls of the Catacombs, or the simple inscriptions there to be read.

The history of these 'Catacombs,' to use the name* by

---

* This name properly applies only to one particular cemetery beneath the church of St. Sebastian, which from early times was known as 'Ad Catacumbas' (this last probably a barbarous corruption of a Greek word). This particular cemetery was easily accessible, and was still known and visited at a time when all the others had passed into oblivion. Hence it was that, when the older cemeteries were discovered in the sixteenth century, the special designation of that one cemetery became a generic term applied to them all.

which they are popularly known, abounds with an interest all its own, quite apart from any reference to the controverted questions of these our own days; though upon these also, as we have already intimated, their evidence is of the highest value. We speak of their history absolutely; but we should rather say their history as far as at present it admits of being written. For all that as yet has been determined concerning them, is confessedly imperfect. And though there is much that may now be regarded as conclusively established, there is also much that still is, and probably will yet remain, subject for conjecture, rather than for well-grounded and certain conclusion.

The 'Roma Sotterranea,'* edited by Dr. Northcote and Mr. Brownlow, is a compendium of what has been written on the subject by Cavaliere De Rossi of Rome, more particularly of a work, as yet incomplete, the title of which they have preserved in their own volume. No one living is so fitted to be the historian of the Catacombs, as the distinguished Roman antiquary we have just named. But the language (Italian) in which his book is written, and in these days of 'short and cheap' publications, we fear we must add its size and cost, nay, even the exactness of its research and great learning,— all these combine to deter many English readers from making acquaintance with its contents. And this being so, we think that the compilers of the volume before us have done good service, in

---

* Roma Sotterranea; or, Some Account of the Roman Catacombs. Compiled from the works of Commendatore de Rossi, with the consent of the Author. By Rev. J. S. Northcote, D.D., President of St. Mary's College, Oscott, and Rev. W. R. Brownlow, M.A. Longmans, 1867.

laying before the English public a summary of the results of De Rossi's investigations. Their book would have been more valuable if they had adhered more religiously than they have done to his guidance. For in spite of the deep importance to doctrinal questions, now controverted, of the monuments with which De Rossi has to deal, yet has he, as far as we have observed, the rare merit of stating his facts exactly and impartially, precisely as he finds them, and drawing theological conclusions (when he does so at all, which is not often) upon a statement of *all* the facts, not of a few such out of many, and these selected and arranged, so as to suit a predetermined conclusion.

We greatly regret, on many grounds, that we cannot extend the same praise to the compilers of the volume now before us. Had they confined themselves to questions of archæological research, as does, for the most part, the learned writer whose works they have epitomised ; or if, embarking on questions of theology, they had treated of them with the exactness of statement and representation, the fulness of research, the strictness of logical inference, of which his archæological writings at least present an admirable example,—had they made it their one end and aim to present fully and impartially to their readers all the facts, within their knowledge, which were of importance to the questions they discussed,—had this been so, we at least should have welcomed heartily the great addition which they might have made to the limited knowledge, that most of us have, of the true history of the early Roman Church. But, as things are, it is impossible to read through their volume, after studying those of De Rossi, without being reminded again and again of the loss we have sustained, in exchanging the guidance of a genuine Roman archæologist for that of an English (*and* Roman) divine.

In saying this, let us not be misunderstood. The book edited by Dr. Northcote may be regarded as made up of two parts, and presenting two distinct characters. The greater part of the volume is devoted to questions of historical and antiquarian research, concerning the construction of the Catacombs, their relative dates, their pictorial ornamentation, and the like. And in this portion of their work, in which theological questions are only very indirectly and remotely involved, the editors have trodden carefully in De Rossi's steps; and have done their own part, in translation and arrangement, extremely well. And in spite of the defects upon which we are about to dwell, we gladly commend this first part of their book as the best available summary of the facts of chief importance in the history of the Roman Catacombs. It is in the later part of their book, where their subjects are such as to command the interest of a far wider circle of readers, that the present editors have conspicuously failed. How, indeed, being what they are, should they have done otherwise than fail ? For in these later chapters (their Book IV.), they deal with controversial questions, which for many centuries past have been, as they still are, at issue in Christendom. And these are questions upon which (as we shall shortly see) the monuments of primitive Christianity bear a testimony the very reverse of that which a Roman controversialist would desire. And, accordingly, if men enter upon the study of the Catacombs, as these editors seem to have done, with a primary view to find there testimony in behalf of modern Romanism, they set themselves to a task involving one of two alternatives. Either they must shut up their books, and lay aside their pen, as soon as they have attained to anything like an accurate knowledge of their subject; or they must acquire (as indeed they seem to have done) that peculiar faculty, which was pithily described by one of old time. They must combine two seemingly inconsistent powers—that of being blind to what all other men see, and that of seeing what to all but themselves is invisible. They have to deal with facts of Christian antiquity. But a constraining necessity is upon them that those facts shall be *Romanised*. Unconsciously therefore (of *intentional* misrepresentation, it is unnecessary to say, we do not for a moment accuse them), they conceal both from themselves, and from others, all that is out of harmony with Roman prejudices, and they import into what is before them ideas utterly unknown* to the ages with which they have to deal.

One of two alternatives, we said. But we were wrong. For yet a third course is possible, and this was actually followed—to his credit be it said—by another author (Mr. Hemans), whose work† is now before us. We have no personal knowledge of the writer, and we repeat only what we have heard stated as matter of notoriety, when we say, that at one time, like Dr. Northcote, he became a 'convert' (so called) to Romanism. Having done so, he

---

* An amusing instance of this (a matter trifling in itself, but like a floating straw indicative of the set of the stream) will be found at p. 138, where the writer speaks of St. Lucius (Bishop of Rome) as *reigning* at Rome in the year 252 A.D.

† A History of Ancient Christianity and Sacred Art in Italy. By C. J. Hemans. Williams and Norgate, London. 1866.

devoted years of study to the literature and the art monuments of antiquity, particularly of those at Rome itself, with a view to strengthening himself in the new position which he had been led to take up. And he studied with such thoroughness of research (of this his book gives evidence, in spite of many minor defects), and to such unexpected results, that he found himself compelled, by the force of evidence which he could not resist, to recall the verdict which he had already practically pronounced, and to retrace the steps which, when less well informed, he had taken. And this is the more notable, because one cannot read his book without seeing, that all his sentiment, poetical and artistic, is still strongly enlisted on the side of the Roman Church, in many features of her system by which most English Churchmen would be repelled. He condemns upon historical and monumental evidence, but he condemns unwillingly. And the very sympathy he shows for the system which he condemns, proves the more conclusively the strength of the conviction on which his adverse judgment is based.

Returning now to the 'Roma Sotterranea' of Dr. Northcote, it may be well to say, that the more controversial part of the work is that, which will be of the highest interest to our own readers. And, for ourselves, we wish it to be understood, that we intend now to devote our inquiry to such matters only, arising out of our present subject, as have a direct bearing upon questions of Christian doctrine or of discipline. Purely antiquarian subjects may best be discussed from a purely antiquarian point of view. And upon these we shall not now enter. But we shall endeavour to carry with us, in our theological inquiries, that spirit of impartial investigation, that scrupulous exactness of statement and representation, in which antiquaries too often carry the palm over theologians. And while we fully admit, that, in dealing controversially with the facts of antiquity, we approach them with the expectation of finding very different conclusions warranted from those to which Dr. Northcote would lead his readers, we shall in all cases be careful to bring forward full authority for every fact alleged. And so, even if by any we shall be supposed to write as advocates, rather than in a spirit of dispassionate judgment, our readers may at any rate have, between Dr. Northcote and ourselves, the evidence that on both sides is available, and upon that evidence base their own conclusions.

Yet, before embarking upon our own immediate subject, it will be well to give here a brief description of the special sources of testimony to which we are about to appeal, these being of a kind which, up to this time, have attracted far less attention than they deserve.

In the principal cities of Italy, in Southern France, and here and there in parts of Africa and of the East, there have been preserved to our own time monuments of primitive Christian art, which reflect in a most remarkable manner the prevailing tone, and the distinguishing characteristics, of the successive centuries from which they date. The earliest of these (some few of those in the Roman Catacombs) date, in all probability, from a time but little later than that of the Apostles. And, from that time onward, we possess a series of monuments of the most varied kind, frescoes, mosaic pictures, sepulchral inscriptions, sculptured sarcophagi, carvings in ivory, ornamented glass, illuminated books, coins, medals, works in bronze and other metals, which constitute a pictorial history of Western Christendom, from the earliest ages to the close of the fourteenth century.* Specimens of these will be set before our readers, few in number, but sufficient to indicate their importance as bearing upon questions of the greatest interest to all religious men at the present time.

Of the many and varied works of art of which we speak, none are of greater interest to ourselves than the series of monuments, either above ground or below it, which are still to be found at Rome. These are of various kinds. But those with which mainly we are now concerned, are the rude frescoes upon the walls of the Catacombs, and the mosaic pictures, dating from the close of the fourth century onwards, which cover the walls of some of the oldest churches at Rome and Ravenna.

THE CATACOMBS.

And first it may be well to say *what* the Catacombs are, —viz., places of Christian sepulture. That, in very exceptional cases, particular chambers in the Catacombs were either constructed, or adapted, so as to make them available for Divine worship, we have clear evidence. But if we would interpret the earlier pictures of the Catacombs aright, we must constantly bear in mind, what apparently never

---

* From this period onward, Christian art in the West has followed its own rules, instead of being subordinated wholly (as in the East it still is) to the direct reproduction of religious ideas after traditionary forms. Monuments of modern art lose in historical value, as direct expressions of contemporary belief, in proportion to what they have gained in æsthetic beauty.

occurs to Dr. Northcote, that we are contemplating expressions of Christian faith, by primitive believers *committing their loved ones to the grave*, not entering churches or chapels prepared for modern Roman worship, and therefore (*inter alia*) for the worship of the Virgin Mary. Judging from the way in which Dr. Northcote interprets monuments, it is evident that, in his view, the one thing of which the faithful would think in the hour of their bereavement, was *the jurisdiction over other churches implied by the Papal pallium!** Or again, that, in the eyes of believers then, Christ, our Blessed Lord, the *Resurrection* and the *Life*, was of such small esteem, His virgin Mother in such sense all in all, that if she and her Divine Infant appear in the same representation, we may assume that *He* is represented '*simply with a view to showing who she is.*'

The actual construction of the Catacombs (or rather the commencement of their construction) dates, in some cases, from the very earliest period of the Roman Church. One consular date (in an inscription which was removed from its place, and whose locality therefore cannot now be determined) is of the year 72 A.D., the third year of Vespasian. And in the cemetery known generally as that of S. Lucina, there are two inscriptions with consular dates, belonging to

---

* This seems scarcely credible even in a Roman controversialist. But the reader may judge for himself by referring to p. 310. Dr. N. there refers to a representation of the *ascent of Elias to heaven* on a sarcophagus (it may be seen also among the frescoes of the Catacombs, see Aringhi R. S. tom. i. p. 565), a scene in which Christian mourners would see a pledge of the sure and certain hope of that new life, of which their own loved ones were inheritors. His comment is, '*It would certainly have reminded Roman Christians of the pallium, the symbol of jurisdiction worn by the bishops of Rome,*' &c. &c.

the years 107 and 110 A.D. These older cemeteries were enlarged, and new ones were constructed, as time went on. But, with a few exceptions only, the *main construction* of the Catacombs dates from the three first centuries; their partial enlargement, and alterations in detail, extend to a further period of about 500 years (*circa* 850 A.D.), soon after which time they were closed up and forgotten, till the time of their re-discovery in the year 1578.

A separate question altogether, and for our present purpose a more important one, is involved, when we have to assign dates to the various pictures (for the most part very rude, but from their subjects exceedingly interesting) with which the walls, in portions of these cemeteries, are covered. For it is scarcely necessary to say, that, in determining the time when some subterranean chamber was first constructed, it by no means follows that we determine also the date of the pictures, or of the inscriptions, which now may appear upon the walls. This question of date can generally be determined only by internal evidence, leaving room for considerable difference of opinion, within certain limits. But there are some general conclusions upon which all investigators are practically agreed, and these we shall take as our guides in investigating such questions as those now before us.

All are, as far as we know, agreed in saying, that what De Rossi calls the 'Ciclo Biblico,' *i.e.*, the definite series of purely Scriptural subjects represented in many of the Roman Catacombs, belong to an earlier period of Christian art than those of special saints, martyrs, Bishops of Rome, and of other Sees, which are also there to be found. And there are many reasons for thinking, with Signor

De Rossi, that the pictures of this 'Scriptural Cycle' are, with few exceptions, to be referred to a period not later than the third century of our era.

The more special marks, however, whereby relative date may be determined, may best be illustrated by actual examples, such as will shortly come before our readers. Yet we may say, speaking generally, that the latest date to any of the pictures in the Roman Catacombs, is the middle of the ninth century, whereas, in the mosaics and frescoes of churches above ground, we have a series, which commences indeed shortly after the close* of the fourth century, but which, *in the form that they now present*, may belong to any period between the fourth century and the present time. The two series, that of the Catacombs, and that of the churches above ground, mutually illustrate each other; and it is only by such comparison that their true history can be determined, and their great historical importance be appreciated.

With these few data to start with, we will, without further preface, join issue with Dr. Northcote upon one of the three controverted questions for which he invokes the evidence of these early monuments. Those questions are,—the worship due (according to the Roman Church) to the Mother of our Lord; the divinely ordained pre-eminence of the Roman See,† as being the See of St. Peter; and the doctrine of the Sacraments,‡ particularly that of the 'Mass.' One of these questions, the first, will more than suffice for our present consideration. We may

---

* Exception is to be made, probably, for some few remains dating from the time of Constantine.

† See Part II. of this volume. ‡ See Part III. ibid.

possibly deal with other questions at some future opportunity.

Writers who had preceded Dr. Northcote in speaking of the doctrinal evidence of the Catacombs, had noted the marked contrast between primitive and modern Rome, in all that relates to the blessed Mother of our Lord. One of these writers, after personal examination of the Catacombs (such of them as are now shown), stated, that he 'had only seen a single certain specimen of a painting of the blessed Virgin in all the Catacombs, that this was of a comparatively late date, and that it was idle to attach much importance to so singular an exception.' Upon this Dr. Northcote says, in effect, that the writer in question evidently knows nothing about the matter, as such paintings are '*very numerous.*' And, in justification of his remark, he refers to two facts. He speaks first of the frequent occurrence of 'Oranti,' figures standing with outstretched hands, in what was of old *the ordinary attitude of prayer.* Among these he says, is a figure of a woman, which is frequently* found as a companion to the Good Shepherd, and which 'a multitude of

---

* '*A figure of a woman*' (the Virgin Mary, according to Dr. Northcote) '*frequently found as a companion to the Good Shepherd.*' As a comment upon these words, we append the following analysis of twenty examples (*all* that are figured by Aringhus) in the Catacombs, in which the 'Good Shepherd' is so represented as *in any sense* to be described as accompanied by an Orante.

In five of these instances, this figure of the Shepherd occupies the centre of the decorated roof of a sepulchral chamber, and there are *four figures* of Oranti in the surrounding compartments. In two out of these five examples, half of the Oranti *are men*, and the others women.

In yet five more cases, there are *two* Oranti, one on each side of Our Lord (as the Good Shepherd). And in these five, either both are women or one of them a man, the other a

considerations' leads him to believe was 'intended for our blessed Lady, or else for the Church, the Bride of Christ, whose life upon earth is a life of prayer, even as His holy Mother is similarly employed in Heaven.' Of the two interpretations, he rather inclines to the first. His reasons for doing so he gives at some length. We need not examine them in detail, the simple facts being these :—
These figures, of which examples are here given, are of frequent occurrence, as Dr. Northcote states, and represents sometimes men, sometimes and more commonly women, *in an attitude of prayer.** Not unfrequently these ' Oranti' are found (dressed as men, as women, or as children, as the case may be)  upon the actual *loculus*, the stone that encloses the grave. Is a Caianus,† or a Respectus,‡ taken to his rest in early boyhood?—a youthful 'Orante' is seen upon his tomb, a bird§ beside him, and on the other side, yet another bird,

---

woman (in one case evidently man and wife, see Aringhi R. S. tom. ii. p. 209).

In yet nine instances more, the figure of the Good Shepherd is seen, where *in some part or other of the same chamber* occurs an Orante, perhaps as one out of many figures on a ceiling, or in part of the same Arcosolium. [In one at least of these (*ibid.* ii. p. 257) the Orante is *a man.*] And in *one only example* do we find *one* female Orante side by side with a figure of the Good Shepherd, such as will answer to Dr. Northcote's description. As to this exceptional instance, which is *certainly* not a figure of the Virgin Mary, see below, p. 17.

* There was a special reason for *this* attitude of prayer, rather than that of kneeling, should be represented in a place of sepulture, viz. that this 'standing' to pray was specially connected with the thought of Resurrection. — Justin, ' Resp. ad Orth.' c. 6.

† Aringhi R. S. tom. i. p. 606.

‡ Ibid. tom. ii. p. 259.

§ Typical, probably, of the soul of the departed. The *two* birds are on the tomb of Caianus.

bearing *an olive branch*, pledge of peace and of new life to one escaped from the troubled waves of the world. Or does

Ornamented Glass* with Male and Female Oranti.

a wife, bereft of her husband, now 'in peace,' commemorate†
her tender love for her own ' Leo,' and his approved worth?

---

* For fuller particulars see description in my 'Vestiarium Christianum,' p. 247.

† 'Leoni dulcissimo marito cojux Urso se biba (i.e. *viva*) benemerenti in pace.' (Aringhi R. S. tom. ii. p. 135.) For other examples of *male* Oranti, see tom. ii. pp. 63, 105 (four men, two of them named, see Marriott's 'Vest. Christ.' Pl. vi.), pp. 109, 183, 257. And for the woodcut above, see 'Vest. Christ.' p. lxxxiv. and p. 247.

—once more a male Orante is figured upon his tomb. Is it again a Fautina,* a Decia,† or a Marcella,‡ who is commemorated?—the veil upon the head of the Orante on each tomb would mark clearly, even if the inscription were wanting, that it is wife, or mother, or daughter, whose memory is here fondly cherished. In a multitude of other instances, where sepulchral chambers (*cubicula*), or portions of them, have been set apart for special use, one or more Oranti, male or female, or both together, form part of the decoration of the chamber. With these facts before them, few reasonable persons, I suppose, would come to any other conclusion than that to which Bosio, Aringhus, and others, constantly give expression, viz., that these Oranti serve to commemorate the faithful departed.

This interpretation, however, finds no favour with Dr. Northcote. He speaks of it as a supposition which '*some have entertained*,'—one that '*possibly may be sometimes correct*.' But 'in the majority of instances,' he 'feels certain that it is inadmissible.' He is apparently not aware that there are such things as *male* Oranti (he never, as far as we have observed, alludes to their existence). And accordingly, his only doubt is, whether these figures are intended 'for our blessed Lady, or else for the Church, the Bride of Christ.'

We ourselves, after a careful examination, can find but one Orante, properly so called, in all the Catacombs, which can, with any probability, be interpreted as referring to the Virgin Mary. But while we state this without any hesitation as our own opinion, we will add, that for any controversial

---

* Aringhi tom. ii. p. 262.   † Ibid. p. 262.   ‡ Ibid. p. 258.

results dependent on the question, there is no reason whatever that we should wish to impugn the very different opinion of Dr. Northcote. The very contrary. A figure of the Virgin Mary, *undistinguished by any conventional attributes from other women*, herself standing in the attitude of prayer*—let this be contrasted with the same subject as we shall see it represented six centuries later—the Virgin Mother then crowned as a queen, seated upon a heavenly throne, which she shares with our blessed Lord, or uplifted by Seraphim and Cherubim, as the Queen of Heaven, and *herself the object of man's worship*; this it is precisely (as we shall shortly see) which constitutes the difference between Christian art (and Christian belief) in the first five centuries, and Roman Mariolatry in the ninth, in the twelfth, or the eighteenth century.

We purposely confine ourselves as far as possible, in the present paper, to matters strictly pertinent to the special subject now under consideration. We, therefore, do not now enter at greater length upon the subject of these Oranti. But in connexion with this question, we have to point out, by a remarkable instance, how very slight a change, by even

---

* Such a representation does occur in several examples of the Vetri Antichi, or ornamented glasses figured by Garrucci ('Vetri Ornati,' &c. Pl. ix. 6, 7, 10, 11), and after him by Northcote, R. S. Pl. xviii. These glasses, with few exceptions, belong to a period of very degraded art. Those now in question we should assign to the fifth century. Roman antiquaries generally speak of them as of the fourth century at latest; but, as far as we can ascertain, they have very little reason to show for their opinion. But there are very strong reasons (of a technical kind, in reference to the use of the nimbus) for assigning many of them to the fifth, if not to the sixth, century. [Dr. Littledale, however, assures us that the art of making these glasses *was lost* at the end of the fourth century. How he knows that we are not informed.]

a slight omission, will entirely alter the character of a monument; and how entirely writers, such as Dr. Northcote, may (though quite unintentionally) mislead their readers, when they deal with archæological evidence, but do so at second hand, without competent archæological knowledge of their own.

Our readers will have observed, that in the words already quoted (above, p. 12) from Dr. Northcote, he lays stress upon the fact, that an Orante *is frequently found as a companion to the Good Shepherd;* and he adds an expression of his strong belief, founded on a 'multitude of reasons,' that this is intended for the blessed Mother of our Lord. If our readers will turn to his Plate viii., reproduced, as he states it is, from Bosio, they will find what is *apparently* the strongest confirmation of the statement that he had made. They will see an Orante represented side by side with our Lord (symbolised as the Good Shepherd), and forming with Him one composition, in which the juxta-position of the two figures was evidently designed. The picture, *as given*, is just what Dr. Northcote could most wish to prove his point. We ourselves came upon it accidentally, just after a careful examination of all the pictures in the Catacombs, as given by Bosio and Aringhus. Almost the last sentence that we had written, in summing up the results of the investigation, was this: 'In one only example do we find a single figure of a female so placed side by side with the "Good Shepherd," as to form with Him what was evidently intended to be a studied and significant juxta-position, and to make up, between the two, a complete picture. *And in this one exceptional instance, the Orante is clearly marked out as a Christian martyr by the "attribute" of an instrument of*

C

torture, a scourge loaded with lead or iron,* *which is painted on a large scale beside her.*' Our astonishment may be imagined, when, on turning to Dr. Northcote's Plates, the moment after writing this, we found this very fresco referred to (in the catalogue) as the *Virgin Mary* and the Good Shepherd; and *the one feature which was specially characteristic of it, serving at once to determine its meaning, had been removed from the picture, and not the slightest reference made anywhere to its existence.* Had this remarkable feature in the picture been preserved, any skilled antiquary would at once have seen, that the picture could not possibly be intended for the Virgin Mary. And even ordinary observers could scarce have failed to feel, as it were by intuition, that Dr. Northcote's interpretation could hardly be the true one. But in Dr. Northcote's work the picture appears catalogued as 'The Good Shepherd and the blessed Virgin,' and a reference is made to Bosio, p. 387. We ourselves felt pretty certain, on seeing this reference, that Bosio would not bear out this description. We turned to his pages, and found exactly what we had anticipated. 'Una Donna orante,' says that writer, 'a woman in the act of prayer,' without one word as to any even possible reference to the Virgin Mary.

What do our readers suppose to be the explanation of this extraordinary misrepresentation? It is one, we are glad to be able to say it, which explains entirely how Dr. Northcote came to be himself deceived as to the real facts of the case, while the Roman artist employed (pro-

---

* 'Flagellum quoddam ad corpus excruciandum,' is the description of Aringhus.

bably not an archæologist at all) was, of course, equally
guiltless of any intentional misrepresentation. The answer
may best be given in Dr. Northcote's own[*] words : ' It is
no news to those who received our prospectus, inviting
them to subscribe to the work before publication, but it is a
fact which was unaccountably omitted in our Preface to the
volume itself when published, and therefore is new to your
Reviewer, that all the twenty Plates, as well as the Map,
were prepared for us by De Rossi himself, executed under
his own eye at the Cromolitografia Pontificia in Rome, and
the impressions sent to us from that city exactly as they
now are. . . . . Eighteen of the drawings for these Plates
were taken from the originals. For Plates VIII. and XI.,
he had an order from us to provide a specimen of Noah
in his Ark ; the Three Children in the Fiery Furnace ;
the Raising of Lazarus ; and an *Orante*. [I have the correspondence before me as I write.] When sending me the
proofs of the impressions, he apologised for the different
and inferior style of these ; but said he did not understand
us to want any *special* instances of these subjects, and
therefore he had not hesitated to spare himself trouble by
taking them from books instead of going to the Catacombs

---

[*] In a letter to the Editor of the 'Christian Observer' (No. 384, Dec. 1869, p. 942). I take this opportunity of renewing the expression of my regret, that in the first edition of this paper (which was a review of Dr. Northcote's book) I spoke in language of strong condemnation in reference to the misrepresentation here pointed out, which I should not have used had I been aware of the facts subsequently stated by Dr. Northcote. I should perhaps add, what I learn from the same letter, that Dr. Northcote did not himself draw up the Catalogue of Plates in which this fresco is described as 'The Good Shepherd and *the Blessed Virgin*.'

for them; and he wrote on the back of the proofs the references to Bosio which we printed. I neither looked into Bosio myself, nor was at all aware, until I read the article in the "Christian Observer," that the necessity of getting into the same Plate a representation of Noah and his Ark as well as an *Orante*, had caused De Rossi's artist to omit a single line of the drawing which he copied.'

We dwell upon this point the rather, because it will suggest a very important lesson for those who are obliged to take their knowledge of antiquity for the most part at second-hand, on the authority, it may be, of controversialists engaged in maintaining a particular thesis. The ' scourge ' at the side of this picture is what context is in a quotation from an ancient author. This context, so to call it, is omitted, first, by the copyist in ignorance of its importance, and then left unnoticed by Dr. Northcote, who knows nothing of its existence. And, accordingly, he publishes the picture in question, in perfect good faith, but *in a shape which entirely misrepresents its true meaning*. This is precisely what may be seen illustrated in almost every page of much of the controversial Divinity that is put forth now, and, for that matter, in the controversial Divinity of every age, as far as we have observed. Sentences, or half-sentences, as the case may be, can be quoted with the greatest ease from Fathers in East and West, from Inscriptions and the like, to prove conclusions the most diametrically contradictory the one of the other, when they are adopted (as controversial writers constantly do adopt them) at second-hand, and without stating, probably without knowing, the context in which they occur. The omission of a concluding clause, the slight colouring of a difficult expres-

sion, which is given with unconscious bias in the course
of translation from ancient into modern languages, the
slight variations of expression introduced by late (and often
ignorant) copyists, and the various readings of MSS.
thence resulting, the introduction, into the text of an
ancient author, of marginal annotations, expressive of the
changed ideas which had possession of later students—
these, or any one of these (to say nothing now of intentional omissions, or conscious falsifications), are often quite
sufficient to make an ancient author, *as quoted*, appear to
affirm the very contrary of what, on fuller examination of
the original (where the true texts can be determined), we
shall find that he actually does say. We shall have to
notice many examples of this in the present treatise. Flagrant examples of such carelessness (we use too light a
term) abound in the 'Catenæ of Patristic Testimonies,'
and of the earlier English Divines, which have been
produced of late years among ourselves in reference to the
controverted questions of the day.

We are glad to return to the point from which we have
digressed, and to resume our investigation of the subject
upon which we are engaged. Quitting the discussion of these
Oranti, Dr. Northcote proceeds to say, that whatever may
be thought of the cogency of his arguments on this first
head, 'the question of Our Lady's position in the most
ancient field of Christian art by no means depends upon
them. If these paintings do not represent her, *yet she
certainly appears in more than a score of other scenes, where
her identity cannot be questioned.*' We are sorry to find
ourselves continually finding fault, but again we are obliged
to say, that Dr. Northcote evidently forgets the right

meaning of words. This imposing phrase of '*more than a score of other scenes*,' means only that the purely Scriptural subject of the adoration of our blessed Lord by the Magi is represented more than twenty times (as he states shortly afterwards) in various parts of the Catacombs. One scene it is, and not twenty, though that one again and again represented with slight variations of treatment. One[*] of them may be seen below.

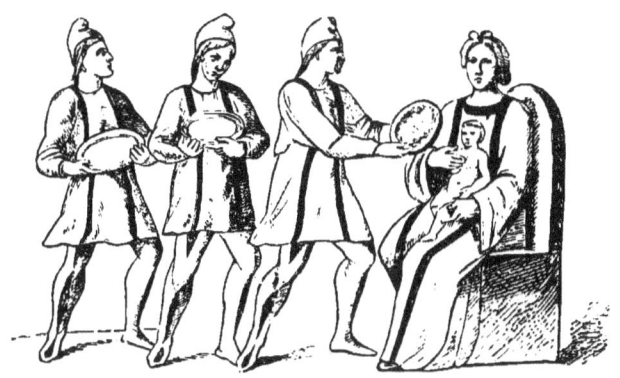

And what is the scene thus repeatedly dwelt on by the Church of Rome as once she was? Is it one, which, like those shortly to be set before our readers, exhibits the mother of our Lord as herself an object of worship to the faithful? The very contrary. Among the various Scriptural subjects on which these early Christians loved to dwell, this of the adoration of the Magi was prominent, as an emphatic testimony to the Divinity of our blessed Lord,

---

[*] From the Cemetery of SS. Marcellinus and Petrus. Aringhi t. ii. p. 117.

and as the earnest of the coming in of the Gentiles into the one fold of Christ. In this picture they were reminded * how these Magi, the first-fruits of the Gentile Church, when they saw the young child and His mother, *fell down and worshipped Him*. A later monument will show us what Roman art taught in the twelfth century. Our readers will there see two Popes, who, like those Magi of old, are represented as in the presence of that young Child and His Mother, and they, as will be seen, fall down and worship *her*.

Such are the facts in regard of the '*more than a score of scenes*' referred to by Dr. Northcote. But, besides this one scene thus marvellously multiplied by our author, there are really two or three other 'scenes,' represented in the Catacombs, in which the blessed Virgin is depicted.

---

* We do not say this without direct evidence of what really was the feeling of early Christendom in this matter. Our readers may refer to any or all of the following passages, and they will see (what but for Dr. Northcote's mode of arguing might well be deemed scarcely to need proof) that the teachers of early days dwelt with one voice upon this subject of the adoration of the Magi, as a proof of the *Divinity of our Lord*, without any the slightest reference to any worship or adoration due to the blessed Virgin herself. See Justin Martyr, Dial. cum Tryph. Migne, P. C. C. tom. vi. p. 654, *al.* 174; St. Irenæi contr. Hær. lib. iii. c. ii.; St. Jerome in Esaiam, lib. vii. c. xix.; St. Ambrose in Evang. Luc. lib. ii.; St. Augustine (his Epiphany Sermons, *passim*). We need not refer to writers in the West, extending beyond the fourth century, such as Leo the Great, Petrus Chrysologus, and Fulgentius, though they too all hold similar language. Among Eastern writers, it is sufficient to name Clement Alex. (Pæd. ii. 8); Origen (lib. i. c. Celsum, p. 46); Chrysostom in his Homilies on St. Matthew (Migne, vol. i. p. 609 *sqq.*), and St. Basil the Great, Homil. in Sanctam Christi Generationem, pp. 600, 601, ed. Bened. vol. ii. [This Homily, however, is probably not St. Basil's, though of early date.]

In one of these* (not described by Dr. Northcote) is probably represented the Annuntiation, in which the angel Gabriel (a human figure, without wings or other attributes, such as were assigned at a later period to the angels,) is seen standing before a seated female figure, and, with extended hand, addressing her. Perhaps the oldest of all these representations, however (De Rossi believes it to be almost of the Apostolic age), is that which is represented below. The natural, and, as we incline to believe, the

true, interpretation of this picture, recognises in it the Holy Family, Joseph on the left hand (spectator's left), the Holy Child, and His Mother; while the Star that is seen above

---

* In the Cemetery of S. Priscilla. The interpretation above given is that commonly received by antiquaries, and is probably, though not with absolute certainty, the true one. See Bottari, Sculture e Pitture sagre, etc. Tav. clxxvi.

(to which Joseph, if such he be, is pointing) serves to determine the general subject of the picture beyond all possibility of mistake. Roman Catholic writers, however (for reasons on which we need not here dwell), generally modify this explanation in one particular. De Rossi suggests that the figure, of which we now speak, may be the impersonation of one of the Prophets of the old Covenant (probably of Isaiah), pointing onward to the Star of Bethlehem, and the Virgin Mother with her Holy Child, as the great subject of prophetic witness. ['The spirit of prophecy is the testimony of Jesus.'] For ourselves, we see no necessity for this explanation. But if any prefer it to the other and simpler interpretation, we are in no way concerned, for any controversial reasons, to quarrel with his judgment. Here, however, as in other cases, Dr. Northcote contrives to put himself in the wrong, simply because he is bent upon improving the occasion for his own special purposes. He calls special attention to the fact that the Blessed Virgin *does not enter here into the composition of an historical or allegorical scene as a secondary personage, but herself supplies the motive, so to speak, of the whole painting.* This criticism will probably appear to our readers to be true in a certain sense, at any rate intelligible, when they view the picture as given by Dr. Northcote, or as it is here sketched in our own woodcut. One who only knew the picture from such representations, might naturally imagine it to be complete in itself; a picture, probably, of considerable size, and occupying the most conspicuous place upon the wall of some sepulchral chamber in the Catacombs. But in all these expectations he would be wholly mistaken. These figures, in their original position, form a very small portion of a piece of decorative work, which, with the single exception of this group, might have been found in the tomb of the Nasos, or any other purely Pagan building. [The figure of the Good Shepherd there traced was classical before it became Christian.] But the criticism in question will be very differently judged by one who views the picture with its actual surroundings, as it is given * by De Rossi. For the three figures which, as here given, at once arrest attention, as might a large picture of the same subject by Raphael, in any modern collection, are, in the original, obscurely placed, so as not even to face the spectator; as we look at them, their position is *horizontal*, not perpendicular. And these circumstances, combined with that of the small scale on which they are drawn, give them the appearance of forming a subordinate part of a merely ornamental design; and that to such a degree, that none but an accurate observer would be likely to notice their real character. And these particulars, to one who has studied the subject with any accuracy, will constitute a strong argument for the extreme antiquity of the work in question. For it is notable, that in the *very earliest* period of Christian art in the Catacombs, there is little or nothing that has an *exclusively* Christian character; but the older pagan forms of decoration are adhered to, sometimes, as the subjects indicate, by way of decoration, and nothing more; while in other cases, as in figures of a Shepherd, or of Orpheus charming

---

* 'Imagines Selectæ Deiparæ Virginis,' Pl. iv. (in which the *context* is given), compared with Pl. i. [Mr. J. H. Parker, a careful observer, and experienced antiquary, assigns this picture to the year 523 A.D.]

wild beasts by the sweet tones of his lyre, a symbolical reference was conveyed.

Let the reader turn from this criticism of Dr. Northcote's to the actual drawings, as they are reproduced, with the greatest care, by De Rossi,[*] and he will see for himself by what *tours de force* of imagination modern Romanism is discovered, by such as are determined to find it, among the records of primitive antiquity.

To sum up briefly this portion of our subject, the facts, as even Dr. Northcote himself would have to admit, are these. In those earliest decorations of the Catacombs, which De Rossi and other Roman Antiquaries believe (and probably with good reason) to be before the age of Constantine, representations of the Virgin Mary *occur only in such connexion as is directly suggested by Holy Scripture.* One picture there is of the Holy Family at Bethlehem (that already represented); one (probably) of the Annuntiation; and there are upwards of twenty (we here follow De Rossi) of the Adoration of the holy Child by the Magi, in all of which, of course, the blessed Mother of our Lord is one of the persons represented. If, in deference to Dr. Northcote's opinion, or upon any other grounds, any should be inclined to think that some of the Oranti figures may have reference to her, even then the statement that follows will be in no way invalidated. With that statement we sum up our investigation of the subject as regards the Christian art of the first three centuries. In no one picture of those which even Dr. Northcote himself could claim as antecedent in date to the age of Constan-

---

[*] See note in preceding page.

tine, is there anything which would appear strange or out of place, on doctrinal grounds, in an illustrated Bible, put forth, let us say, for the use of English Sunday Schools by the Society for Promoting Christian Knowledge. And this being so, our readers may judge what amount of evidence, in favour of modern 'Marianism,' is to be obtained from the witness of really primitive Christendom at Rome.

Fourth Century.

One picture there is in the Catacombs, not yet described, which may perhaps be as early as the fourth century. We ourselves believe that it should be assigned rather to the fifth century than the fourth. But as we wish to meet upon common ground of fact, as far as may be, those from whom we differ in our conclusions from those facts, we will assume that it belongs to the century immediately succeeding the three already examined.

The picture of which we speak,* is a fresco in the Cemetery of St. Agnes on the Via Nomentana. It is a picture of the Virgin Mary and Holy Child; the picture here, for the first time, being in the character of a *portrait* of the two, as distinct from the suggestion of a historical (and Scriptural) subject. In point of style, it departs widely from the older type, and is of Byzantine character, probably painted (as most of the later work at Rome was) by a Byzantine artist. Neither the Holy Child, nor the Virgin, have the nimbus; the latter is in the attitude of prayer (like that of the Oranti

---

* De Rossi, 'Imagines Selectæ, etc.' Tab. vi. Northcote, p. 257. Students of antiquity should further observe the surroundings of the picture as shown by Bosio, p. 451; Aringhi t. ii. p. 209.

already described). A growing taste for costly ornament is indicated in the addition (here first seen) of a necklace of jewels about the neck of the Virgin. On either side is the sacred monogram, which spoke to early Christians at once of Christ, and of Christ crucified.

Here again, though there is great degradation, in point of taste, in the figure of the Virgin Mary as compared with that seen in the Holy Family at Bethlehem above figured (p. 24), yet there is nothing to which, on doctrinal grounds, any English Churchmen need for a moment object.

What do our readers suppose to be Dr. Northcote's comment upon this fresco? It is scarcely credible that a man of real piety, as we doubt not he is (though of superstitious piety), should bring himself so to write. He says, seriously, that the Divine Infant '*is placed in front of his virgin mother simply to show who she is.*' And he evidently thinks that there is a strong argument in proof of Mary worship in the fourth century, in the fact to which he calls special attention, viz., that 'The Christian monogram on either side *is turned towards her.*'* What a picture is here of the kind of comment which passes current for conclusive argument, when men go to antiquity with their heads full of modern Romanism, and come away again, bringing back precisely what they had taken with them!

For ourselves, we need not dwell further upon this picture, though it is one of considerable interest as bearing upon the history of art at Rome. In respect of our own theological inquiry, we have only to note, that in this picture

---

* As the Holy Child is standing before the Virgin Mary, the monogram could not well be otherwise placed than it is. Being 'turned towards' our Lord, it is also turned towards the Virgin.

(whatever be its real date) we pass, from the representation of Scriptural *history*, to the representation of Scriptural *personages* as such. This transition is one which is not without significance as bearing upon the gradual development of Image-worship in the Church. But in itself, this picture, like those earlier frescoes already considered, presents nothing that on doctrinal grounds can be objected to. Far from this being the case, if we place ourselves in the same position as those earlier Christians, all unwitting as they must have been of the ages of gross ignorance and superstition which were approaching, we can enter into and share the feeling of devotion, and of true Christian faith, with which they, in committing their departed ones to the grave, would find their one comfort in the thought, recalled to them by pictures such as these, of the unfailing love, and ever present power, of Him who was born of Mary. It was the truth of the Incarnation which they embodied in their pictures of the Virgin mother and her holy Child. 'Christ crucified,' they recalled, even in the emblematic letters inscribed beside Him; Christ the Good Physician, of body and of soul, in their oft-repeated pictures of the healing of the sick, or the giving sight to the blind; Christ the Bread from Heaven, in the miracle of the loaves; Christ the Prince of Life, in the raising of Lazarus from the grave; Christ the Star risen out of Jacob, and the Desire of all nations, in the star-led Magi, laying their offering at His feet in Bethlehem; Christ, above all, under that form which to Christian hearts is the tenderest and most loving embodiment of their Lord, the Good Shepherd, bearing back upon His shoulders the lamb, that, but for Him, had been lost.

We pass now from these memorials of primitive faith in

the Catacombs to a new series of monuments, and of far other character, in the Churches above ground, from the fifth century of our era to the present time.

Character of the Later Monuments.

We have been occupied hitherto with monuments the date of which can only be approximately determined, but of which (with the exception, perhaps, of the last described) there are the strongest reasons for believing that they are, at any rate, antecedent[*] to the year 400 A.D. We proceed now to consider some later works, the date of which can be determined much more exactly. And as introductory to this part of our subject, we will quote a very significant sentence from Dr. Northcote himself. Speaking of the difference between the earlier and the later representations of 'St. Joseph,' he states that the later artists (from the fifth century[†] onwards) probably followed

---

[*] In saying this, we state what is our own belief upon a disputed question; and we do so the more readily, because it places us in accord, as to questions of fact, with those Roman controversialists whose deductions from those facts we impugn. We are glad to be able thus far to meet them on common ground. But some antiquaries, of considerable repute, attribute to the fourth and fifth centuries frescoes which De Rossi (followed by Dr. Northcote) considers to be of the second and third.

[†] 'From the fifth century onwards.' We know of no works of art in the West, embodying unmistakably these Apocryphal legends, which can with any probability be assigned to a date earlier than 500 A.D. The earliest example known is the Diptych of Milan, figured and fully described in Bugati, 'Memorie di S. Celso Martire,' App. Tav. i. ii. There is little doubt that this dates from the sixth century. The Annuntiation is there represented just as it is described in the Apocryphal Gospel of St. James (Fabricii Codex Apocr. Nov. Test. tom. i. p. 91). Another early example (probably

legends concerning him *which occur in the Apocryphal Gospels*, especially that which bears the name of St. James the Less, and those on the birth of Mary and infancy of our Saviour. 'These legends had been quoted by St. Epiphanius, St. Gregory Nazianzen, and other writers of the fourth century; and allusions to them, or even whole scenes taken from them, occur in the artistic monuments of the fifth and succeeding centuries. *Before this time Christian artists seem strictly to have been kept within the limits of the Canonical* Books of holy Scripture.* Afterwards it was probably considered that there was no longer any danger to the integrity of the faith, and greater license was given both to poets and artists.' Thus far Dr. Northcote. Whether this assumed consideration of probabilities was verified in the course of time, our readers will shortly be able to judge.

With this much of preface, we may now proceed. We are now to emerge from the Catacombs, and leave unnoticed those later † pictures, there existing, whose date can only be approximately determined,‡ and we proceed

---

not earlier than the sixth century) is to be seen in the Church of S. Giovannino at S. Maximin in Provence. The Virgin Mary is there described as Menester (Minister) Ecclesiæ Hierusalem.

* 'Canonical' from the Roman point of view, Dr. Northcote, of course, means. He is speaking of Canonical Scriptures of the *New* Testament, to the exclusion of the Apocryphal Gospels, and such-like books, which found circulation in the West during the fifth century, and were formally condemned by Gelasius, Bishop of Rome, A.D. 495.

† 'Later pictures.' See particularly Aringhi R. S. t. ii. p. 354-5 (very interesting on archæological grounds, but of no doctrinal importance), and the latest of the pictures figured by De Rossi in his 'Imagines Selectæ Deiparæ Virginis.'

‡ Together with these we pass over also the 'Vetri antichi,' the ornamented glasses found here and

to speak of some other monuments, whose date admits of being closely fixed. The objects, of which we now speak, are the mosaic decorations of churches at Rome and Ravenna, the frescoes on the long-buried walls below the Church of St. Clement at Rome, and one or two others that are less well known.

Of these monuments there are some few, which date from the early part of the fifth century. And these mosaics, executed, as we know them to have been, under the immediate superintendence of the highest ecclesiastical authorities, in Rome or Ravenna, as the case might be, are, from that circumstance, of especial value as indications of received doctrine. The simple records of family affection, which abound in the Catacombs, picture to us, in their few touching words of love, and faith, and hope, how in very truth, to the humblest Christian, death had been robbed of its sting; how the grave had become the gate of peaceful * rest; and death, as men deem death, only a blessed sleep † to them that rest in the Lord. But the elaborate mosaics with which, from the close of the fourth century onwards, so many churches, both of East and West,

---

there in the Catacombs. Of their date we have already said a few words. A full treatment of the subject would require a treatise in itself. But when all were said that could be, on either side, the main argument of our present paper would be in no way dependent on, or affected by, the conclusion reached.

* 'In peace,' 'received into peace,' 'committed to the ground in peace,' 'lieth in peace,' 'rests in peace,'— these are recurrent forms in the inscriptions of the Catacombs. And here and there, but much less commonly, are such expressions as ' In pace requiescat.' (Aringhi R. S. tom. ii. p. 140.)

† The day of death is often '*dormitio*,' 'a falling to sleep.' The same word is often used of the place of burial.

were decorated, though they lack this personal interest, have a value all their own, as being deliberate expressions of theological belief. They are little less than embodied Creeds, reflecting from century to century the prevailing tone of opinion on the part of those of highest authority in the Church. Bearing this in mind, we may proceed now to consider what are the facts presented to us, on examination of the series of monuments of the fifth and later centuries, which immediately succeed, in historical order, those earlier frescoes, of the 'Biblical Cycle,' in the Catacombs.

Mosaics at Rome and Ravenna from 400 A.D. *to* 600 A.D.

The character of the elaborate mosaics which date from this period is well described by Seroux d'Agincourt in his 'Histoire de l'Art par ses Monuments.' [In this case, as in other citations from modern authors, we purposely quote from Roman Catholic writers, as being free from any suspicion of 'Protestant prejudice' in what they write.] Describing[*] some of the more important mosaics dating from the fifth century, he writes as follows :—' In the mosaics before us, what most deserves praise is the earnestness with which the Christians of that age sought to make art subservient to the greater honour of God. . . . . All the pomp of a heavenly triumph is displayed in the composition of a mosaic in the Church of St. Paul "extra muros." It adorns that portion of the interior which was known to Christians as the "Triumphal Arch." This was situated, in this instance, as in most of the Basilicas and

---

[*] Peinture, Décadence, tom. ii.p. 30. For fuller details, and ancient authorities, see Ciampini V. M. t. i. p. 199.

more important churches, above the principal altar, and formed a majestic termination to the great nave, and was immediately followed by the Arch of the Tribune.* These two arches, enriched on both sides, both the one and the other, with mosaics, were generally full in view of the faithful as they entered. The Saviour appeared on the Triumphal Arch of this Church in all His glory, seated upon His throne, and receiving the homage and adoration of the inhabitants of heaven. *Solio medius consedit avito.* It was after such a manner that emperors of Rome, after victories won, found the representation of them reproduced on the triumphal arches erected in their honour by the gratitude of their people.'

We would ask our readers to bear these particulars in mind, while noticing the list that follows. It comprises all the mosaics of importance to our present subject, dating from the years 400 to 600 A.D., in the collections of Ciampinus and Seroux D'Agincourt, and in another, consisting of original drawings (once the property of a Pope), to which we have access.

The earliest in point of date are the original † mosaics in the Church of St. Maria Major, dating from the year 433 A.D., or shortly after. Those of which we now speak are on the upper walls of what we should call the chancel

---

* By the Arch of the Tribune is meant the apse-like termination of the Roman Basilicas, at what would correspond to the 'East end' of one of our own churches. Accordingly, this arch, and the 'Triumphal Arch' above described, are what would at once meet the eye of worshippers on entering the church, as D'Agincourt observes.

† They are now intermixed with many, of much later date, in other parts of the church.

36   THE CULTUS OF THE VIRGIN MARY.

arch, the 'Arcus Triumphalis' just described. We find here a series of Scriptural subjects * bearing upon the truth of the Incarnation and of the Divine nature of our Lord, which culminate (over the centre of the arch) in a symbolical designation of our Lord, as the Lamb, derived from Revelation, cap. iv., v. There is here no suggestion whatever of the Virgin Mary being an object of adoration, still less of her sharing the heavenly throne of Christ. Not only so, but, in the picture of the Adoration of the Magi, what may be called the *natural* arrangement of the picture is sacrificed, for the sake of more clearly expressing divine truth. The Holy Child, with angels in attendance on Him, is seated *alone* upon a throne of state; His own higher dignity, and that of the angels, being marked also by a nimbus upon their heads. The Virgin Mary has a subordinate, though honourable, place at one side of the principal group; and neither here, nor in any other of the scenes represented, is the nimbus, or any such mark, assigned to her. We have engraved this particular group, and we invite especial attention to it, as of the highest value to the historian of primitive doctrine. For the mosaic was given to the Church by XYSTVS EPISCOPVS † (so

---

* Very imperfectly represented by Ciampini V. M. i. p. 200. One of the groups (the Annunciation) is well figured by D'Agincourt, 'Peinture,' Pl. xvi. No. 4. But this group, and others of the same composition, are very exactly represented in the private collection above spoken of once the property of Pope Clement XI. It is from this that our own illustration is taken. The Annunciations made both to Zacharias and to the Virgin Mary, the Adoration of the Magi, the Presentation in the Temple, the Murder of the Innocents, the Questioning with the Doctors, and the Death of John the Baptist; such are the subjects represented.

† Sixtus III. Bishop of Rome from 432 to 440 A.D.

THE ADORATION OF THE MAGI.—(*From a Roman Mosaic, c.* 435 A.D.)

named in the mosaic itself) *within two or three years of the acts of the Council of Ephesus being promulgated*. In that Council the title of 'Theotokos'* was vindicated for the Virgin Mary, as a protest against the heresy of Nestorius. The entire composition of the mosaic had direct reference to the doctrinal questions which then agitated the Church. And the group now before our readers, more forcibly than any other evidence that could be produced, proves what was the mind of the Roman Church, in the middle of the fifth century, concerning the honour due to our Lord, and to the Virgin Mary, respectively. It is evident that, as in the Acts † of that Council, so in this picture, *as it was originally arranged* (how it was *afterwards* treated we shall yet have occasion to say), the object proposed was that of *vindicating the Divinity of the Son of Mary* against those who by implication denied it, and was not, what later perversions have made it to be, that of exalting the Virgin

---

* Theotokos, *i. e.* one of whom God was born. See following note.

† The opinion that was to be condemned is most simply expressed by Cyril Alex. himself (Nestorius' principal opponent). He represents the Nestorians as using the following language:—'He who by the nature of His own Being, and in very truth, was the Son, and as such was free, He, the Word of God the Father, who was subsisting in the form of Him who begat Him, and was equal unto Him, *took up His dwelling in a man born of a woman.*' In other words, the Nestorians maintained, according to the words which S. Cyril either puts into their mouth, or actually quotes, that He who was born of Mary was not Himself God, but that *God the Son took up His dwelling in the man that of Mary had been born.* In direct contradiction to this heretical statement, the title Theotokos served to assert, that He to whom Mary gave birth *was God, not a mere man* in whom the Godhead might afterwards abide. [For the words above quoted see Labbé, Concil. tom. iii. p. 32. They occur in the Letter of Cyril, addressed to the Egyptian Monks, § 14.]

Mary herself to all but coequal dignity with her Divine Son. And accordingly, in the original mosaic, here depicted, not the 'glories of Mary,' but the glory of our Lord, is evidently the central aim of the whole. Notice, as bearing upon this, the arrangement of the group before us. In every other representation of this particular subject, with which we are acquainted, the Holy Child is, as naturally might be expected, held in the arms of His mother. To the simple faith of an earlier age, merely human pictures such as those already delineated,* sufficed to recall at once all that to the faith of a Christian was implied in the thought of the star of Bethlehem, and of that Holy Family to which it points. But in the fifth century, at the period of which we now speak, more than this was thought to be required, as a protest against heretical teaching. What was desired now was, that art itself should minister to the assertion of the Divinity of Him who was born of Mary. And accordingly the Holy Child is now seated *alone* (apart from His mother) upon a throne, angels being in attendance upon Him, as though waiting to do His bidding. The Virgin Mary *shares not this His throne*, but is in a subordinate position † at one

---

* See pp. 12 and 14.

† The accurate drawings here reproduced enable us to correct a mistake shared by Ciampinus and Mr. Hemans. They speak of the Virgin Mary as *standing*. This is not so. She is seated, but on a *chair* of some kind, as far as one can judge, and in a subordinate position, while the Holy Child is seated on a spacious throne. The detailed description by Ciampinus, and the drawing which we now publish for the first time, will enable antiquaries to arrive at a true conclusion concerning the whole. More particularly we would call attention to the fact mentioned by Ciampinus, that there was originally yet another figure on the extreme left of the picture (probably the *third* of the Magi), which had all but disappeared, even

side; Joseph (probably) on the other. And while the angels, and our Lord, have the nimbus about the head, the Virgin herself is without it. What makes this absence of the nimbus from the head of the Virgin the more significant, is the fact, that, in other portions of the mosaic here described, Herod, *as being a King*, has the nimbus. This attribute had been a designation of *royalty*, and of *divinity* (under the Empire the two ideas were not very accurately distinguished) before it was adopted into Christian use, and in the earliest Christian monuments this meaning was still preserved. And from this monument that appears clear, which from the evidence of contemporary literature we might also infer, viz. that to the Virgin Mary neither queenly nor divine honours were assigned, even as late as the fifth century of Christendom. And the later evidence, which follows, shows that even this period must be considerably extended, before we shall find traces, in Roman churches, of either of those two ideas.

A few years later in date than the mosaics last described, are those in the Church of SS. Nazarius and Celsus* at Ravenna, originally constructed as a mausoleum. There are here repeated representations, symbolical or personal, of our Lord; *none whatever of the Virgin Mary*.

All but, if not quite, contemporary with the last, are the

---

in his time, in consequence of alterations in the building. I should add that the seated figure (*spectator's right* of the throne), which is evidently that intended for the Virgin Mary, so little corresponded with what Ciampinus, as a Roman Catholic, would naturally expect it to have been, that he interpreted this figure as representing the third of the Magi, and the standing figure (which is really that of a man) on our Lord's *right hand* he assumes to be intended for the Virgin Mother.

* See Ciampini V. M. tom. i. c. xxiii.

mosaics, again on the 'Arcus Triumphalis,' of the Church of St. Paul on the Via Ostiensis,* presented by Leo the Great (A.D. 441). Here, again, it is the 'Triumph' of the ascended Saviour that is represented, according to the description given in the Revelation of St. John (cap. iv., v.). The four living creatures,† the four-and-twenty Elders, holding crowns (*i.e.* victors' garlands) in their hands, SS. Peter and Paul—all these are represented, *but in no way whatever does the Virgin Mary appear.*

The same remarks will apply, *mutatis mutandis*, to other mosaics‡ at Ravenna, of the years 451 and 462 respectively. There is much here to recall our Lord and His Apostles to the minds of the faithful. *The Virgin Mary is nowhere represented.*

Not even in the sixth century, *a period of rapidly increasing barbarism in Italy*, is any change yet to be found in the prevailing character of these more public§ monuments of the Church. To this period belong numerous mosaics, both in Ravenna and at Rome. Among the former we may

---

* See Ciampini V. M. t. i. c. xxiv. A good representation of these will be found in D'Agincourt, 'Peinture,' Pl. xvi. No. 6.

† Identified in the mosaic with the symbolic designations of the four Evangelists.

‡ See Ciampini V. M. tom. i. cc. xxv. and xxvi., and Plates lxx. to lxxv.

§ The later Vetri Antichi, on the other hand, whether they be assigned to the fourth, fifth, or sixth century, indicate that at the time of their execution, whatever that was, there was among private persons at Rome a considerable development in the 'cultus' both of the Virgin Mary, and of martyrs such as St. Agnes. There is nothing *more* of honour traceable in the representations of the Virgin Mary than in those of St. Agnes and St. Lawrence. But both one and the other, in these more individual expressions of devotional feeling, present a marked contrast to the public monuments we have to describe.

42   THE CULTUS OF THE VIRGIN MARY.

enumerate those* of the Church of St. Vitalis (*circ*. 550 A.D.), of St. Maria† in Cosmedin (A.D. 553), of St. Apollinaris‡ (A.D. 570). At Rome itself we have mosaics of about the same date, in the Church of SS. Cosmas and Damianus§ (A.D. 530), and in that of St. Laurentius ‖ (A.D. 578). Among a multitude of Scriptural subjects, or Scriptural personages, there represented (none others occur, *in these more public monuments*, till late in the sixth century), there is but one¶ instance, to our knowledge, of the Virgin Mary being figured at all, and then only in the scene of the Adoration of the Magi. And it is very noteworthy, that in every instance** of mosaic decorations, of this or of earlier centuries, placed on the 'Arcus Triumphalis,' or on the 'Arch of the Tribune,' it is our blessed Lord, in every case, who, either by symbolic†† designation or by direct representation, is set forth as at once God and Man, and, as such, as the object of religious worship to the faithful; and, with the one exception of the historical [scriptural] representations of the

---

* Ciampini V. M. tom. ii. c. ix. Pll. xix. xx. xxi.
† Ibid. c. x. Pll. xxiii. xxiv.
‡ Ibid. c. xii. Pll. xxv. xxvi.
§ Ibid. c. vii. Pll. xv. xvi. xvii.
‖ Ibid. Pl. xxvii. 1.
¶ S. Apollinaris, at Ravenna. Ciampini, t. ii. Pl. xxvii. The 'one only' of which we speak, is exclusive of those mosaics of Sixtus III. A.D. *c.* 435) already described.
** See Ciampini, t. i. Tab. xlvi. lxviii.; t. ii. Tab. xv. xvi. xvii. xix. xxiv. xxviii.
†† 'Symbolic designation.' Paulinus, Bishop of Nola (*flor. circ.* 420 A.D.) and St. Nilus of Egypt (*flor. circ.* 440) will answer as well as any could for the feeling of the Church in these matters of sacred art, in West and East, early in the fifth century. Students of early art should compare the Epist. xii. (ad Severum) and Poema xxvii. of Paulinus, with the letter of St. Nilus to the Prefect Olympiodorus. (Lib. iv. Epist. lxiii. Romæ, fol. 1668.) Both letters are of great interest, as on other grounds, so more particularly for their bearing on the history of Christian art; and

St. Maggiore already described, *in no one of these instances is the Virgin Mary in any way represented.*

And thus we are brought to the close of the sixth century, a period at which, in art, as in literature, we find proofs of rapid deterioration from the higher standard of earlier times, but in which *the public monuments* of the Church were as yet primitive and Scriptural in character, and without any the slightest trace of idolatrous worship offered to any creature, in derogation of that due to the three persons of the blessed Trinity.

We shall find manifest traces of a change in the character of these monuments in the century that follows. But before proceeding to speak of these, we may briefly notice one, which in character, as well as in date, belongs to the transitional period which we have now reached, though not locally connected with the other monuments above described.

The picture which our readers have before them is from a Syriac Book of the Gospels, written and illuminated at Zagba, in Mesopotamia, at the close of the sixth century (A.D. 586), and purchased nine centuries later by an agent of the Medici for their library at Florence. Of this library

---

we regret that space will not allow of our quoting them. But we may state one conclusion to which they point, viz. that while the nave of a church was decorated with stories from the Old and New Testaments (for the instruction, says St. Nilus, *of those who cannot read Scripture*), yet in the chancel (as we should now call it) Christ alone was repre- sented, and that not personally (in His form as man), but symbolically, by the figure of a lamb, or by a cross. [This last is the only deco- ration St. Nilus will have in the Hie- rateion, the Sacrarium of Western writers.] This cross, as described by Paulinus, was surrounded by a corona, or victor's chaplet, just as we see it in numerous early sarcophagi.

it still forms one of the most cherished treasures. The middle and upper part of the picture before us, with which alone * we are here concerned, contains a representation of the Ascension. And it will be seen, that here, as in almost all the later mediæval representations of the same scene, whether in East or West, the Virgin Mary is made the central personage in the picture, although in Holy Scripture we have not the slightest intimation of her having been present. And after what has been already said on the subject of the nimbus, our readers will see what is implied by a fact, trivial indeed in itself, but suggestive of the tendencies of the time from which this picture dates. We find that, in this picture, our Lord, the Angels, *and the Virgin Mary*, have the nimbus, while the Apostles are without it. In all other respects, the older traditions of Christian art are still observed. The Virgin is in an attitude of adoration, standing as in prayer, not seated on a throne of glory, and herself (as in later pictures we shall see her) the object of adoration to others. Though she occupies the central place, with the Eleven on either side of her, and is marked out as distinguished above them by the nimbus about her head, yet do we find as yet no traces of those apocryphal stories concerning her, which had already come into existence, and which, in some parts of

---

* In the lower compartments of the picture are reproduced, on a much smaller scale, two other illustrations from the same ancient source. One is of the Crucifixion, in the other are figured Eusebius, Bishop of Cæsarea, and Ammonius of Alex- andria (engraved in 'Vest. Christ.' Pl. xxvii.). For further particulars concerning this MS. see 'Assemani Bibliotheca Medicea,' Florentiæ, fol. 1742, where the illustrations are engraved and described.

the West, about this time, found expression in Christian art. Still less do we find anything approaching to those blasphemous representations of which Western art has been prolific in later ages.

From 600 A.D. to 800 A.D.

In proceeding now to speak of the monuments of the two centuries immediately following, we will quote, as being exceedingly apposite to our purpose, the words of a foreign writer, to whose authority we have already made appeal. Seroux d'Agincourt, describing* the gradual degradation of art in the successive centuries of our Christian era, writes as follows of the seventh:—' In the seventh century . . . . the custom was introduced of representing in churches persons who were the objects of a special "cultus" [*d'un culte particulier*, of a special worship or reverence other than that paid to God Himself].' He then refers to particular mosaics in which occur figures of St. Agnes, St. Sebastian, and St. Euphemia. And then describing another, in which was a figure of our Lord, he writes : ' Christ is here seen as if in act of blessing, but the figure, which is but a half-length, is without dignity, *and is lost as it were in the crowd of images produced by emblematic representations of the Evangelists and of saintly personages who fill the principal space.*' What a comment is here unconsciously given upon the tendencies of the age of which the writer speaks!

Numerous mosaics dating from this seventh century are figured by Ciampinus and others. The earliest in date is

---

* For these quotations see vol. ii. p. 37, of the ' Histoire de l'Art,' &c.

of the year 623 A.D., in the church of St. Agnes, restored and decorated by the Roman Popes Symmachus and Honorius I. Here, for the first time, the arch of the tribune is found to be occupied, not by our Lord, but by saints (St. Agnes, and the two bishops to whom was due the restoration of the Church). *And these figures take the place, which in earlier times would have been occupied by the Saviour, with angels and apostles on either hand.* The barbarism of the inscription forms an instructive comment upon the picture itself. Some twenty years before this, St. Gregory the Great had told us, that he himself knew nothing of Greek, and that at Constantinople there was no one who could make sense out of a Latin letter requiring translation into Greek. And by the inscription now before us we may judge what was now that '*purity of Latin speech*' boasted * of, as this at least had been, at Rome in St. Gregory's time.†

---

* Joannes Diaconus 'Vita D. Gregorii,' lib. ii. c. 13.

† We give the description exactly as we find it in Ciampinus, V. M. t. ii. p. 105:—

'Aurea concisis surgit Pictura metallis,
Et complexa simul clauditur ipsa dies.
Fontibus e nibeis [*i.e.* niveis] *credas aurora subire*
Correptas nubes ruribus aura rigans.
Vel qualem inter sidera lucem proferat Irim
Purpureusque pavo ipse colore nitens.
Qui posuit [potuit?] noctis vel lucis reddere finem

Martyrum e bustis hinc reppulit ille chaos.
Sursum versa nutu quod cunctis cernitur usque,
Præsul Honorius hæc vota dicata dedit.
Vestibus et factis signantur illius ora
Excitat aspectu lucida corda gerens.'

The Pontifical inscriptions of the fifth and sixth centuries are some of them bad enough, in all conscience. But what can be said, what thought, of Latin such as this, at the very centre, and in the Patriarchal See, of Latin Christendom? Archbishop Manning will no doubt tell us that it was not written '*ex cathedrâ.*'

With such evidence before us of the barbarism of the Roman Church at this time, we shall not be surprised at finding, even in the public monuments of this century, proof of a marked change in the feeling of the Church in reference to doctrinal questions, and of declension from the purity of primitive faith. In the Chapel of St. Venantius,* the mosaic decorations of which date from 642 A.D. or thereabouts, the one figure which is so placed as at once to catch the eye of worshippers thoughout the Church, is that of the Virgin Mary. She appears here as the central figure, with six Apostles on either side of her. Both she and the Apostles have a nimbus exactly resembling that assigned to our Lord and the two angels who attend on Him. It is, however, with a view, probably, to mark the greater dignity of these celestial personages, that they have been drawn on a much larger scale than the Virgin Mary and the Apostles, who occupy the lower, and more generally visible, part of the composition.

Once more we quote D'Agincourt. It is thus that he describes the characteristics of Christian art in the period that immediately followed. 'In the eighth century,' so he writes ('Peinture,' vol. ii. p. 38), 'the carelessness and ignorance of the times often mixed up in the same composition subjects utterly alien the one from the other .... At this period the fervour of Christian people for the worship ("culte") of the Mother of God was continually increasing. *The homage paid to her was no longer distinguished from that rendered to the Lord of all.*' So writes the Roman Catholic historian of Christian art. But we are

---

* See Ciampini V. M. tom. ii. c. xv. Tab. xxxi.

bound to say that we do not ourselves know of any monuments* of the *eighth* century, which bear out this very strong language, which, however, is strictly applicable, as we shall see, to the centuries that follow.

The Ninth and three following Centuries.

The period at which we have now arrived is one which well deserves attentive study, as on other grounds, so especially upon this, that in the four centuries which elapsed between the age of Leo III. and Charlemagne (A.D. 800), and that of Pope Innocent III. (*sed.* 1198-1216), the doctrine and ritual of the Roman Church were gradually elaborated and stereotyped by a series of councils, to whose decrees the divines assembled at Trent in the sixteenth century appealed † as being nothing less than the teaching of 'the Church of God.'

The first of the monuments we have now to notice dates from an early period of the ninth century. It is a mosaic ‡ in the Church of St. Cecilia, restored and decorated by Pope Paschalis the First (817-824). Here we find a marked evidence of the advance made (if advance we

---

* A point of transition towards the more pronounced representations of the ninth century will be found figured in Ciampini 'De Sacris Ædificiis,' Tab. xxiii. Pope John VII. is there represented approaching the Virgin Mary, 'venerabiliter curvus.' The Virgin herself has the nimbus, and has *a royal diadem;* but she is still standing, and in the attitude of prayer. These date from the beginning of the eighth century.

† Catechismus ad Parochos, pp. 139, 140. Romæ, fol. 1566.

‡ Figured and described in Ciampini V. M. t. ii. c. xxiii. Tab. xliv. By Seroux D'Agincourt, Pl. xvii. No. 15, and also in the Collection of original Drawings once belonging to Pope Clement XI., already spoken of.

can bear to call it) in the publicly recognised worship of the Virgin Mary. The arch of the tribune is occupied by a gigantic figure of the Virgin, seated on a gorgeous throne. She holds the Infant Saviour in her arms. But the Pope [Paschalis himself, as the *square nimbus* about his head indicates], who kneels before the two, directs his worship, *not to the Infant Saviour, but to the Virgin Mary*. He is *embracing her feet*, as he kneels in an attitude of adoration. The Pontifical Latin is here again significant—*Virgo Maria tibi Paschalis Præsul honestus condidit hanc aulam lætus per sæcla manendam.* Another church, that of St. Cecilia, also owed its mosaic decoration to the same Pope Paschal (*circ.* 820 A.D.).* And here we may note some significant changes made in the traditionary representations of the worship of Christ on the Arcus Triumphalis. The four-and-twenty elders, with their white robes, and crowns in their hands, are still in their wonted place. But above, and in the very centre of the whole, instead of a figure of our Lord alone, personally or symbolically represented, *the Virgin Mary, wearing a royal crown, is seated as a Queen, upon a throne, bearing the Holy Infant on her knees.*

With this may be compared two other mosaics of nearly the same date; one in the Cathedral Church of Capua;† one in the Church of St. Maria Nova at Rome, in which ‡ the Virgin Mary, with all the insignia of a Queen, is set forth as the most conspicuous object for the worship of the faithful.

---

* Ciampini V. M. tom. ii. c. xxvii. Tab. xi.; D'Agincourt, ' Peinture,' Pl. xvii. No. 14; and a drawing in the collection of Pope Clement XI.

† Ciampini *ubi sup.* Tab. liv.

‡ Ibid. Tab. lvii. (Photographed, from a drawing of Pope Clement's, in 'Vestiarium Christianum,' Pl.xxxviii.) Compare D'Agincourt, ' Peinture,' Pl. xvii. No. 13.

But we pass hastily over these, in order to dwell in more detail upon a picture, somewhat differing from these in character, which was only discovered a few years ago, and which since then has often been the subject of keen controversy.

There is a special interest attaching to this picture, because, like so many other monuments of both the art and the literature of antiquity, it has been grossly misrepresented, and is even now employed, we believe, to serve the purposes of Roman controversy.

This picture of 'the Assumption' (for such it probably is) was discovered only a few years ago, on the buried walls of perhaps the oldest church in Rome, that of St. Clement. A church so named has long been shown, as many of our readers doubtless know, and has been reputed among the most ancient buildings of Christian Rome. But in the course of some repairs that were found necessary in the year 1858, a crypt was discovered below the floor of the church, this crypt being no other than the primitive Church of St. Clement, half buried and half destroyed. On the ruins of this, a comparatively modern church had been constructed, in (we believe) the twelfth century. On the walls of this buried church, frescoes were found, one of which is now presented to our readers. The subject is the 'Assumption,' as we have already observed; and though Roman antiquaries, such as De Rossi, have at once recognised the true date of the fresco, which is actually inscribed upon it, as we shall see, yet proselytising ecclesiastics at Rome long remained in ignorance (so we are bound in charity to suppose) of this date, and displayed this fresco again and again to English visitors as giving proof

that the Roman doctrine concerning the Virgin Mary, and especially concerning her Assumption, had been recognised in the primitive Church from all but Apostolic times. 'The Church of St. Clement, even as known hitherto,' (so it was * argued,) 'was one of the oldest Christian Churches at Rome. Here is a church more ancient still,—so ancient as to have been buried beneath the ground, and altogether lost to sight and knowledge for hundreds of years. The very construction of the walls gives proof of an all but Apostolic antiquity; and here, upon those walls, providentially preserved for the conviction of Protestants, and for the establishment of the faith of Catholics,—here are proofs of what was the belief of the Church while, it may be, the voices of the two princes of the Apostles were still sounding in the ears of their surviving disciples.'

This ingenious statement, like many another similar argument that has been set in currency of late years among ourselves, can only be acquitted of far graver fault on the ground of a scarcely excusable ignorance. For what are the facts of the case—facts which at Rome, the very centre of archæological study, might have been ascertained at once from persons competent to give an opinion? Our readers have before them the opportunity of judging these facts for themselves, and that upon evidence furnished by the very persons † whose opinions we are now combating. And first,

---

* It is right to add, that the present writer is not a personal witness as to this. He is only retailing at second-hand the general purport of what he has heard stated by others. [I will add, also, that since the first edition of this paper I have seen, by a description of these mosaics published not long since by the custodians of the church, that they do now recognise their true date.]

† Our illustration is reproduced

let it be noted, that the figure on the left-hand (*spectator's left*) occupies the place which, in pictures of this kind, was conventionally assigned to *the giver* of the mosaic, or of the fresco, as the case might be. Observe, further, the contrast between the 'nimbus' about the head of this figure (it is shaped like a square piece of board), and the ordinary circular nimbus of the figure on the spectator's right. This 'square nimbus,' as it is sometimes called, was, in the middle ages, a conventional mode of marking out a distinguished personage *while still living*,* whereas the circular nimbus was reserved as a mark of honour after death.

Now let us note, before going further, how many clear indications of date there are before us, even independently of the inscriptions which we have yet to consider. The *shaven crowns* of 'St. Vitus,' and of the corresponding figure on the left, would have been regarded, even as late as St. Jerome's time (close of fourth † century), as a mark proper to the priesthood of some heathen superstition.

---

mechanically, and with mechanical accuracy, from a photograph published by the custodians of the church.

* John the Deacon, writing in the ninth century, at the very time from which this picture dates, is the first writer who notices this custom. Describing a picture of St. Gregory the Great which was extant in his time, he says,—'Circa verticem *tabulæ similitudinem, quod viventis insigne est*, præferens, non coronam.' The earliest existing monument, known to the writer, in which it occurs, is on a head (mosaic) of John VII., dating from the beginning of the eighth century. (Ciampini 'De Sacr. Ædif.' Tab. xxiii.)

† S. Hieron. in Ezek. xliv. (Opp. t. iii. p. 1029. See 'Vest. Christ.' p. 30.) 'By this it is clear that we ought not to have shaven heads, like the priests and worshippers of Isis and Serapis; nor yet, on the other hand, to wear long flowing hair, which is for the luxurious only, for barbarians, or men of the sword.' · · · And again, 'Heathen superstition has its shaven heads.'

The earliest known examples in art of the *bare crown*, by way of tonsure, are of the sixth century. Again, the use of the circular nimbus in representing a personage such as St. Vitus, and the square nimbus seen in the same picture, point to the sixth century as the *very earliest* to which the picture could with any probability be referred. And on all these grounds any one even moderately acquainted with the data of Christian archæology would at once say, that the first glance of the picture, independently of its inscriptions and of its *subject*, marked it as being at any rate later than the year 500 A.D.

But this is not all. There are two inscriptions on the fresco before us, which, if this picture is to be trusted, fix the date, beyond all posssibility of mistake, to the middle of the ninth century. The first of the two inscriptions is thus worded:

QVOD HÆC PRÆ CVNCTIS SPLENDET PICTVRA DECORE
COMPONERE HANC STVDVIT PRESBITER ECCE LEO.

It is not as a specimen of mediæval Latinity that we quote these lines, but as an introduction to a second and somewhat later inscription, about the head of this same 'Presbiter Leo.' Represented here as the giver of the fresco, at a time when he was 'Presbyter Urbis' (a 'Cardinal,' he would now be styled), this second inscription speaks of him by his later title as *Sanctissimus Dominus* * *Leo Quartus*

---

* This title of 'Dominus,' as an *official designation* for the occupant of the Roman See, was first assumed, we believe, by Leo III., at the beginning of the ninth century. It appears in art monuments for the first time in the mosaics of the famous 'Triclinium Lateranum.' See 'Vestiarium Christianum,' p. lii. and Pll. xxxii. xxxiii.; and Pl. vi. below.

Papa Romanus. And we are thus able to fix the date of this picture to the middle of the ninth century, to a period shortly preceding the Pontificate of Leo IV. (845-855).

We give this date upon the evidence (professedly *photographic*) furnished by Roman authorities. But the photographic picture (reproduced in these pages) was taken, *not from the actual fresco*, but from a drawing intended to represent as exactly as possible its true state. And we observe that Mr. J. H. Parker of Oxford, who has devoted himself of late more especially to Roman archæology, both Christian and classical, has photographed the fresco itself by means of lime light, and he believes the inscription to refer to Leo IX. (1048-1054). He gives (in his printed description) the inscription about the head of Leo as follows :—

DOM. LEO P. M. ROMANVS,

and an inscription below, which, he says, is only partly legible, thus :—

PARCVS (? PARIES) IIS SPLENDET PICTA DECORE LEO
PONTIFEX HANC STVDVIT PRESBYTER ECCLESIAM FIERI.

In the photograph (published at Rome) which we ourselves have reproduced, the abbreviated inscription is SS. DOM. LEO QRS. PP. ROM. (*i. e.* Sanctissimus Dominus Leo Quartus Papa Romanus). If Mr. Parker's date be the correct one, our own case is even stronger than before. But here, as throughout, we have preferred taking the Roman controversialists *on their own ground*, for the saving of unnecessary argument.

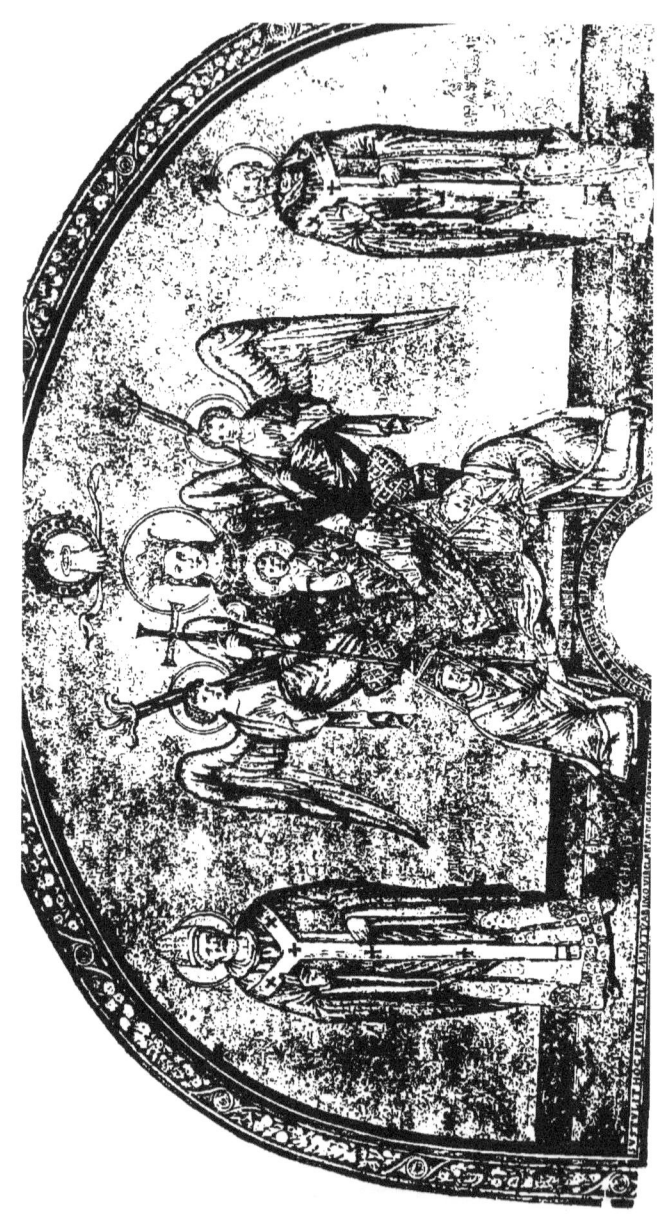

And thus we find that this picture of the 'Assumption,' appealed to with such confidence, by Roman controversialists, as an evidence of all but Apostolic antiquity for the doctrine in question, proves nothing more than that (at the earliest) *after a lapse of* 800 *years*, and 300 years or more after the utter decay of primitive learning in Italy, this doctrine* had at length obtained public recognition upon the walls of a Roman church.

Twelfth Century.

If anything were wanting to complete the contrast between the Christian Rome that once was, and the Marian Rome of mediæval and of modern times, the want might be supplied by mosaics of the twelfth century, such as those of which a speciment is here given. Let our readers contrast this with earlier pictures, such as those figured above, pp. 22 and 24.

The mosaic picture here reproduced (see opposite) was commenced by Pope Calixtus II. (1119 to 1124), and completed by Anastasius IV. (1153, 1154). And these two Popes are represented kneeling at the feet of this 'Queen of Heaven,' and embracing them in an attitude of adoration.

And thus by successive steps, such as have now been placed before our readers, the contradiction is made complete, between the teaching of Holy Scripture and that of mediæval Rome. In Holy Scripture we are told, and in the earlier pictures of the Catacombs we are again and again

---

* For the literary evidence bearing upon this subject see Appendix (C) at the end of this volume.
† For other examples from the tenth to the fourteenth centuries see Seroux d'Agincourt, 'Peinture,' vol. v. Pl. xviii.; and 'Vestiarium Christianum,' Pl. xlv.

reminded, how the Magi, divinely guided, came where were the young Child and His mother; and how, so coming, they fell down and worshipped *Him*. In this crowning monument of Roman superstition we see two* Popes represented as coming, like those Magi, into that holy presence; and they, so coming, fall down and worship *her*.

Fifteenth Century.

One example must suffice, out of the many to which we might refer, in connexion with our present subject, in the fifteenth century. It will bring before us, at a single glance (and a single glance upon a subject so repulsive is all that we will venture upon), the horrible depravity which, in the very centre of Roman Christendom, and on the very throne, as Romanists hold, of St. Peter, could coexist with extravagant devotion to the so-called 'honours of Mary.' We will not trust ourselves to use words of our own here, but will rather quote the description of one who writes simply

---

* Our readers will ask how *two* Popes come to be represented as each having the 'square nimbus,' indicating that the person represented was then living. The answer is suggested in what we have above stated, therein following Papebrochius ('Acta Sanctorum,' Maius, Propylæum, p. 320), who accounts for this peculiarity by the fact (whether *known* or *presumed* I do not feel sure) that Calixtus began the mosaic, and represented himself, but that Anastasius completed it, and put his own effigy opposite to that of Calixtus. He also expresses his belief that the large figure (*now* that of the Virgin) was originally intended for our Lord by Calixtus, but that Anastasius made considerable alterations in it, and so substituted the Virgin Mary for the Saviour. [A significant change!] The mosaic is also figured in Muratori, 'Rerum Italicarum Scriptores,' t. ii. p. 417. Our own representation is reproduced, by photography, from a drawing in the collection of Pope Clement XI.

as an historian of art :—'*One of the frescoes in the Vatican represents Giulia Farnese in the character of the Madonna, and Pope Alexander VI. (the infamous Borgia) kneeling at her feet in the character of a votary.*' The same writer goes on to say, ' Under the influence of the Medici, the churches of Florence were filled with pictures of the Virgin, in which the only thing aimed at was an alluring, and even meretricious beauty. Savonarola thundered from his pulpit, in the garden of S. Marco, against these impieties. He exclaimed against the profaneness of those who represented the meek mother of Christ in gorgeous apparel, with head unveiled, and under the features of women too well and publicly known. He emphatically declared, that if painters knew, as well as he did, the influence of such pictures in perverting simple minds, they would hold their own works in horror and detestation. Savonarola yielded to none in orthodox reverence for the Madonna, but he desired that she should be represented in an orthodox manner. He perished at the stake, but not till after he had made a bonfire in the Piazza at Florence of the offensive effigies : he perished—persecuted to death by the Borgia family.' *

Eighteenth Century.

Before we conclude, we are bound to take notice of a remarkable monument at Rome, which may well be thought

---

* Jameson's 'Legends of the Madonna,' 2nd edit. (Longmans, 1857), Introduction, p. xxxi. The whole passage is well worth consulting, as showing, by the evidence of art, that of which there is abundant evidence in literature, how baneful was the fruit of the classical revival, where there was no better Christianity to deal with it than that which prevailed in Italy in the fifteenth century.

entirely subversive of the conclusions to which the facts, above stated, all point. A series of mosaics is shown at Rome as dating from the fifth century. One who saw them for the first time would be struck with the remarkable confirmation of modern Roman doctrine which they afford. In a picture of the Worship of the Magi, in one of the oldest churches now remaining, there is to be seen now, what we have at this moment in exact facsimile before us —the Virgin Mary marked out by a *golden* nimbus (peculiar to our blessed Lord and to herself), and so exalted in celestial honour above the four angels (probably archangels) who are behind the throne of Him, who was at once Son of Man and Son of God. For the angels have a nimbus, it is true, but it is of a bluish white, suggestive of light; but it is not of gold, as is that of the Virgin. Not only so, but the dress of the Virgin herself is such as was only assigned to a Queen; viz. a golden tunic and scarlet shoes (with these, however, a large black 'palla,' suggestive of altogether other ideas).

What do our readers suppose to be the real worth of this seeming testimony to the *antiquity* of the doctrine now inculcated at Rome? After reading what has been already before them, they will probably anticipate the reply. This mosaic, so eloquent in its testimony to the catholicity of modern Romanism, is nothing less than the mosaic of Xystus III. already described and figured (see pp. 36, 37), not as it originally was drawn, but *as it was rearranged* in *the time of Boniface XIV., so as to bring into conformity with modern teaching what had, up to that time, borne unmistakable testimony against it.*

Our readers will naturally ask, on what evidence we can

A REMARKABLE MONUMENT IN ROME. 59

prove that the representation given above (p. 37) really represents more truly the *older state* of the mosaic, than the mosaic itself, as it may now be seen at Rome? We reply, that we have two nearly contemporary, but independent and unimpeachable, witnesses of what the mosaic was some 200 years ago: one being Ciampinus, a Roman archæologist of acknowledged authority; the other being no less a person than Pope Clement XI. The former of the two, Ciampinus, in his 'Monumenta Vetera' (t. i. p. 200), gives an engraving of the whole series of mosaics, of which this of the Worship of the Magi forms a part. This, however, is so barbarously executed, that we could not have appealed to it with any confidence had it stood alone. Fortunately, however, he has given us an elaborate verbal description of the whole; and his description, coupled with his engraving, entirely bears out, in every point of importance, the exactness of the drawing supplied by Pope Clement. The latter, when Cardinal Albano, formed a large archæological collection, and among them some twelve large volumes of drawings, two of which consist exclusively of ecclesiastical monuments. After the lapse of a century or more this collection was purchased, at Rome, for an English monarch; and from this source now comes to light, yet half a century later, the drawing which we have exactly reproduced above. To make this subject complete, we lay before our readers an exact representation (p. 63) of the present state of the mosaic. It will be instructive to the student of antiquity to observe how slight a modification of an ancient monument will suffice to give it a meaning *the exact opposite* of that which the original was calculated to convey. (See above, pp. 36 to 40.)

Recapitulation.

Our historical survey has already occupied so much space, that it may be well briefly to recapitulate that, which, in greater detail, and with all necessary reference to authorities, has now been brought under review.

1. *First four Centuries.*—Of all the pictures in the Catacombs, the date of which can be referred to the first four centuries of our era, there is not one, in which the Virgin Mary is represented, which is not purely Scriptural in its character. Even if (which is doubtful) some of the figures known as 'Oranti' had reference to her, these figures precisely resemble others in which ordinary persons, recently deceased, were represented, whether men or women. Christian art at this time, to use Dr. Northcote's own expression, *was kept strictly within the limits of the canonical books of Holy Scripture.* (See pp. 11 to 32.)

2. *Fifth and Sixth Centuries.*—In the more public monuments of Rome and Ravenna, which date from 400 to 600 A.D., there is nothing inconsistent with those earlier pictures of the Catacombs. On the contrary, in the one monument of them all which was evidently intended formally to embody the faith of the Church, as proclaimed in the Council of Ephesus just previously, the natural arrangement of the scene, in the Adoration of the Magi, is purposely departed from, in such a way as to mark that the Virgin Mary, however near to our Lord in respect of His incarnation, *had no place upon the throne which belongs to Him and to Him alone.* (See pp. 32 to 45.)

In less important works of art, such as might be dictated rather by private fancy than by the deliberate judgment of the chief representatives of the Church, we find at this time, in one or two instances here and there, traces of legendary fables concerning the Virgin Mary, and in others (as the 'Vetri Ornati,' or ornamented glasses) indications of considerable advance, on the part of some, in the honours paid to her, as to other Saints. (See n. §, p. 41.)

3. *Seventh and Eighth Centuries.*—*Side by side with convincing proofs of a rapidly progressing barbarism in Italy at this time*, we find now, even in public monuments, figures of saints, and of the Virgin Mary, intruded into those portions of the older churches, which had hitherto been exclusively devoted to proclaiming the glory of the risen Saviour. Now first, according to the chief historian [*] of Christian art, the homage paid to the Virgin Mary was not to be distinguished from that rendered to the Lord of all. (See pp. 45 to 48.)

4. *Ninth and later Centuries.*—In the ninth century, for the first time—a period of the greatest barbarism in Italy, though of a brief revival, under the auspices of Charlemagne, in France and parts of Germany—there appear upon the walls of churches, at Capua and at Rome, representations of the Virgin Mary enthroned, and in all the splendours of royal estate, in dress of purple and gold, a golden crown upon her head, and scarlet shoes upon her feet.

Now for the first time is the apocryphal legend of the Assumption embodied in representation upon the same walls.

And from this ninth century onwards, in an age which

---

[*] See above, pp. 47, 48.

Roman Catholic* historians of the greatest repute have denounced as the most horribly corrupt, and the most barbarously ignorant, of all which a Roman annalist has, with shame and confusion of face, to describe,—in this age we find one step of advance after another made in the exaltation of the Virgin to heavenly and divine honours. And the whole series culminates in mosaics such as those of the twelfth century, in which the worship, that of old had been offered to God alone, is diverted from our Lord to be bestowed upon Mary; or, worse yet, in a picture yet 300 years later in date, in which, upon the walls of the Vatican Palace itself, and by the orders of a Pope, the worship of Christendom is embodied under the guise of an Alexander Borgia kneeling as a votary at the feet of a Giulia Farnese. (See pp. 48 to 59.)

Contrast these with the beautiful and purely Scriptural

---

* See the passage quoted from Cardinal Baronius in 'Vestiarium Christianum,' Introduction, p. lxxxiii. note. I add here a passage, less generally known, from the 'Chronographia' of Genebrardus, Archbishop of Aix (lib. iv. p. 553) :—' Infelix dicitur hoc sæculum, exhaustis hominibus ingenio et doctrina claris, sive etiam claris principibus, et pontificibus, in quo nihil fere dignum memoria posteritatis gestum sit; unde ferunt tunc repertum fuisse quoddam monstrum capite canino et cæteris membris humanis, quod statum illius temporis mirifice referret.' And again :—' Hoc quidem infelix quod per annos CL., Pontifices circiter L., a Johanne scilicet VIII. . . . . . ad Leonem IX. usque, qui primus a Deo vocatus velut alter Aaron antiquam pontificum integritatem e cœlo in sedem apostolicam revocavit, a virtute majorum prorsus defecerunt apostatæ apotacticive, potius quam apostolici.' This language was too truthful to be acceptable at Rome, and it brought both the Archbishop and his book into disgrace. In all the later editions of the 'Chronographia' (an abridgment of Universal History) a Church History by Arnaldus Pontacus (a somewhat unscrupulous Romanist) is substituted for that of Genebrardus.

picture, which De Rossi, in common with ourselves, places first in the whole series of these monuments (*supra*, p. 24), and our readers will be able to judge of the gulf which separates the Marian Rome of the ninth and all later centuries, from the Christian Rome of the second.

The conclusions which, we venture to think, any unprejudiced reader would draw from the evidence hitherto produced, will be found confirmed by the literary evidence, alleged more in detail in the Appendices (A to C) at the end of this volume.

THE MOSAIC OF XYSTUS III. (above, p. 37, AS ALTERED IN THE EIGHTEENTH CENTURY.

[The nimbus of our Lord, and of the Virgin Mary, is of gold: that of the angels white, or light blue. The dress of our Lord is white with a black stripe; that of the Virgin, cloth of gold, with scarlet shoes. The outer mantle black. None of these colours, in the dress of the Virgin, are found in the original mosaic, as described by Ciampinus, and as drawn in the Collection of Pope Clement XI.]

PART II.

MONUMENTS OF CHRISTIAN ART,

HAVING REFERENCE TO THE SUPREMACY

CLAIMED FOR

The See of Rome.

NOTICE.

The two Papers which follow were written as an Exercise to be read in the Divinity School at Oxford. I have added some additional matter since that time, but the pressure of other duties, to which I was bound to give precedence, has prevented my recasting them entirely, as I could have wished to do, before publication. I mention this in order to account for some peculiarities in the form of these Essays, for which I must ask the indulgence of my Readers.

Eton, Feb. 19, 1870.

THE SUPREMACY CLAIMED FOR THE SEE OF ROME.

THE literary monuments bearing upon questions now and for some time past disputed within the Church, have been under the examination of Divines and Historians ever since the revival of learning. But there is another large class of monuments, those of early Christian and Mediæval art, to which, in this country at least, as far as I have observed, very little attention has been given. There is, however, scarcely one, if one, of the many questions now most prominent as matter of discussion among Churchmen, upon which these monuments of art have not important evidence to give. What that evidence is upon one such question, that of the Supremacy claimed for the See of Rome, it will be my object to show in the present paper.

I propose to set before you, in their historical order, a series of monuments bearing upon this question, either in representation the most exact that can be obtained, or by description where that cannot be.

The Diptych of St. Paul.

First in the whole series is an Ivory Diptych (see Pl. iv. the 'Diptych of St. Paul'), to which I venture to think that a very great historical interest attaches, while it may claim a high place, on artistic grounds, among the monuments of primitive Christendom.

This 'Diptych,' technically so called, is formed upon the model of those Imperial and Consular* Diptychs, of both old and new Rome, many of which, dating from the third century onwards, are preserved in the principal Museums and Cathedral Treasuries of Europe. That now before you has been known hitherto only to a very limited number of persons interested in archæological study, and by them under the title of 'The Naming of the Beasts in Paradise.' In the only published work, that of A. Duval, in which it is figured (one leaf only), it is described (quite wrongly, as you will see), as a Consular Diptych. Its date may be determined with great confidence, as at any rate not later than the year 400 A.D., even if we have regard only to the beauty of its execution. And on grounds of historical probability, we may reasonably doubt whether after that time St. Peter would have been represented (as here in all probability he is), as in a position secondary to that of St. Paul. Before proceeding further, I may mention all that I have been able to learn as to the history of this monument. I find it first noticed as forming part of the collection of Baron Denon, who was one of the *savans* employed by Napoleon I. from time to time in carrying off treasures from Museums and Libraries, in countries subjected to his power. And amongst other places, I find evidence that he was at Rome with the

---

* Specimens of these Consular Diptychs may be seen in Plates xxii. and xxiii. of my 'Vestiarium Chris- tianum;' and many more in Gorius (' Thesaurus Veterum Diptychorum,' 3 vols. fol. Florence, 1759.)

THE TWO LAVES OF THE DIPTYCH

revolutionary armies, and interesting himself (whether on public or on private account, or on both), with its archæological treasures. And I think I shall not be wrong in thinking, that it was there and then that he became possessed of this Diptych, whose true character, however, he does not seem to have perceived. After his death it was figured as forming part of his collection by Amaury Duval.* It is now in the hands of M. Carrand of Lyons, and has been reproduced in facsimile by the Arundel Society, from a cast taken from the original by Mr. Nisbet. I shall be very glad of any assistance in tracing its earlier history. Such works as these were almost, if not altogether, confined to the two cities of Rome and Byzantium, in early times. And this, from its representing an incident in St. Paul's voyage to Rome, and the two Apostles, SS. Peter and Paul, who were specially connected with the Roman church, was originally produced, we may feel sure, at Rome, probably as an offering for the church of St. Paul. (See Ciampini De S. Æd. cap. vi.)

Its true character you will, I think, have no difficulty in determining. On the more important of the two sides of the Diptych (that on the *spectator's right*), three scenes are represented, having reference, each of them, to events in the life of St. Paul. In the centre is the scene described in Acts, xxviii. 1-6. You may see the fire of dried wood burning near the Apostle's feet (St. Paul himself is seen standing at the *spectator's left*); the viper is falling from his hand; and in the centre of the group is seen Publius, the chief officer of the island, holding up his hands

---

* Monuments des Arts du Dessin, 4 vols. fol. Paris, 1829.

in astonishment at what he sees. A soldier is in attendance on him, who occupies the last place on the *spectator's right*.

Below this group is yet another, having reference to what is recorded somewhat later in the same chapter of the Acts (ver. 9). Two out of those 'many which had infirmities in the island,' are there represented. And the same soldier who had appeared above as in attendance upon Publius, is seen here again, evidently bidding these sick persons go to St. Paul, to whom he points, for the healing that they need.

Postponing for a moment any reference to the uppermost of the three groups, I will ask you to observe, in passing, the other leaf of the Diptych. If that had stood alone, as an isolated picture, we might perhaps accept the interpretation implied in the title, 'Adam naming the Beasts.' But, as it is, we may with good reason assume, that this side of the Diptych has an intended reference to the other. And, if we regard the two as mutually related, we shall probably be led to the conclusion, that in the one picture we see placed before us Man, and the lower animals, as they were before the Fall, brought about as this was through the guile of that serpent, who, with malice concentrated in his features, is here entering the peaceful Paradise before him. In the other we may see suggested the restoration of humanity through the power of the kingdom of God, whose triumph over that of the serpent is embodied in the miracle of Melita. In two words, *Paradise lost through the malice of the serpent, and Paradise reopened through Him who crushed the serpent's power*—these appear to be the leading ideas traceable in those parts of the Diptych which have been noticed hitherto.

But I proceed now, from this more general description, to speak in more detail of that upper group of the right-hand leaf, wherein lies, for our present purpose, the special interest of the monument now before you.

No detailed argument will be needed to show that it is no Roman Consul who occupies the middle place in this group, but the same Paul whose features we have already seen pourtrayed among those of the central picture already described. A moment's comparison of the two faces will serve to show their absolute, and evidently designed, identity. The same high, bald head,[*] and peculiar pointed beard, are seen in both groups. And as no one, not even that one foreign Editor already mentioned (A. Duval), has any doubt as to the person intended, when figured on the *spectator's left* in that central group (the person who is shaking off the serpent from his hand), it follows, as matter of certainty, that St. Paul also is the person represented above, as occupying what may be described as an apostolic throne, or chair of state.

---

[*] Compare the description of St. Paul's personal appearance in the 'Philopatris' generally attributed to Lucian. The Apostle is there scoffingly described as Γαλιλαῖος, ἀναφαλαντίας, ἐπίρρινος, ἐς τρίτον οὐρανον ἀεροβατήσας—'the *bald-headed* and long-nosed Galilæan, who mounted through the air into the third heaven.' And in the Apocryphal Acts of the Apostles, edited by Tischendorf, it is said of Dioscorus the shipmaster, who had followed St. Paul to Rome, and was mistaken for the Apostle and beheaded in his stead, that he, too, was bald: καὶ αὐτὸς ἀναφάλαντος ὑπάρχων. (Northcote's R. S., p. 285.) Compare Hieron. Comment. in Ep. ad Gal. i. 18. Dr. Northcote has published a bronze medal, now in the Vatican Library, found by Boldetti in the Cemetery of Domitella, and attributed to the era of the Flavian emperors at Rome. In this the busts of the two Apostles are represented, and they bear a considerable resemblance to those of the Diptych before us.

One of the three figures, and that the most important, is thus at once determined, as being that of St. Paul. But a question still remains, Who are the other two? To this question also an answer can be given; but I willingly allow that, with such evidence as alone is open to us at present, we cannot claim any absolute assent to the solution I propose.

And first for the personage on St. Paul's right, to whom the Apostle appears to be giving Benediction. We have at once a clue to his identification, in the fact of his holding in his left hand a Codex, or bound book, which is no other than the book of the Gospels. This book was, as we know from authorities * of early date, laid on the head of a Bishop at the time of his consecration, as being 'the true Tiara of the Gospel.' Such a book, held in the left hand, as in the monument before you, was, in almost all the early monuments of Christian art, the traditionary attribute of a Bishop, while that of an Apostle † was the older form of a

---

* The Sermon 'De Uno Legislatore,' attributed to St. Chrysostom, and quoted at length in 'Vestiarium Christianum,' p. 53, notes 89 and 90. 'It is commanded that the head of the Priest' [here the *High-Priest*, according to what follows] 'be not bare but covered, in order that he who is head of the people may learn that he, too, hath a Head in heaven. For this cause in the Church also, at the consecration of Bishops ('Vest. Christ.' notes 61 and 90), *the gospel of Christ is laid upon their heads*, that he who is ordained may know that he then receives the true tiara of the Gospel; and may learn this also, that though he be head of all, yet doth he act in subjection to God's laws; though he be ruler of all, yet is he, too, under rule to the law; though in all things a setter forth of the Word, yet himself to that Word in subjection.'

† See further 'Vest. Christ.' p. xli. For examples of the two insignia here spoken of, as proper to Apostles and to Bishops respectively, see ibid., Pll. xxv. (St. Gregory the Great); xxx. St. Cornelius (of Rome)

'Scroll' or 'Roll' of a book (*volumen*), associated in idea with the Scriptures in their original form. This attribute served to designate them as charged on Christ's behalf with messages of the divine Word to man. It is in accordance with this, that, in the Diptych before you, St. Paul holds in his hand a 'Volumen,' or 'roll' of a book, while the Bishop (as I venture now to call him) holds a Codex of more modern form, much such as those still in use.*

Thus far I do not anticipate much difference of opinion as to the interpretations hitherto proposed. But there is yet another personage to be identified; and at this point agreement can no longer be anticipated. As to this, then, let me begin by saying, that if any one were to examine for himself the language of Holy Scripture † (more particularly the Epistle to the Romans and the Book of the Acts), and that of St. Clement's first Epistle, the conclusion he would draw would probably be, that the *actual Founder* (under

---

and St. Cyprian; xxxi. St. Xystus and St. Optatus; xxxviii. (four Apostles); xl. Leo IV.; xli. Tarasius and other Eastern Patriarchs at the Seventh Council; and other later illustrations.

* The following fact is mentioned here as a curious illustration of the way in which mediæval usage, at Rome more especially, has preserved some of the most ancient features of primitive Christianity, even while overlaying and all but concealing them under the accretions of later ages. In the Consecration of Bishops, as prescribed in the 'Pontificale Romanum,' the Book of the Gospels, though it has been displaced in favour of the mitre, from its traditionary pre-eminence, is still laid (and held by an assistant) at the back of the head, and on the neck, of the 'consecrandus.' [Pontificale Romanum Clementis VIII., &c. Paris, fol. 1664, pp. 66, 71, 76, *et sqq.*] I need hardly remind the reader of the delivery of the Bible, as an appointed part of the rite of Ordination to the Priesthood, and of the Consecration of Bishops, in our own Church.

† See the evidence on this point in Appendix (D) at the end of this volume.

Christ) of the Roman Church, was St. Paul; that this Apostle both wrote his Epistle, and arrived at Rome as a prisoner, before St. Peter was in any way connected with the Church that was there; that St. Peter's connection with that Church was mainly through his martyrdom; St. Paul's through a residence there of considerable, though interrupted, duration, before the time of that martyrdom which he shared with St. Peter. He would conclude, that St. Paul would be at Rome not only *an* Apostle, as were others of the twelve, but in a special sense *the**** Apostle of the Roman Church, as being its Founder; but that St. Peter when at Rome was [ἐν ἀλλοτρίῳ κανόνι] within a spiritual domain which already owed a kind of personal allegiance to St. Paul. In a word (if the earliest historical indications are followed rather than late tradition), St. Paul at Rome would be not Apostle only, but Apostle *and Bishop*, occupying a place such as that held at Jerusalem by James the Brother of the Lord.

It is, perhaps, not without significance in this regard, that among the frescoes of the catacombs the only figure of an Apostle which is represented separately from the rest of the twelve, is that of St. Paul, described as PAVLVS PASTOR APOSTOLVS † side by side with a figure of 'the good Shepherd.' In none of the catacombs is St. Peter specially designated by name or attribute.

---

* By 'Apostolus,' when absolutely used, Western writers generally designated St. Paul. So we learn, among others, from St. Augustine, 'Contra duas Epist. Pelag.' lib. iii. cap. iii., '*Apostolus cum di-cetur, si non exprimatur quis apostolus non intelligitur nisi Paulus.*'

† The picture of St. Paul above mentioned is in the Cemetery of St. Priscilla. See Aringhi R. S. t. ii. p. 273.

A conclusion such as this, which results from an examination of Holy Scripture, and of the evidence to be derived from the earliest Christian literature, is one which will exactly account for the peculiar phenomena presented in the earliest monuments of Christian art, in which SS. Peter and Paul are figured. One very remarkable peculiarity of the Roman* monuments is, that, in the numberless instances in which SS. Peter and Paul are represented *on either hand of our Lord*, no definite and unvarying rule of precedence is observed. The *prevailing* rule, to which, in the more public monuments, as the mosaics of churches, there are few, if any, early exceptions, is that *St. Paul is placed at the right hand of our Lord, St. Peter at the left.* But this rule has its exceptions. In the *Vetri Antichi*,† so called, or pieces of ornamented glass, found chiefly in the Roman cemeteries, and on Roman Sarcophagi of the fifth‡ and later centuries (possibly some may be of the fourth), some special attributes are assigned to St. Peter, and marks of precedence over St. Paul indicated; peculiarities, such as any one acquainted with the claims put forward by the Roman Church from the time of the First Council of Nicæa, might have counted with

---

* The types that prevailed at Rome reappear elsewhere; as, for example, in the *Sarcophagi* (fifth and later century) at Milan, and in the South of France. But these last appear to me to be direct *imitations* of the form already stereotyped, so to say, at Rome.

† In two of these, preserved in the Vatican, and figured (to name but one) by Dr. Northcote in his 'Roma Sotterranea,' St. Peter is represented, instead of Moses, as striking the rock to draw out refreshing streams for the people of God.

‡ I am speaking here of those which are appealed to, for controversial reasons, by Roman controversialists.

some certainty on finding in monuments executed at Rome itself.

An enumeration of all the known monuments antecedent to the year 800* A.D., in which the two apostles are represented together, would show that, in a very large majority of cases, *the place at our Lord's right hand is assigned to St. Paul*. And the fact, urged by some Roman archæologists, that in some instances, at least, this place is occupied by St. Peter, is precisely what clenches the argument in favour of the historical conclusion of which I speak. If the rule were invariable that St. Paul occupied the one place, St. Peter the other, there would be some show of probability for the assertion, that in these early times the place of honour was not what it now is; that the *spectator's right*, not the right hand of the principal personage, indicated the place of precedence. But the varying usage in this matter which does, in point of fact, exist, leaves us a choice of only two conclusions. One (which no one at all acquainted with antiquity would be likely to accept), that right and left, in point of precedence of honour, were regarded as matter of indifference; the other, and, as it appears to me, the true one, that *at Rome* there was one ground of precedence for St. Paul (in respect of his special relation, as founder, to that Church), another ground of precedence for St. Peter, in respect of the special position which he occupied in the apostolic body. And so, according to varying circumstances, St. Peter at one time, St. Paul at another, would be represented as standing ἐκ δεξιῶν τοῦ Κυρίου, at the right hand of our Lord.

---

* The old traditionary usage asserts itself, in many instances, even in much later monuments.

And now, though after a long digression, I may return to the monument of which I first spoke, the Diptych of St. Paul. And I think you will admit that it is, at least, not an improbable supposition, that, in the monument before us, we have a record both of St. Paul's voyage to Rome (in the miracles of Melita), and of his subsequent occupation, at Rome, of one of the 'apostolic Sees ;' that while the apostle who occupies the 'throne' (the central figure of that upper group) is undoubtedly St. Paul, the bishop, who stands before him, is to be understood as representing Linus, the first Bishop of Rome; and lastly, that the figure behind the throne of St. Paul, that of one who holds in his hand, as does St. Paul, the 'scroll,' or roll of a book, which is the attribute of *an apostle*, is to be regarded as representing St. Peter*—sharer of the same apostolic

---

* These Essays have been written not without a hope that the evidence they allege upon disputed points may receive a candid consideration from some who may differ, and perhaps very widely, from the conclusions in support of which I write. Any such will be inclined to think that St. Peter *could not*, especially in a Roman monument (assuming that this is such), occupy such a position relatively to St. Paul as is suggested in the text. I will venture, therefore, to ask them to compare with this plate a representation of the Three Persons of the Blessed Trinity on an ancient sarcophagus, figured and described by an eminent Roman antiquary, P. Garrucci. Of the Three Persons one only is seated, and this, according to Garrucci's interpretation, is the Word of God; while He, whom G. identifies with the Father, *stands behind* the seated figure, much as does St. Peter (if such he be) in this diptych. The grounds of Garrucci's interpretation do not admit of being briefly stated. ['Dissertazioni Archeologiche di Raffaelle Garrucci,' vol. ii., Roma, 4to. 1865, p. 1 *sqq.*] Antiquaries acquainted with the treatise will have no difficulty in seeing the analogy between the explanation he gives of the peculiarities of that sarcophagus, and that which I have ventured to suggest for the diptych here described.

office with St. Paul, and united with him in counsel; but not, like him, the actual founder, under God, of the Roman Church, and the immediate head of its line of apostolic bishops.

Before passing on to yet another branch of my subject, I may mention, as strongly confirming the view here maintained as to the relation to the Roman Church of SS. Paul and Peter respectively, that there is a monument (unedited as far as I know), in the Royal Library* at Windsor, the peculiarities of which can only be accounted for, as far as I am able to see, on the hypothesis which I have already suggested. In an ancient mosaic there represented, the two apostles are figured, as usual, St. Paul on the right hand, St. Peter on the left, of our Lord. And while St. Paul holds in his hand the symbol (a roll of a book) which designated him as *an apostle*, St. Peter holds the martyr's 'crown,' or chaplet, which marked him out as one who had witnessed, by his death, for Christ. Now, as both these were alike apostles, both alike martyrs, what more natural explanation of this difference of designation, than that St. Peter's special claim to recognition at Rome was that

---

* In a collection of drawings originally made for Cardinal Albano, afterwards Clement XI. While speaking of this collection I may mention also, what will be of interest to many archæologists, both at Rome and elsewhere, that careful drawings, on a large scale, are there preserved of the famous mosaic of our Lord and the Apostles in the church of St. Pudentiana, showing the principal figures *as they were before the lower part of the mosaic was blocked out by the wood-work of the church*. The figure on our Lord's right hand (commonly interpreted of late as being *St. Matthew*) has the title PAVLVS inscribed near the feet. That on the left of our Lord, PETRVS, in a similar position.

of *his martyrdom;* while, in the case of St. Paul, the thought of his *apostolic bishopric,* so to call it, over the Church, was more prominent than that of the martyr's death, wherewith his life of labour was crowned.

I willingly allow, however, that, as against any clear historical notice, or any really primitive, general, and self-consistent tradition, inferences such as these would weigh very little. But when, as in this case, the traditions concerning St. Peter as specially the *Bishop* of Rome, first appear in the heretical compilation known in the 'Clementine Recognitions,' and then with a distinct party purpose in view; when the later traditions to the same effect (embodied* in the lists of Popes preserved by Anastasius) bear upon the face of them the marks of late concoction in support of the claims to primacy first, and afterwards to supremacy, put forth by the Roman Church; when, as is unhappily notorious, that Church, in support of these claims, had recourse (through ignorance, we may charitably believe) to decrees of the first Nicene Council, *as interpolated by Roman hands*—a falsification, which was at once exposed almost as soon as it was attempted; with all these facts in view, we may, without presumption, claim for these monuments, in their cumulative evidence, a weight far beyond what would attach to any one of them separately. If they fail to convince opponents pledged to a foregone conclusion (which no doubt they will fail to do), they will at any rate afford interesting and valuable indications of truth to all those (I trust and believe they are an ever-increasing number, both at home and abroad) who search into an-

---

* St. Jerome, however, writes to the same effect in one place.

tiquity with minds open to conviction, and with a single eye to the truth, and the truth alone.

I have dwelt upon these earlier monuments at greater length than I had intended, because of their great intrinsic interest. It may be well, however, to say, before quitting this portion of my subject, that in these arguments on the question, whether St. Paul or St. Peter were really the first 'Bishop and Apostle' of Rome, we, who argue against the claims of the Roman Church, occupy a position of almost unfair advantage, if we regard the matter as one of mere intellectual fence. For the debate is one in which, if we prove our point, our opponents have no longer a ground to stand upon. For the whole weight of the Roman position rests upon two assumptions; the first, that St. Peter had not only priority, and in some sense a primacy, of honour and dignity among the Twelve, but *had rule over them* as Christ's vicar upon earth ; and secondly, that he was also the first Bishop of Rome, and *conveyed* (according to Christ's ordinance) *his own* (primacy or) *supremacy* to his successors in that particular See. If, therefore, we show that there is no proof of St. Peter's having been Bishop of Rome at all, their superstructure falls at once to the ground.*
But even if we fail to show this, our opponents are scarcely any nearer than before to the establishing of their own point. For even if it could be conclusively proved that St. Peter, rather than St. Paul, was the true founder of the Roman Church, it does not at all follow that the priority or primacy, which, *in some sense*, has generally

---

* For the early traditions on this subject see Appendix (F) at the end of this volume.

been regarded as attaching to St. Peter, devolves, from him, upon all bishops of the Roman Church. If this primacy were hereditary the Bishops of Antioch must have, at least, as much right to primacy (or supremacy) as the Bishops of Rome; for tradition, which speaks of St. Peter as first Bishop of Rome, speaks of him no less clearly as Bishop of Antioch before he became Bishop of Rome.

And I may add, that the See of Alexandria claimed (as did Rome and Antioch) succession from St. Peter, through St. Mark. St. Gregory the Great expressly recognised this co-ordinate claim of Antioch and Alexandria; and when addressed by a Bishop of Alexandria (jealous of the encroachments of the 'New Rome' on the Bosporus) as being the true 'Universal Bishop,' he peremptorily refused such a title, and declared that any one who presumed to put forward such pretensions would, in so doing, *mark himself out as Antichrist.*

Petrus, or Peter, distinguished from 'Petra,' the Rock.

But it is time now that we proceed to other monuments which yet await our consideration.

And, first, I would refer to an interesting example of the way in which ancient monuments serve to illustrate ancient literature, and to confirm the conclusions to which that literature points. I need not do more than remind those present that, with a very few exceptions, the early Fathers are almost unanimous in interpreting the 'Rock' of Matt. xvi. 18, not of Peter personally, but either of Christ, the true Rock, on whom the Church is built up, or of *the faith in Christ,* as the Son of God, which Peter had professed. The letters of Paulinus, Bishop of Nola (late in the fourth, or early in the fifth, century), describe the mosaic decorations of his own churches; and by comparing his descriptions of those mosaics with actually existing works of art (mosaics and sarcophagi), dating from the time at which he wrote, we find that a prevailing type for the designation of our Lord was one of symbolic rather than of direct representation. He was represented, for example, in the 'Apse' of Paulinus' Church under the figure of *a Lamb, standing upon a rock, from which rock flowed four streams.* This rock is, to Roman archæologists always (as far as I have observed), a 'mountain,' not a rock; and to it, and the four streams thence flowing, they give various interpretations according to circumstances. '*Mount Zion, and the four streams which flow therefrom;*' '*the four rivers of Paradise flowing from the mountain, which designates the Church;*' '*the four streams, which issue from that one head of waters, over which Peter presides;*'* such are a few among the many interpretations that we meet with. But among all modern Roman controversialists I have never found any (and I should be greatly surprised to hear that any could be found) who gives the interpretation which Paulinus himself furnishes in his 'Epistola xii. ad Severum.' In that letter, describing a church which he had himself built and decorated, he says, 'that in the Apse (whether to be spelt Absis or Apsis he professes himself unable to say) there was a *camera musico illusa,* a vaulted roof, decorated with mosaics, and under this mosaic picture (evidently in three compartments, corresponding to the "trichora" of the

---

* So Dr. Northcote.

east end of his church) the following descriptive lines.' [I omit the two first sets of verses, not immediately to our present purpose.]

> '*Regnum et triumphum purpura et palma indicant:
> Petram superstat ipse Petra Ecclesiæ,
> Ex qua sonori quattuor fontes meant,
> Evangelistæ, viva Christi flumina.*' *

The 'Lamb, standing upon a rock' of the mosaic picture, is in the descriptive verse Christ Himself, the Rock of the Church, standing upon a rock; and the four voiceful springs thence flowing are the four Evangelists, the living streams of Christ.

St. Peter as the 'Moses' of the New Covenant, and St. Peter's Chair.

In Dr. Northcote's 'Roma Sotteranea,' a work already noticed at some length in the earlier pages of this volume, we have the advantage of seeing an epitome of all that the most learned Roman archæologists (and some of them are men of very great learning) have collected from the whole field of antiquity, in relation to the controverted questions which most concern the Roman Church. And I cannot help thinking it a very remarkable fact, that all the erudition of Padre Garrucci, the exact scholarship and unrivalled archæological knowledge of De Rossi, the patient and laborious investigations of Cardinal Pitra, should have found

---

* 'The Purple and the Palm are signs of royal estate and of triumph. Standing upon a rock is He who is Himself the Rock of the Church; and from this go forth four voiceful streams, Evangelists, the living Rivers of Christ.'

so little in the field of really primitive antiquity (in the first four, or even five, centuries) which will serve in any degree for an even seemingly solid basis on which to rest the pretensions of the Roman See, or to vindicate for Roman doctrine, such as it has now become, the suffrages of the great teachers of the Church in East and West before the decay of primitive learning.

Some evidence, however, in the field of archæology they have alleged in reference to the question now under discussion, and that of a kind which, to any who may not have made these questions a subject of special study, will probably appear at first sight entitled to serious consideration.

On fragments of ornamented glass (of uncertain date, and of uncertain locality, most of them), and on sarcophagi, or sculptured stone coffins, chiefly of the fourth and fifth centuries, we find, here and there, representations of St. Peter, with attributes which were evidently designed to indicate a special pre-eminence in him as compared with the rest of the Apostolic body. Such, for example, are two ornamented glasses* now in the Vatican, in which a figure, which we should naturally have interpreted as Moses striking the rock in the desert, is identified with St. Peter by the word PETRVS inscribed beside him; and again, in the sarcophagi of which I speak, there is this marked difference between the Christian sculptures there seen, and those of the frescoes in the catacombs, of which we have already had occasion to speak, that in many of the sarcophagi St. Peter† is

---

* Figured by Northcote, R. S., Pl. xvii. As to the date of these glasses, see note p. 16.

† See the engravings of these sarcophagi in Bosio and Aringhi R. S. As regards St. Peter they give the

singled out for representation by unmistakable allusions (such as the cock crowing beside him); and in one or two, *to him alone among the Apostles*, and in common only with our Lord, is assigned the 'virga potestatis,' the rod or staff, symbolical of *power.**

Nor is this all. This idea of St. Peter being the Moses of the New Covenant, occupying a place towards God's people under the New Dispensation like to that of Moses under the old—this idea finds support, not in the language of Bishops of Rome, in whose mouth it would carry little weight, as being alleged in support of their own claims, but in that of an Egyptian monk† and Presbyter, in no way interested (*so many would suppose*) in supporting any special claim to pre-eminence on the part of St. Peter.

---

following results:—He is represented together with St. Paul six times (but of these some are open to doubt); in the scene of the Denial (symbolised by the cock crowing), five times; his arrest, six times (one or two of these doubtful); as holding the rod of power, once. The contrast here presented with the older representations of the 'Scriptural cycle' in the Catacombs (in none of which is St. Peter specially designated) is very significant.

* Northcote, R. S., Pl. xix.; Bosio, R. S., p. 295.

† St. Macarius of Egypt, *circ.* 391 A.D. In his tenth Homily he writes:
—'In the times gone by, Moses and Aaron, having the priestly office (τὴν ἱερωσύνην ἔχοντες), endured many troubles. But Caiaphas occupying their seat (καθέδρα, or seat of authority, comp. Matt. xxiii. 2), himself persecuted and condemned the Lord. Yet did our Lord, out of honour to the priesthood (*i. e.* to the priestly office of Caiaphas), suffer it to be done [according to his word]. In like manner the prophets were persecuted by the Jewish people. Afterward Peter succeeded Moses, having had entrusted to him the new Church of Christ [in contrast this to the old *Church* that was in the wilderness] and the true priesthood. For now there is a baptism of fire and of Spirit [in contrast to the baptism in the cloud and in the sea " unto Moses "], and a circumcision which is wrought in the heart.' [S. Macarii Ægyptii Homiliæ, ed. J. G. Pritius, Lipsiæ, 12mo. 1693.]

All this sounds very *Roman* indeed to our ears when we first hear of it. But in point of fact, it is exactly what any one acquainted with the history of the two Sees of Rome and of Alexandria would have expected antecedently to find, in monuments, whether of art or of literature, *dating from the fourth and fifth centuries*. And the wonder is, not that two or three isolated facts such as these can be alleged, but that much more of like kind has not been discovered.

The explanation of the facts now alleged, and of much that would otherwise be inexplicable in the history of the Church from the fourth century onwards, is this. When, at Nicæa, in the year 325 A.D., the whole Church, both Eastern, Greek, and Latin, met together in representation, for the first time, at a General Council, and met again, some fifty years later, at Constantinople, questions of precedence and of privilege between the various 'Apostolic Sees' naturally arose, which it was necessary to settle. Constantinople, the 'New Rome,' had no claims whatever on ground of antiquity, or of Apostolic foundation, to take rank even on the same level with, far less to take precedence of, the ancient Apostolic Sees — Rome, Alexandria, Antioch, Ephesus. But if weight and importance in the Christian world, *as it then was*, were to be considered, as well as prescriptive dignity, there were two great cities which held first place in the whole Roman world (the οἰκουμένη), to which as the seats of empire, in East and West respectively, it was natural for a Council, held under Imperial auspices, to assign first place of precedence in the united Councils of the Church. Rome, as ennobled by the blood of Apostles, and being one of the Apostolic Sees, had a higher title to precedence in the eyes of Churchmen than any Imperial dignity could bestow; but had the advantage of combining both Imperial and Ecclesiastical claims. And she, therefore, clung to the style of 'Apostolic See,' which, by degrees, became ' *The Apostolic See;*' while Constantinople, whose claim to precedence, when first advanced, was really that of her *Imperial* position in the Roman οἰκουμένη, assumed after a while the title of the '*Ecumenic* See,'—a name which, when its true import was, ere long, forgotten, became a source of bitter strife between that Church on the one hand, and Rome on the other, *Rome being supported by those other Apostolic Sees which Constantinople had displaced.**

Bearing all these circumstances in mind we shall better understand the language of the famous Canons of the first and the second General Councils (Nicæa, 325, and Constantinople, 381 A.D.). In the first of these the ancient Metropolitan (and Apostolic) Sees were recognised in the

---

* This is well illustrated by a letter of St. Leo's (Bishop of Rome from 440 to 461), written in reference to the Council of Chalcedon and its Canons. He makes it matter of complaint that the See of Alexandria should have lost her privilege of second place (*secundi honoris privilegium*), and the Church of Antioch her dignity as the third See in Christendom. He adds:—
'Let not the rights appertaining to Provincial Primacy be violently done away; nor the Metropolitan Bishops be defrauded of the privileges that of old were established. Let not the See of Alexandria lose aught of that dignity which she attained *through the holy Evangelist Mark, the disciple of blessed Peter.* And let Antioch, too, maintain the rank which by the Fathers was assigned to her (*in paternæ constitutionis ordine perseveret*). [Quoted by Dupin, 'De A. E. D.,' Dissert. iv.] This standing alliance between Rome and the displaced Sees of Alexandria and Antioch, is perhaps the true explanation of a fact which has been the puzzle of Roman antiquaries and Ritualists, viz. that *at Rome* was celebrated, for many centuries, the Festival of *the See of St. Peter* (Cathedra Petri) *at Antioch*.

following terms (Canon Nic. vi.),—' Let the ancient customs hold in Egypt, and Libya, and Pentapolis, so that the Bishop of Alexandria have authority (ἐξουσίαν—jurisdiction) over all these; seeing that to the Bishop also that is in Rome this* is of established custom. In like manner, also, in Antioch, and in the other [eparchies] provinces, the privileges of the several churches shall be preserved.'

Τὰ ἀρχαῖα ἔθη κρατείτω, τὰ ἐν Αἰγύπτῳ καὶ Λιβύῃ καὶ Πεντα- πόλει, ὥστε τὸν Ἀλεξανδρείας ἐπίσκοπον πάντων τούτων ἔχειν τὴν ἐξουσίαν· ἐπειδὴ καὶ τῷ ἐν τῇ Ῥώμῃ ἐπισκόπῳ τοῦτο συνηθές ἐστιν· ὁμοίως δὲ καὶ κατὰ τὴν Ἀντιοχείαν καὶ ἐν ταῖς ἄλλαις ἐπαρχίαις τὰ πρεσβεῖα σώζεσθαι ταῖς ἐκκλησίαις· Καθόλου δὲ πρόδηλον ἐκεῖνο, ὅτι εἴ τις χωρὶς γνώμης τοῦ μητροπολίτου γένοιτο ἐπίσκοπος τὸν τοιοῦτον ἡ μεγάλη σύνοδος ὥρισε μὴ δεῖν εἶναι ἐπίσκοπον.

Such was the language of the Church in her first General Council. Little more than fifty years afterwards, the following new arrangement was made, having reference, evidently, to changes which had been brought about, and to dangers which had been experienced, in the meanwhile. The Second Canon of the Council of Constantinople is as follows : ' *Bishops having metropolitan jurisdiction* (τοὺς ὑπὲρ διοίκησιν ἐπισκόπους) *shall not interfere with Churches beyond their own border, nor bring confusion upon the Churches.*'

---

* 'This,' *i. e.* jurisdiction such as this over the comprovincial Churches, 'the Ecclesiæ Suburbicariæ,' as they were called (*suburbicaria loca* in the versio Prisca of the Nicene Canon). These Churches were those of the ten provinces comprised within the Diœcesis Romæ; viz. 1. Campania; 2. Tuscia et Umbria; 3. Picenum suburbicarium; 4. Sicilia; 5. Apulia et Calabria; 6. Bruttii et Lucania; 7. Samnium; 8. Sardinia; 9. Corsica; 10. Valeria. [See the authorities for this in Gieseler's ' Ecc. Hist.' vol. i. p. 431, note 3.]

Then, after mention of Alexandria, the 'East' (*i.e.* the Diœcesis Orientis) with Antioch as its head, 'the Dioceses' of Asia, of Thrace, and after reference to the Canons of Nicæa already quoted, the Third Canon adds: '*Yet the Bishop of Constantinople shall have precedence of honour* (τὰ πρεσβεῖα τῆς τιμῆς) *next after the Bishop of Rome, because of its being New Rome.*'

Exactly seventy years after this, at the Council of Chalcedon (A.D. 451), being the fourth General Council, a yet further step in advance was made good by the Imperial or 'Ecumenical' See, when (ἴσα πρεσβεῖα) equality of privilege and honour was decreed to the two Sees of Rome and Constantinople; yet with a concession of 'priority' to the older See.*

I have been making a long digression, but thus much was necessary in order to explain why it was that in the divisions by which the Eastern Churches were rent asunder, the see of Alexandria is constantly found in deadly feud with that of Constantinople, and as constantly appealing, not without effect, to 'Old Rome' for succour against her foe; and again how it is that at Alexandria (*deriving Apostolical foundation from Peter through St. Mark*) there is to be traced something of the same exaltation of St. Peter's privileges as at Rome itself.

I may add further, that we have clear evidence to show that the language of the Nicene Canon (quoted above, p. 86) was far from satisfying the ideas which the Roman Church even then entertained of their own right to a 'primacy' of honour and privilege. They put their own

---

° For fuller details concerning the Councils, see Appendix (D).

interpretation upon that Canon, and in their own Latin version headed the Canon itself with the superscription, or perhaps the marginal annotation, '*Ecclesia Romana semper habuit' primatum*,' or '*De primatu Romanæ Ecclesiæ.*' Before long, however, the Roman Canonists, having nothing but their Latin version of the Canons to refer to, came to think this inscription to be a part of the actual Canon of Nicæa itself, and as such quoted it, both in controversy with the African Churches, and afterwards at the Council of Chalcedon, in support of the Roman claims.

This falsification (which was probably quite unconscious in the first instance, the result of ignorance not of deliberate fraud, like many of the other falsifications with which the history of the Roman See abounds) was of course at once exposed at Chalcedon by the production of the genuine acts. But what, for our present purpose, it is of importance to note, is, that from the time of the first Council of Nicæa onwards, the Church of Rome was thrown on her defence, as it were, with regard to the position of primacy which she claimed, so that 'Peter,' and the 'succession from Peter,' would be constantly in the mouth of her Canonists—more particularly after the Council of Constantinople, and when the seat of *Empire* had been completely transferred to Constantinople.

These things being so, we see at once the reason why, *at Rome itself*, in the glass cups, which on other grounds we have had reason to assign (many of them at least) to the fourth and fifth centuries (some few of them perhaps to the sixth), we should find Peter occupying a very different position to any that was assigned to him in the earlier 'Biblical Cycle' (dating from before the conversion of Constantine): and why similar 'Petrine' developments are manifest in the sarcophagi, which are also, with few exceptions, to be assigned to the same period as these ornamented glasses.*

Bearing these things in mind we shall see, that the very few facts of archæology which Roman writers (as *e.g.* Dr. Northcote) can allege in support of Roman claims, amount to nothing more than proofs of what was already notorious, that the Bishops of Rome from the fourth century onward (even in the third we have traces of the same feeling) '*contended*,' to use the words of Firmilianus, that they *had succession from Peter*, and tried to found a claim thereupon, first to primacy, and afterward, as time went on, to supremacy in the Church. How utterly inconsistent with Roman ideas of *supremacy by Divine right over the whole Church*, is the language of those General Councils which I have quoted, I need scarcely be at pains to point out.

There is yet another matter to which great importance has been attached by some Roman Catholic writers, viz., the question of the antiquity or otherwise of the so-called 'chair of St. Peter,' preserved with great veneration at Rome. I will not enter upon the question at length, because now that the facts are ascertained (by the removal of its bronze covering, at the Pope's orders, in 1867), it is found to involve matter of purely archæological interest. It is *not* an Episcopal 'throne' or 'Cathedra,' such, for

---

* I adopt here, as probably the true explanation of this falsification, what the learned Gallican, Dupin, has suggested, 'De Antiq. Eccles. Discip.' Dissert. iv. p. 325.

example, as that assigned to St. Paul in the Diptych already figured, or in other early ecclesiastical monuments, but is a *sella gestatoria*, a kind of portable arm-chair, such as was used in old times as a mark of dignity by Roman Senators.

The original oak chair is very ancient, and it is adorned with ivory plates representing the labours of Hercules. If this be, as Roman archæologists contend, the material *Cathedra Petri* sometimes referred to by ancient authors (in some we read of a '*sella gestatoria*'), the conclusion would be one singularly in accordance with the view maintained throughout in this paper, viz., that the 'Cathedra' or Apostolic See (Sedes Apostolica) at Rome was really St. Paul's rather than St. Peter's. For in existing monuments we should have one (that lithographed above, Pl. iv.) showing St. Paul seated on an Apostolic throne, in the act of Benediction, and another, this much-talked-of 'Chair of St. Peter' proving to be (even if genuine) nothing more than a Senator's chair (a kind of sedan-chair) suited for out-door use.*

---

* A kind of fatality seems to attend upon Dr. Northcote and his co-editor as soon as they attempt to make controversial use of the archæological facts before them. Mr. Brownlow, who writes a Dissertation on this Chair of St. Peter, quotes two lines from a Poem against Marcion, 'usually appended to the works of Tertullian, and which from internal evidence clearly belongs to the third century.' *Hac Cathedra, Petrus qua sederat ipse, locatum Maxima Roma Linum primum considere jussit.* Mr. B., with a disregard of quantity, of grammar, and of lexicography, which is quite Pontifical (see above, p. 46), renders these words, 'In this Chair, in which Peter himself had sat, *he ordained Linus first to sit with him* [*as Bishop*] *established in Great Rome.*' What will De Rossi say of such scholarship as this, on the part of his English representative?

The Fresco of Cornelius Papa and St. Cyprian.

Quitting now this portion of my subject, I will ask your attention in the next place to another monument, of considerably later date, which I have had lithographed for the illustration of this paper.

Its outward appearance I need not describe, for you can judge of this yourselves. I have only therefore to state its history, and point out its subject. Its significance in reference to our present question will then be readily appreciated, without any detailed comment on my part.

The personages represented are St. Cornelius, 'Pope of Rome,' and his contemporary St. Cyprian 'Pope of Carthage.' I use these terms advisedly, as being at once historical and monumental. The first term, PAPA ROMANVS, was used officially even at Rome itself, as late as the middle of the ninth century. In the companion picture to this for example ['Vestiarium Christianum,' Pl. xxxi. representing S. XYSTVS of Rome, and a Bishop (probably 'Optatus') of some other See], this very title of Papa Romanus [*] is employed. And for other Sees I need hardly

---

[*] The word Papa (in some of the earliest inscriptions Pappa or Pappas) was originally a term of affection, equivalent to Father. So Furius Dionisius Filocalus, an artist employed by Damasus (*sed.* 366–384), speaks of himself as being *Damasi sui Pappæ cultor atque amator*. In another inscription (the Deacon Severus) we read of *Papa suus Marcellinus*. (De Rossi, 'Insc. Christ.' t. i. p. cxv.) St. Perpetua, in the Acts of her Martyrdom, addresses Bishop Optatus in the words '*Tu es papa noster.*' (Ruinart. 'Acta sincera,' ed. Paris, p. 92.) And in like manner both St. Urbanus, Bp. of Rome (Laderchi 'Acta S. Cæciliæ,' t. i. p. 12), and St. Antony, who was but a Presbyter (Mabillon, 'Analecta,' t. iv. p. 104), were both known to their own flock as '*Papa*

remind you, that the Patriarchs of Alexandria were as commonly designated by this title as the Patriarchs of Rome; and that the same word 'Papa' was frequently used in reference to Bishops of other less important Sees, as those of Carthage, Rheims, Lyons, and others.

But while the personages represented in the fresco before you are Bishops of the third century, the fresco itself (on the walls of the 'Catacomb' or cemetery of St. Callistus) dates* from the time of Leo III., the close of the eighth or early in the ninth century. I may note further, that the picture appears to have been a restoration, or rather if I may use the term, a palimpsest—traces of still earlier frescoes (probably of the same subject) being found by De Rossi under these, which he himself discovered only a few years ago. And with these few facts premised, I need only ask you further to observe, as bearing upon our present subject, that there being four Bishops represented in the two frescoes ('Vest. Christ.' Pll. xxx. and xxxi.), of whom two are Bishops of Rome, one a Bishop of Carthage, and the fourth a Bishop of some unknown See *other*† than Rome, *precisely the same costume and insignia are attributed to all the four.* In the monument before us, buried as it was beneath the ground for a thousand years, discovered

---

suus.' (Quoted by De Rossi, R. S. t. ii. p. 200.) St. Germanus, Patriarch of Constantinople (eighth century), speaks of Leo and of Vigilius as being ' Popes *of Rome*' exactly as does the fresco here in question. (Scti. Germani, etc., de Sanctis Synodis, ap. A. Mai, Spicil.)

* I adopt the opinion advocated by De Rossi, and, as I believe, now commonly received.

† The first letter of his name [O] remains on the fresco, and this, as De Rossi observed, is sufficient to show that it is *not* a Bishop of *Rome;* for no Bishop of Rome, from first to last, has borne a name of which O was the first letter.

by a Roman archæologist, published to the world under the auspices of the present Pope, as one of the first-fruits of the Cromolitografia Pontificia, we find preserved to us the record of a time, when, neither by title* nor by insignia, were Bishops of Rome distinguished from other Bishops, even when figured, as are these four, in a place of burial especially appropriated to the occupants of the Roman See.

Mosaics of the Triclinium Lateranum.

The series of Monuments figured next in order to that last described, are of the same, or all but the same, date as the last, in point of actual execution. But in another point of view there is a wide difference between them. For that last reproduced the ideas (probably also reproduced, with slight changes only, the actual artistic work) proper to four or five centuries before. But these that we now see, are a genuine embodiment of the ideas concerning 'Church and State,' the spiritual and the temporal power, which prevailed at Rome at the beginning of the ninth century.

In the woodcut given on the following page, I have fortunately been able to reproduce the most important por-

---

* In the official Cemetery of Bishops of Rome in the third century, we find such inscriptions as these:—**ANTEPWC EΠI**(σκοπος) **KOPNHΛIOC EΠICK**, and the like. And so Xystus III. (*sed.* 433–440), in an inscription put up by himself [in the church of S. Maria Maggiore: Ciampini 'Mon. Vet.' t. i. p. 203], describes himself as Xvstvs Episcopvs. For further particulars see 'Vest. Christ.' p. 218, note 448; p. 92, note 167; and for the title 'Pontifex Maximus,' n. 304, p. 146.

tion of these mosaics, in a shape more authentic* than any in which it has been published hitherto.

These mosaics were originally placed on the walls of the

Triclinium Lateranum, a great banqueting-hall (used also as a place of meeting for Roman 'Lateran' Councils) which

---

* The woodcut here given is from a coloured drawing in the collection of Pope Clement XI., now in the Royal Library at Windsor. For the history of these mosaics see Nicolai Alemanni De Lateranensibus Parietinis Dissertatio Historica, Romæ, 4to. 1625. To the eye of an archæ- ologist, one little matter of detail will at once mark out *Pope Clement's version* (so to call it) as the true one. The pallium worn by Leo III. is arranged *in the Greek fashion* in the genuine picture, but after a later *Roman* fashion in the same picture as edited by Alemannus. Note, too,

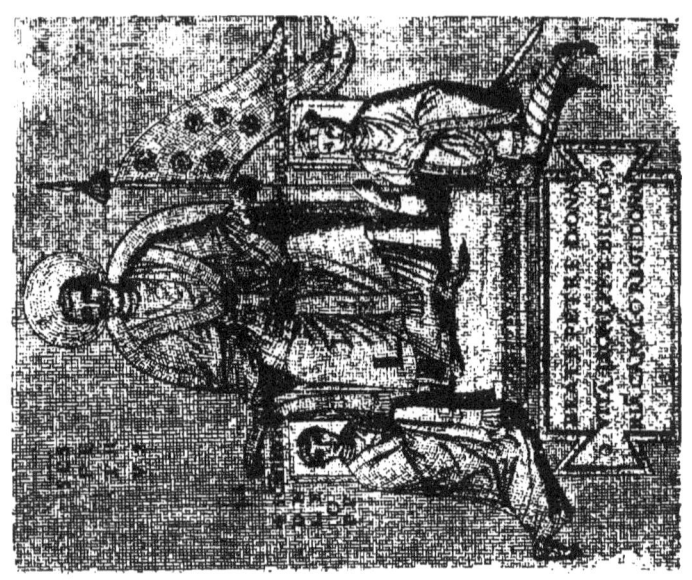

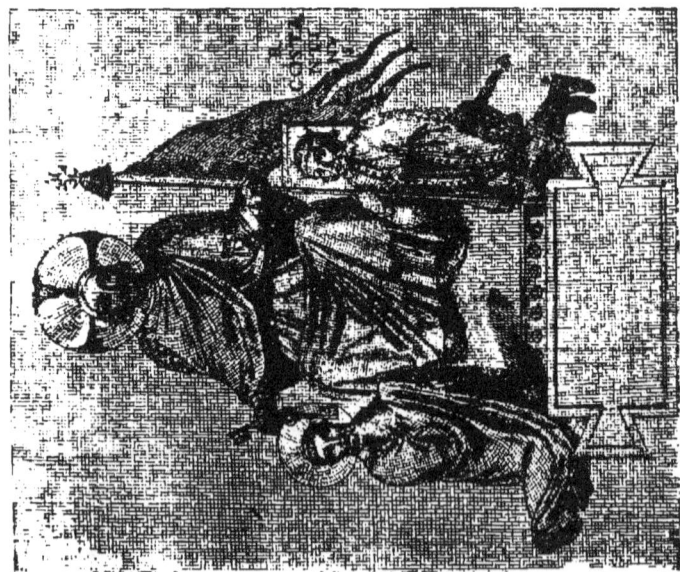

MOSAICS OF THE TRICLINIUM LATERANUM. 97

Leo III. built about the time of the Coronation of Charlemagne. Great portion of the building was restored later in the same century by Leo IV.—a small portion of the walls, and fragments (I believe) of these mosaics are still in existence. The general arrangement of the whole apse of the Triclinium is shown in 'Vest. Christ.' Pl. xxxii. ; the two most important groups, as represented by Alemannus, in Pl. vi. of this volume, and one of these again (containing what are probably contemporary representations of Leo III. and Charlemagne) in the woodcut above. The two groups of which I speak (Pl. vi.) tell their own tale. That on the *spectator's left* represents our Lord, bestowing with His right hand the keys on St. Peter (regarded as representative of the Roman Church), and with His left giving the 'Vexillum,' or standard of empire, to Constantine. In the group on the right St. Peter occupies the place corresponding to that of our Lord in the other. He is depicted (in accordance with Roman ideas at that time) as the representative through whom, under Christ, all power, both spiritual and temporal, was derived to the Roman Church; but whereas, at a later time, we shall find both these powers concentrated in the person of the Pope, *we have here their division recognised*, the pallium, as the symbol of ecclesiastical jurisdiction and of spiritual power,

---

that this last editor has thought it necessary to put *the keys* on the lap of St. Peter, while nothing of the kind appears in the other drawing. Of *additions*, such as this last, I find conclusive evidence in many of the Roman monuments, restored as they have been from time to time ; and each restorer, sometimes each editor, making slight but significant changes to suit the ideas prevailing in his own day ; and these more often (I fully believe) through inadvertence, and want of archæological knowledge, than from any deliberate or conscious misrepresentation.

being bestowed on Leo III., the vexillum, as the symbol of Imperial power, bestowed on Charlemagne. And it is in accordance with this distinction, that while the Emperor is here represented as wearing the *diadema imperii*, or Imperial crown, the Pope is content with the *corona sacerdotii*,* the tonsure, which he shared in common with other Priests and Bishops of his time.

Contrast this with the representations of a Pope (Eugenius IV.) in those monuments which stand last in the series before you below (Pll. viii. ix.), and you will see at a glance how rapid were the developments of the intervening centuries—how wide the interval which separates even the successful ambition of a Leo III. from the unbounded pretensions to universal sovereignty in things temporal and spiritual, put forth, and for a time successfully, by the later Popes, and now being claimed once more, to what result God knoweth, and God alone, by Pius IX. and the Roman Curia.

The Donation of Constantine.

The mention of this marked difference between the Papacy of even Leo III. and that of Hildebrand and the later Popes, leads us naturally to the mention of that wonderful instance of successful forgery, pregnant with results of untold importance to Europe, the false Decretals, which

---

* There is precisely the same distinction of insignia in other mosaics (believed by Ciampinus and others to have been contemporary pictures) in which Charlemagne and Leo III. appear together. There are coloured drawings of these in the collection of Pope Clement XI., photographs from which are in my possession.

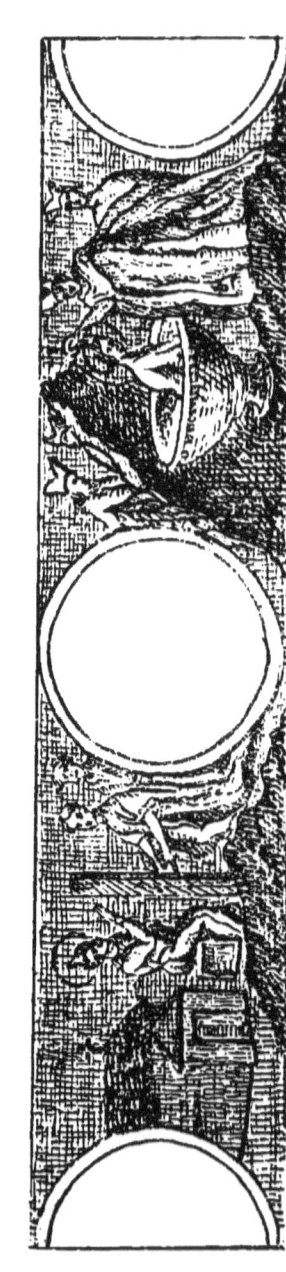

REX BAPTIZATUR ET LEPRAE
SORDE LAVATUR.

REX INSCRIPTURA SYLVESTRO
DAT SUA JURA.

bridged the intervening space. I have succeeded quite lately in finding, what I believe to be the only representation in mediæval art of the so-called ' Donation of Constantine ;' and this you will find reproduced, exactly as I found it, among the illustrations* before you. We are able to determine the date of this monument, on archæological grounds, with certainty, to a time *not earlier* than the twelfth century. The form of the mitres in the ' Baptism of Constantine ' is alone sufficient to determine this.

That among the innumerable monuments of Roman art dating from the fourth century onwards, some of which, as those of the Triclinium Lateranum just noticed, have direct reference to Constantine—that among these no reference whatever should have been made to a transaction so momentous, *if only it had been real*—that Anastasius again, who records all the offerings made by Constantine to the various churches in Rome, even to the number of the pounds weight of the candlesticks and other such things— that he, too, should know nothing of this 'Donation'— these two facts would alone constitute the strongest possible evidence of the utterly fabulous character of the whole story, even if other evidence were wanting. A work lately published,† and widely circulated both in this country and on the Continent, has entered so fully into the literary history of the forged Decretals, that it is unnecessary for me to enlarge upon that topic.

I pass on, therefore, to the last in the series of monu-

---

* This Plate (vii.) is an exact copy of that given by Ciampinus in his ' De Sacris Ædificiis,' Tab. ii., figg. 3, 4. The mosaics in question were upon the ' zophoros,' or frieze, of the Lateran Basilica.

† ' Janus.'

ments which I have to describe. And these, as they are the latest in date of those here figured, so are they also, to the shame of Western Christendom it must be said, a most conspicuous example of the habitual, and in this case it must be feared, the conscious and deliberate misrepresentations, through which, from the fifth century down to this present time, the pretensions of the Roman See have been maintained.

THE BASSI RELIEVI FROM THE GREAT GATES OF ST. PETER'S AT ROME.

The Pope's Supremacy, temporal and spiritual.

In describing these monuments I will first state briefly what are the subjects represented, and then point out, as concisely as may be, the gross misrepresentations of historical fact which are there embodied.

These four plates, then, give an exact picture of some of the principal relievi on the great bronze gates of St. Peter's at Rome. Their immediate subjects are sufficiently indicated by the titles printed under each—of one, the Coronation of the Emperor Sigismund; of the others, the principal events of the Council of Florence (previously of Ferrara), the first session of which was held at Ferrara on Wednesday, January the 8th, in the year 1438.* And the general idea which, evidently, it was intended herein to set forth, is that of the union in the person of the Pope, as God's vicegerent upon earth, of supreme power, *both temporal and spiritual.*

---

* Raynaldus, ed. ann. 1438, § 2.

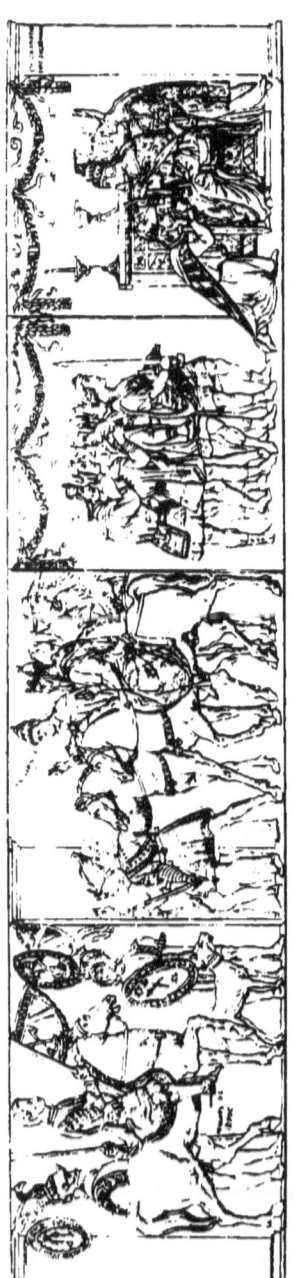

THE VOYAGE OF THE EMPRESS

Departure from Constantinople. The Reception at Ferrara

The Coronation of Sigismund.

His supremacy of temporal power is indicated in the scene of the Coronation of Sigismund, who kneels humbly, as you see, at the Pope's feet, to receive at his hands the Imperial crown, which it is for the Pope to bestow or to withhold, at his good pleasure. It is probable that this scene may not incorrectly represent* the submissive attitude to which the German Emperors had in the course of time been reduced. And a suggestive contrast for the ecclesiastical historian will be found, in comparing the scene here represented with that of the Coronation of Charlemagne by Leo III., as described by contemporary writers. One† of these tells us how, at the time of the coronation, 'Carolus more antiquorum Principum, a Leone Pontifice *adoratus fuit.*' And this *adorare*, though we are not to suppose with certain moderns that it expressed, necessarily, in ancient times, all that is implied in our own word to '*adore*,'‡ does here express the ceremonial kiss of *duty*, as distinct from the mere *osculari* of brotherly affection. Another old writer (quoted as above by Alemannus) has exactly hit the meaning of the term, when, versifying the words I have just quoted, he says : —

---

* It is worth noting, however, that representations such as these vary considerably, *according to the authority from which they proceed.* In French monuments, executed, I doubt not, under other than Papal auspices, a Pope may be seen officiating at the coronation of a King of France ; and there it is the King who sits, while the Pope stands.

† Auctor Annal. Franc. apud Alemannum de Lateran. Pariet. p. 76.

‡ See further on this word, Appendix (A) at the end of this volume.

'Post laudes igitur dictas et summus eundem
Præsul *adoravit, sicut mos debitus olim
Principibus fuit antiquis.*'

A 'Papa Romanus,' in the ninth century, thought it natural '*adorare*,' to give *the kiss of duty*, to the Emperor whom he had just anointed and crowned. Three centuries later, Popes had learnt to require from Emperors the menial services of a groom.

The Council of Florence.

But I must not linger on this portion of my subject, but go on to speak of the other monuments relating to the Council of Florence.

The first in the series is that which for our present purpose is of chief interest. In the larger portion of it, that on the *spectator's left*, we see the transit from Constantinople to Venice, and the landing of the Emperor (who wears the καμηλαύκιον, or peculiar shaded helmet of the Byzantine Emperors), and of the Patriarch Joseph, who is seen, in mandyas and cowl, immediately behind the Emperor. In this part of the plate there is nothing to call for special remark. But it is scarcely possible to conceive a greater concentration of direct misrepresentation of fact, within two or three square inches of space, than we shall find in the small portion of this plate which yet remains to be described.

The subject here represented is that of the formal reception by the Pope, at Ferrara, of the Greek Emperor and the Patriarch of Constantinople. And if we had no other evidence of what really happened than that which is here given us on the infallible authority of Eugenius IV.

(if anywhere careful of exact truth we might well suppose to be so *here*, in a matter affecting the whole constitution of the Church and of the Roman See, and the relations of Eastern and Western Christendom), the conclusion we should come to would be this. We should suppose (I have only to appeal *oculis fidelibus* for what I say) that the Pope was seated on his throne, wearing the triple crown of sovereignty in things of heaven, things of earth, and things under the earth—that the Greek Emperor then came humbly into his presence, that he left his own Imperial crown in the hands of an attendant, on entering the presence chamber, in token of humility, and in acknowledgment of the supreme sovereignty of God's earthly Vicar—and then bowed himself on one knee at the Pope's feet, as though to sue for the pledge of forgiveness, which the Pope, without rising from his throne, is graciously pleased to bestow. And while the Emperor thus acknowledges his superior in the person of St. Peter's representative, the Ecumenical Patriarch, as Joseph would have styled himself, is seen in attendance, standing humbly and expectantly, at the door of the presence chamber, till it shall please the spiritual monarch of the world to notice the humble Bishop who awaits his pleasure.

Such is the picture by which Antonio Filarete of Florence, at the command of Eugenius IV., has perpetuated, in unblushing bronze, the fictions of which an infallible Pope is capable. From Roman historians of the time (to say nothing now of the Greeks), we have full details of what really did happen on the occasions referred to; and these accounts prove conclusively that what actually occurred was *the exact opposite* of what is here represented, and that in every particular, from first to last, almost without a single exception.

What actually occurred was this. The Emperor reached Ferrara on the 4th of March. We may well imagine the endless questions of ceremonial etiquette which would have arisen, had a formal reception in public audience been given to him on this occasion by the Pope. And it would seem from the conflicting accounts of the Latins and the Greeks, that the diplomatists on either side must have come to the determination of avoiding altogether difficulties which they could not more directly surmount. A Roman Cardinal (Andreas à Santa Cruce) wrote as follows of what occurred :* 'On the 4th of March the Greek Emperor entered Ferrara with a large train on horseback. All the Cardinals then at Ferrara went to meet him, outside the city, accompanied by a large body of Prelates. The Emperor was conducted under a golden canopy to the Apostolic (Papal) Palace, and went on horseback up to the Pope's chamber, by a way which had been made in the Palace, in old times, by the Marquises of Ferrara. When he had duly paid his respects to the Pontiff (*exhibita Romano Pontifici debita* † *reverentia*) he was conducted in similar state to the Palace (known

---

* Raynaldi Annal. ad ann. 1434. No. 6.

† This is a conveniently vague term. Roman and Greek ideas of the amount of ceremonial reverence to be shown by an Emperor to a Pope would differ considerably. Palæologus, however, throughout (as was natural under the circumstances) was much more complaisant both in these matters of ceremony, and in matters of grave doctrinal importance, than were the Patriarch and the other Greek Bishops. In the authentic copy of the final Decree of the Council (now in the British Museum) *the Emperor alone* signs on the Greek side, the Pope and a host of Latin ecclesiastics on the other.

as " Paradise ") which had been prepared for his reception.' So speaks the Cardinal, describing, if I mistake not, the *intended* programme of the ceremonial. The Greek Phrantzes,* deriving his information from the Emperor's Brother, the 'Despotes' of the Morea, who was present on the occasion, gives the following account of what actually occurred : 'When the Pope heard that the Emperor had reached the gate, he rose, and *took a walk*, and as he was thus walking up and down (*spatia facientem*, apparently in the grounds attached to the Palace) the Emperor accidentally came upon him ; and when he would have fallen on his knees, the Pope would not permit him to do so, but embraced him, held out to him his right hand, and kissed him, and placed him at his left hand (*ad sinistram suam collocavit*).' All this, as Raynaldus observes, 'nonnihil discrepat' from the representation on the bronze gates of St. Peter's, that now before you. ' Visitur in æneis valvis basilicæ S. Petri, Eugenii jussu conflatis, efformata effigies, qua Pontifex ipse papali thyara redimitus, Imperatori nudo capite altero genu provoluto manum porrigit, *a quo nonnihil discrepat Phrantzes*.'

But the contrast between fact and representation of fact, which is not small in this case, is far more flagrant, and far more significant also, in regard of the Patriarch of 'New Rome.'

It had been arranged, as I have already said, by the Diplomatists on either side, that the Patriarch should make his entry four days after the Emperor. And as the whole question of the relative position of East and West, of Old and

---

* Quoted in Latin by Raynaldus, *ubi supra*.

New Rome, might have been seriously prejudiced by any unguarded concessions, in the matter of public ceremonial, on an occasion so remarkable as this, it was not only natural, but right, that the whole programme should be made matter of careful arrangement and concert between the two parties, or rather the two Churches, chiefly concerned. On all such occasions, as in the East from the remotest antiquity, so in the traditionary public etiquette of Western Courts, both in mediæval and modern times, one main point of ceremonial observance is that of the *going out to meet* persons of great dignity, at specified distances from the place in which they are actually to be received. The distance to which this 'Hypantesis' extends, and the rank of the high officials who form the procession, vary according to the rank of the person to be received. Hence it will be readily understood, that when an Emperor was to be received, the Roman Cardinals made no difficulty in going out to meet him, because in so doing they did but acknowledge, what even they were not prepared to deny, that an Emperor of Constantinople was a more exalted personage, in point of worldly dignity, than a 'Prince' of the Roman Church. But when they found themselves called on to go out to meet the Ecumenical Patriarch, a question of precedence was involved, which, to the Greeks at least, was not a mere matter of personal dignity, but of serious ecclesiastical importance. The view of the Cardinals was, that they were fully the equals of the Patriarch. But the latter, representing, as in some sort he did, the Eastern Churches generally in their relation to those of the West, was far from admitting any such equality. And upon primitive principles he was right in so doing.

Greeks, and other Easterns, who took their stand on the Canons of the 'most holy Ecumenical Synods' of the first eight centuries of Church history, could know nothing of 'Cardinals' as having any recognised precedence, as such, in the ecclesiastical hierarchy. To their eyes Cardinals were Bishops, Priests, or Deacons, as the case might be, holding various offices in the court of the Patriarch of 'Old Rome.' And it is evident that, at this period at least, at the first opening of the Council, the Greek Patriarch was determined to maintain the position conceded to his See in the Councils of the fourth and fifth centuries. According to Byzantine tradition the two Sees of Old and New Rome were of equal dignity in respect of their Patriarchal rights— and to New Rome in the East, as to Old Rome in the West, a primacy belonged, but with a concession of ceremonial precedence to the older See. To this view we find Joseph and his Churchmen adhering throughout these opening scenes of the Council. And it will be clear to you at once that the Patriarch would seriously have compromised his position, if by any public act he had recognised the Cardinals as his own equals. Had he done so, the conclusion would have been patent, that, in admitting his equality with Cardinals, he must be, by his own confession, *greatly the inferior of a Pope*.

These considerations will account for what took place on the occasion which is, I can hardly say *represented*, in the plate before you. The Patriarch had stipulated that all due formalities should be observed in the details of his reception. The proper officials were to meet him at specified places; and more particularly he required that the *Cardinals* should meet him outside the town, so as to escort him with due ceremony to the place where the Pope awaited his arrival. As to the Pope again, it had been arranged that he and the Patriarch should have precisely the same number of officials in attendance on them (they were limited to *six* each—'*ultra Cardinales*,' however, says Raynaldus). These and other details had been matter of concerted arrangement ('conventus') between the two potentates, and the Pope appears to have carried out his own part of the programme to the satisfaction of all parties. Not so the Cardinals. Their failure to perform their part caused a delay of a whole day in the proceedings. At the time that had been appointed for the Patriarch's solemn entry, Archbishops, Bishops, and other Prelates, were present in large numbers to meet him—the Marquis of Ferrara and his son were also in their place—but Cardinals there were none. What excuses, if any, were made for their absence, we are not told. But the Patriarch was determined to hold his own. He knew perfectly well what their absence meant, and he therefore quietly remained in the place he had then reached (the 'portus quo naves Ferrariam applicant'), refusing to enter Ferrara unless the programme of the ceremonial were properly carried out. The result was, that the next morning, 'by order of the Pope,' two Cardinals (*the two juniors, Deacons*, Raynaldus adds) were in attendance. They met the procession, but evidently in very ill humour; for Raynaldus tells us that they rode up, and without either 'bending their bonnets' to the Patriarch, or any other salutation of civility, said, '*Reverendissime Pater, Dominus noster Papa misit nos ut associaremus paternitatem vestram ;*' and then, putting themselves on either side of him, rode on into the city. The Pope remained seated, in a private chamber, till the Patriarch arrived, with the Cardinals placed (*constitutis*) at his right hand. The Patriarch was seated *in scabello*,* at the left of the Pope; and after a brief conversation he was escorted, with the same attendance as before, *the two Cardinals excepted*, to the palace assigned as his residence.

I have dwelt, in more detail than I could have wished, upon these matters, because I could not otherwise bring out, as clearly as the truth of history requires, the egregious misrepresentations of fact embodied in the monument before you. I need not, however, describe in detail the other plates of this series. What I have already said will be sufficient for the purpose now before me. I do not wish to add to the burden of the charges of forgery, interpolation, falsification of every kind, which attach to the history of the Roman See. As Christians ourselves, the shame of these things redounds in a measure upon us. The history of this Council would present only too suggestive a theme for reproach, if such were the object in view. For myself, in the present paper, I purposely confine myself to such points only as are directly suggested by the art-monuments on which I undertook to comment. But I will not conceal my opinion, that the circumstances of these our own days are such, even as regards our own Church, that it does become a duty to examine, without passion and without prejudice, but yet thoroughly, and, as far as may be, exhaustively, the grounds on which rest the claims now put forth on behalf of the Roman See.

---

* As to this, and other details of interest concerning the Council of Florence, see the original authorities quoted in Appendix (E).

One great difficulty in doing so is, that the personal history of many of the Popes from the ninth to the fifteenth century (one which is intimately connected with their claim to vice-gerency on God's behalf over the whole Church, and their infallibility), involves details so horrible, that it is impossible to reproduce them for general reading, even under the cover of a learned language.

But when we find that the more learned among the members of the Roman Church itself find themselves constrained to lay before the world the utter hollowness of these claims—when the abettors of those claims, instead of appealing, in answer to their opponents, to Scripture, to authentic History, to the text of Councils or of Fathers, can do nothing but declare, through an irresponsible tribunal (the Council of the Index), that the writings of those who question her infallibility or her supremacy are heretical, and to be shunned, under pain of excommunication, by all good Catholics—we have a virtual admission on the part of 'Romanists' themselves (I purposely use the term in its distinctive sense), that their claims do not admit of support, unless the calm judgments of historical truth can be suppressed, and the verdict thence resulting be drowned in the loud acclaims of an excited assembly. It may be that now at Rome, as in another great city 1800 years ago, the voice of Apostolic truth may so be drowned for awhile; it may be that in this assembly, of which as of that former one we read, that the 'more part know not wherefore they be come together,' all appeal to Scripture, to antiquity, to reason, may be overborne by a cry as false, and soon to be found as false, as that '*Great is Diana of the Ephesians!*' that was heard of old by the space of two hours. Men may, if so they will, stop their own ears against the voice of truth; but the time is past when falsehoods can be forced upon the belief of Christendom by dint of the acclaiming voices of a packed assembly. Let us pray Him, who is indeed the Head over all to the Church, who worketh out His predestined purpose through paths, and by instruments, that we men wot not of, that He will overrule, to the fulfilment of His own will, the counsels of rulers, whereinsoever they are against the Lord, and the blindness of peoples, whereinsoever they are in error; and that He will bless for good, as He alone can bless, every effort, however humble, for the promoting of His true kingdom upon earth, and for the restoration to a distracted Christendom of '*Peace through the Truth.*'

PART III.

THE AUTUN INSCRIPTION,

HAVING REFERENCE TO THE DOCTRINES OF

Baptism, the Holy Eucharist,

AND

The State of the Faithful after Death.

NOTICE TO THE READER.

The Dissertation that follows is a combination of Two Papers, one of which (relating exclusively to questions of Archæology) was read lately before the Society of Antiquaries; the other (as already mentioned) was written some few months ago, as an Exercise for the Divinity School at Oxford.

THE AUTUN INSCRIPTION.

CHAPTER I.

INTRODUCTION.

To few, if any, of those now present, need I make any apology for bringing under notice the exact representation, now in your hands, of the Inscription found at Autun thirty years ago. It is of exceptional interest, on many grounds, to the student of Christian antiquity ; and of its important bearing upon theological questions now, as for centuries past, debated in the Church, there have been some remarkable proofs, in quite recent times, among ourselves. If apology were needed at all, it would rather be for my own presumption in entering upon a task which, for the last thirty years, has exercised the ingenuity of some of the first scholars and most learned divines in almost every nation in Europe.

But in dealing with subjects such as these, the attainments of one generation form the starting-point of the generation that follows. And I should not feel that any labour I have bestowed on this particular monument were at all inadequately repaid, even were I able to do no more than to publish it with that perfect accuracy of representation which photography alone makes possible, and to bring under the notice of English students generally the results hitherto reached by those who have devoted themselves to its elucidation.

To some present the history of the Inscription itself may be unknown, or only imperfectly known; and it may be well, therefore, as a first step, very briefly to state what that history is.

It was found* in the year 1839, buried in the soil of an ancient cemetery, in the immediate vicinity of the town of Autun, once the capital of Gallia Æduensis. The modern name is an abbreviation of Augustodunum,† or 'Augustus Town;' a name which replaced the older Celtic name Bibracte, by which this place had previously been known.

The marble, some portions of which have perished altogether, is twenty-one inches in width, and half an inch less in length. The letters are as nearly as possible seven-eighths of an inch in length. There are marks on the back of the block, indicating that it was once fastened with iron clamps to the wall of some building. Dom. Pitra (now Cardinal), who at the time of its discovery was resident close by, in a seminary of which he was the Master, was the first‡ to make the Inscription known to the world. And

---

* For full particulars as to this, see Pitra, 'Spicil. Solesm.' i. p. 554.

† For the history of the town, ancient and modern, see the article 'Autun,' in Zidler's 'Universale Lexicon,' and the authorities there quoted.

‡ In the 'Ann. de Philos.' 2ᵉ sér. t. xix. p. 195, 1 Sept. 1839, with the initials 'L. T. C.' For later communications from the same pen, see ibid. 3ᵉ série, t. i. p. 165; t. ii. p. 7; t. iii. pp. 7, 85; t. v. p. 165; t. vii. p. 232.

from that time to this it has served as a subject for scholars, antiquaries, and theologians, and has now quite a literature* of its own, and that of the most varied character; Frenchmen, Italians, Germans, countrymen of our own, descending in succession into the field, whether for careful research, as some, or for the support of some pre-conceived opinion in matter of modern controversy, as others.

For myself I propose, first, to inquire, with all the exactness that I may, into the archæological history of the monument, and then to consider its bearing upon theological questions.

And as a first step in the investigation, it may be well to translate the Inscription itself into letters of more ordinary shape than those seen in the photo-lithograph now in your hands. In doing so, I confine myself to those parts of the Inscription which can with certainty, or all but certainty, be determined. We can better judge of the more doubtful readings, and of the purely conjectural restorations

---

* See particularly the 'Spicilegium Solesmense' (edited by Pitra), vols. i.–iii.; and to the various writers there quoted add Garrucci (Rafaele), 'Monuments d'Epigraphie ancienne,' Paris, 4to. 1856, 1857; F. Lenormant, 'Mémoire sur l'Inscription d'Autun' (' Extrait des Mélanges d'Archéologie '), Paris, 1855; J. P. Rossignol,' Explication et Restitution de l'Inscription Chrétienne d'Autun;' 'Revue Archéologique,' 13ᵉ année (1ᵉ série), Paris, 1856, p. 65 *sqq.* and p. 491 *sqq.* (this last being a bitter attack upon the treatise of Garrucci last mentioned); Kirchoff, in the 'Corpus Inscript. Græc.' tom. iv. No. 9890. The Bishop of Lincoln (Dr. C. Wordsworth), whose Dissertation on this monument is printed in the 'Spicil. Solesm.' t. i. p. 562, had not before him at the time an accurate representation of the actual text. After seeing a photographic copy of this, he has seen reason to withdraw some of the conjectural readings which he had suggested in writing to Dom. Pitra; and I hope to be able to add his last corrections in the Appendix to this volume.

proposed for the two last lines, when the whole history of the monument shall have been clearly set before us.

Ἰχθύος ο[ὐρανίου ἅγ]ιον γένος ἤτορι σεμνῷ
Χρῆσε * λαβὼν ζωὴν (or πηγὴν) ἄμβροτον ἐν βροτέοις
Θεσπεσίων ὑδάτων· τὴν σὴν, φίλε, θάλπεο ψυχὴν
Ὕδασιν ἀενάοις πλουτοδότου σοφίης,
Σωτῆρος δ' ἁγίων μελιηδέα λάμβανε βρῶσιν.
Ἔσθιε πινάων † (for πεινάων) Ἰχθὺν ἔχων παλάμαις.
Ἰχθύι χε . . . . ἆρα λιλαίεο δέσποτα Σῶτερ
ευ (or σu) . . . . τήρ σε λιτάζομε ‡ φῶς τὸ θανόντων.
Ἀσχανδῖε πάτερ, τῷ 'μῷ κεχαρισμένε θυμῷ
σὺν μ § . . . . οισιν ἐμοῖσιν
Ι ‖ . . . . . μνήσεο Πεκτορίου.

And the general meaning will be this :—

'Offspring of the heavenly Ichthus, see that a heart of holy reverence be thine, now that from Divine waters thou hast received, while yet among mortals, a fount of life that is to immortality.

---

* Either for ἔχρησε, or (as λιτά-ζομε for λιτάζομαι, in ver. 8) for χρῆσαι (1 aor. imp. mid.).

† First suggested by Garrucci (having a photograph of the text before him), and approved by Kirchoff, on the evidence of the same photograph. The older restorations (πῖνε λαβὼν—πῖν' ἀήρ—πῖν' ὑγίαν—πῖνε τεαῖν—πῖνε ἑνοῖν) are too long for the space to be filled up, and are open to objections on other grounds.

‡ For λιτάζομαι, by an 'Itacism' of frequent occurrence in epigraphic Greek.

§ Probably σὺν μητρὶ γλυκερῇ καὶ ἀδελφειοῖσιν ἐμοῖσιν (Franz), or σ. μ. γ. καὶ πᾶσιν τοῖσιν ἐμοῖσιν (Rossignol), or σ. μ. γ. σὺν τ' οἰκειοῖσιν ἐμοῖσιν (Pitra).

‖ Probably ἰχθὺν ἰδὼν υἷον μνήσεο Πεκτορίου.

Quicken thy soul, beloved one, with ever-flowing waters of wealth-giving wisdom, and receive the honey-sweet food of the Saviour of the saints.* Eat with a longing hunger, holding Ichthus in thine hands.'

'To Ichthus .... Come night unto me, my Lord [and] Saviour [be Thou my Guide] I entreat Thee, Thou Light of them for whom the hour of death is past.'

'Aschandius, my Father, dear unto mine heart, and thou [sweet mother, and all] that are mine .... remember Pectorius.'

With thus much said by way of introduction, we may proceed now to consider some preliminary questions, the solution of which is necessary to a right understanding, and the more complete restoration, of the Inscription before us.

And first, it will be well to state, in some detail, what were the ideas more particularly associated in the thought of Primitive Christendom with that Ichthus symbol which is so prominent in the monument before us.

---

* For ἁγίων Wordsworth reads ἁγ' ἰών, a reading which is adopted from him by Kirchoff.

† Assuming the reading to be λιλαίεο, *i. e.* literally, 'long thyself' (to me), and so 'let thine own love bring thee nigh.' See further as to this below, p. 137.

CHAPTER II.

THE SYMBOLISM OF THE WORD ΙΧΘΥC.

THERE are two ways in which we might seek to determine what this symbolism was. One, which would be a very interesting, but a very laborious way, that of examining in detail the various monuments of ancient Christian art, in which this symbol is employed. It would be impossible, however, even to attempt this within present limits. The other is that of referring to the statements concerning this symbolism, contained in the literature of antiquity. This latter source of evidence itself extends over an immense field,* but it admits of being at least summarily stated here.

In doing so, I will exclude all secondary and more far-fetched symbolisms, of which there are many, and confine myself to those which have a direct bearing upon our present subject. What we are now concerned with, for the elucidation of this Autun Inscription, is the application of this symbol of the Fish, first, to our blessed Lord, and, secondly, to Christian people generally.

---

* See more particularly the great collection of authorities brought together in the third volume of the 'Spicilegium Solesmense.' But these require careful verification, as they are not always accurately cited.

1. *The Term* IXΘYC, *or* '*Piscis*,' *in reference to our Lord*.

In the language of Christian writers, both in East and West, from the second century onwards, our Lord is spoken of as IXΘYC, as 'Piscis,' 'Piscis noster,' and the like, and that for a variety of reasons.

First, in respect that the fish, blessed on more than one occasion to the feeding of great multitudes, or of His own Apostles (John, xxi.), by our Lord while on earth, was regarded as a type of that heavenly food, His body offered on the Cross, which He gave for the life of the world.* And, according to the mystical interpretation of Scripture adopted by many of the Fathers, the 'broiled fish,' together with a piece of honeycomb, of which our Lord partook with His Disciples after His resurrection, was regarded as a type of Christ Himself, in regard of His passion, when by the fire of tribulation He was, as it were, 'scorched.' This thought, which we meet with first in Melito of Sardis [*Piscis in mensa cum favo mellis positus Christus tribulationis igne assatus*], gave rise to the catchword, so to call it, of this symbolism, '*Piscis assus, Christus passus.*' †

---

* Compare the word spoken by our Lord Himself (John, vi. 51), 'The bread which I will give (*i.e.* as the context implies, which I will give *to* men) is my flesh, which I will give *for* (ὑπὲρ, *in behalf of*) the life of the world.' And again (Mark, xiv. 24, coll. Luke, xxii. 20), ' This is my Body, which is given for you' (ὑπὲρ ὑμῶν, *on your behalf*). 'This is my Blood of the New Covenant, which is shed for you' (τὸ ἐκχυνόμενον ὑπὲρ ὑμῶν, *poured out on your behalf*).

† St. Augustine in Joan. Evang. Tract. cxxiii. '*Fecit prandium Dominus illis septem discipulis suis, de pisce scilicet quem prunis superpositum viderant, huic adjungens ex illis quos ceperant, et de pane . . . . . Piscis assus, Christus passus. Ipse est et panis qui de caelo descendit.*'

Secondly, inasmuch as fish was, in primitive times, very generally in use as an ordinary article of food, as a savoury* accompaniment to the bread, which in some form or other formed the chief staple of food, so under the figure of fish, as well as under that of bread, early writers not unfrequently designated the wholesome doctrine of Christ, and particularly the words of truth contained in Holy Scripture.†

Thirdly, when the practice of figuratively‡ designating our Lord as ΙΧΘΥΣ, or Piscis, had become established, it was not unnatural to connect this thought with that of birth (*i.e.* new birth) in water. The earliest example of this is the well-known passage in Tertullian (De Bapt. c. 1), 'We smaller fishes, after the example of our Fish, are born in the waters, and it is only by continuing in those waters that we are safe (continue in a state of salvation). *Nos pisciculi secundum Piscem nostrum in aquis nascimur, nec*

---

* Compare St. Augustine, 'Duo pisces *qui saporem suavem pani dabant.*' De Div. Quæst. lxi.

† So St. Jerome on Matt. xiv. 17. (Opp. t. iv. p. 60); and again (ibid. t. vii. p. 119), 'In septem panibus et pisciculis Evangelii sacramenta' (*i. e.* mystical types of the Gospel of Christ). Pseudo-Eusebius Emissenus (In Domin. vii. post Pentec. *apud Spic. Sol.*), 'Septem panes, septem libri sunt Veteris Testamenti, quos heptateuchum vocamus; pauci vero pisciculi, pauci libri Novi Testamenti.' Clemens Alex. 'Strom.' lib. vi. (p. 786, ed. Potter.), speaks of the fishes and barley loaves as typi-

fying the προπαιδεία, or preparatory teaching, of Greeks and Jews. And St. Cyril Alex. (In Joan. vi. tom. iv. p. 283), speaks of our Lord as feeding unto life eternal them that believe on Him, with divine and heavenly teaching, both that of the Law, and that of the Evangelists and Apostles. So St. Ambrose (In Luc. ix. No. 80, tom. i. p. 1403, ed. Benedict.), 'Plerique septiformis Spiritus gratiam in panibus definitam, in piscibus quoque duplicis testamenti figuram intelligendam putant.'

‡ Comp. Origen in Matt. (Opp. ed. Bened. tom. iii. p. 584), Χριστὸς ὁ τροπικῶς λεγόμενος Ἰχθύς.

nisi in aquis permanendo salvi sumus.
This is curiously illustrated by the Episcopal Ring, here engraved (twice the size of the original), which belonged to St. Arnulf, Bishop of Metz, in the sixth century.*

Lastly,† Christ Himself, in respect both of His divine and of His human nature, was mystically signified in a way that none but Christians could understand; in reference, not now to fish as mentioned in Holy Scripture, or regarded as a spiritual food, but to the letters, of which the Greek word ΙΧΘΥC is composed, and which form the initials of the titles specially belonging to our Lord, 'I-ησοῦς Χ-ριστὸς Θ-εοῦ Υ-ιὸς Σ-ωτηρ, Jesus Christ, Son of God, Saviour.

2. *The* ΙΧΘΥC *Symbol applied to Men.*

The second of the symbolic usages for the 'fish' of early Christian writers, which we have to consider, is its application to men generally,— to the faithful for one reason, and through one line of association; to the unfaithful and unworthy for another.

---

* See Pitra, 'Spicil. Solesm.' t. iii. Tab. iii. n. 4.

† I speak of this as last in order, because it appears to me, on examination of all the evidence, that this acrostic symbolism was not the foundation out of which all the others sprung (as some eminent archaeologists have held, and as theologians, not being archaeologists, have commonly assumed), but was a comparatively late invention (probably of the Alexandrian schools), founded upon the older accepted symbolisms already attached to the fish in literature and in art.

It will suffice to mention this last, without dwelling upon it in any detail, as this application is one which in no way pertains to the elucidation of the monument before us.

But with the other we are directly concerned. For in the very opening line of the Inscription, we find that either baptized Christians in general (according to one interpretation), or more particularly the Apostles and other teachers of the Divine Word, are spoken of as 'the [holy] offspring of the heavenly IXΘΥC;' in other words, as being themselves ἰχθύες, or, in the language of Tertullian, '*pisciculi*,' in respect of the new spiritual life of which, through Christ, they have become partakers.

The very earliest writer who treats *ex professo* on the allegorical meaning of Scripture, Melito of Sardis (*circ.* 150 A.D.), furnishes us with an authority for this application of the word, and shows on what passage of Holy Scripture this allegorical application was more especially based. 'Fishes,' says Melito,* 'are the holy ones of God : *Pisces Sancti.* For so it is written, " *Traxerunt rete plenum piscibus magnis.*"' John, xxi. 11.

Some of the Fathers even make the symbol, in this sense, more comprehensive still, applying it to mankind generally, as when St. Gregory of Nazianzum speaks of our Lord as having chosen the fishermen (the Apostles), in order that they might bring forth man, the fish, out of the deep (ἵν᾽ ἐκ βάθους τὸν Ἰχθὺν ἀνενέγκῃ τὸν ἄνθρωπον). And so St. Maximus of Turin : '*Palpitantes pisces vivificandi homines.*' Sermo xcvi. (Quoted by Pitra.)

---

* Melito, 'Clavis,' xl. 2. Elsewhere (cap. xii. n. 25) he refers to the same : ' Centum quinquaginta tres—*omnes electi.*'

The language of Tertullian speaking of the baptized as '*pisciculi*,' 'smaller fishes,' in respect of their new birth in the waters of baptism, has been already quoted (p. 122). With this agree some few passages in later writers; as, for example, St. Hilary,[*] St. Optatus,[†] and St. Augustine,[‡] to name no more.

3. *The Symbolism of this Monument.*

The passages now quoted, and the various usages of the IXΘΥC symbol here enumerated, will suffice for the illustration of the monument before us, in which we have both the acrostic IXΘΥC in the initial letters of the five first lines; then, the personal application of the term to our Lord (as in ver. 1); a similar application to Him considered more particularly as the spiritual food whereon they feed, for the sustaining of the new life, who have

---

[*] Hilarius in Matt. ed. Benedict. p. 677; a passage which contains the same thought by implication. 'Ex hominum arte futuri eorum (*sc.* apostolorum) officii opus proditur, ut piscibus e mari, ita hominibus deinceps e sæculo, in locum superiorem, id est, in lumen cælestis habitaculi protrahendis.'

[†] S. Optati Milev. de Schism. Donat. lib. iii. cap. 2. 'Hic (*sc.* Christus) est piscis qui in baptismate per invocationem fontalibus undis inseritur, ut, quæ aqua fuerat, a pisce etiam piscina vocitetur. Cujus piscis nomen secundum appellationem Græ-

cam in uno nomine per singulas literas turbam sanctorum nominum continet, IXΘΥΣ, quod est latinum *Jesus Christus Dei Filius Salvator*.'

[‡] S. Augustini Confessionum lib. xiii. c. 23 (Migne, tom. i. p. 860). ' Homo . . . . accepit potestatem piscium maris . . . . approbat quod recte, improbat autem quod perperam invenerit: *sive in ea solemnitate sacramentorum quibus initiantur quos pervestigat in aquis multis misericordia tua, sive in ea qua ille Piscis exhibetur quem levatum de profundo terra pia comedit.*'

already, through Him, received new birth of the spirit (so in ver. 6); while in the first line either the Apostles (as some think), or the baptized generally (according to the interpretation above followed), are spoken of as 'born of Ichthus,' *i.e.*, as having received new birth from Christ.

With thus much premised for the explanation of the terms employed in the Inscription before us, we proceed now to further matter which yet remains for discussion.

CHAPTER III.

DATE OF THE INSCRIPTION.

WHAT has been said hitherto by way of introduction will suffice as a first step towards the determination of some more debatable questions, connected with the monument under our consideration. And among these we may consider first that of the date to which it may probably be assigned.

There are three main sources of evidence to be relied on in determining these :—the surroundings of the monument itself, considered in reference to the history of the place in which it was found; the palæography of the Inscription, in other words, the form and arrangement of the letters employed ; and, lastly, the internal evidence afforded by style of composition, and by the symbolical language employed.

1. *Local History.*

The surroundings, first, of the monument, and the history of the place in which it was found.

It was discovered, as we have already said, buried in the soil of an ancient cemetery, in the immediate vicinity of Autun. There are some interesting facts connected with the history of this town, which it is of importance to bear in mind in reference to our Inscription. This city was distinguished, I may first say, by a peculiarly Greek culture; and of this there is proof, even to this day, in the fact that Greek words are still preserved in the local dialect of that town and neighbourhood, which are wholly unknown elsewhere. Of this there is a remarkable instance in regard of the very cemetery of which we are now speaking. This is known, locally, not as a cimétière, but as *polyandre*, *i.e.* πολυάνδριον.

And to this last fact I would ask your special attention, as it is one out of many concurrent circumstances which serve to the determining of the true date of the Inscription. The fact itself, curiously enough, was commented on some thirteen hundred years ago by St. Gregory of Tours, in a passage which has utterly puzzled both editors and readers. St. Gregory had himself visited this very cemetery of which we are now speaking, and in referring to it ['De Gloria Conf.' c. 73], he says, that this *cœmeterium* was called by a *Gallic name*, because '*the bodies of many men were buried there.*' '*Cœmeterium Gallica lingua vocitavit eo quod multorum hominum cadavera ibi funerata sint.*' People naturally asked themselves, in reading this passage, what this could possible mean. The purpose of all cemeteries alike being, that '*the bodies of many men*' may be buried in them, it was difficult (nay, more than difficult) to say why a 'Gaulish' name should have been given to this cemetery, because of this not very surprising fact. But all becomes clear when we find that in the local dialect of this town, even to this day, this particular cemetery is known as 'polyandre,' that is, the Greek πολυάνδριον, a place, literally, '*of many men*.' This is interesting in a philological point of view; but I venture to think that there lies wrapped up in this a valuable historical indication of importance to our present purpose. For what is the distinction between the two words κοιμητήριον and πολυάνδριον, between the place of *rest*, as in sleep, and the '*place of many* (men) *bodies?*' The distinction is significant in itself, and of import to our present purpose. The first, 'the place of peaceful rest,' is the *Christian term*, unknown in this sense to classical writers, while the latter word, πολυάνδριον, the 'polyandre' of Autun usage for 1800 years or more, is a classical term,[*] of which, *with this one exception*, there are no traces to be found in Christian language. And how, then, are we to account for this exceptional occurrence? Simply by this, that this ground had been the site of a *Pagan*[†] burial-place long before it was devoted

---

[*] It is interesting to find in the exact meaning of the word an explanation of the word ἄνδρες (*viri*) entering into the composition of πολυάνδριον, rather than ἄνθρωποι (*homines*). The πολυάνδριον was not an ordinary burial-place, but one in which, after a battle, or other the like occasion, a number of grown men (ἄνδρες) were buried.

[†] This is known to have been the case. See Lenormant, 'Mémoire,' &c., p. 1, n. 1. 'Ce Polyandre, *d'abord occupé par les paiens*, était devenu dès les premiers siècles du Christianisme un cimitière chrétien.' Pagan inscriptions have been found there, testifying to the fact.

to Christian use, and consequently had its Pagan designation already assigned to it, and sanctioned by long usage, at the time of its transfer to Christian hands. But when can this transfer have taken place? Surely not till after the public recognition of Christianity by Constantine. True it is, that, even in the three first centuries, Christian communities took advantage of Roman law giving facilities for the purchase of land by '*collegia funeraticia*' (nearly our 'Burial Clubs'), and were enabled thus to obtain land of their own for the purposes of Christian burial. But it is scarcely conceivable that a Pagan burial-place should have been *transferred* to Christian hands till after the public recognition of Christianity by Constantine, early in the fourth century. The earliest historical notice of the place, that of Gregory of Tours, in the sixth century, is such as to confirm the conclusion to which these considerations point. For he mentions, almost in the same breath, two Bishops of Autun; one being Reticius, who was a contemporary of Constantine, and died early in the fourth century; the other Cassianus, who died *at the close* of that century. And as he records ('De Gl. Conf.,' 74, 75) the fact of his seeing in this cemetery the tomb of *Cassianus*, but says nothing of that of Reticius, we have here again a fact which, at any rate, exactly fits in with what I have already suggested.

These facts, then, as far as they go, all point to the conclusion that no Christian Inscription, such as that we are now considering, could have been put up in the 'polyandrium' of Autun before the fourth century, and probably the latter half of it at the earliest.

This conclusion will be further confirmed by what we know of the fortunes of the Church at Autun before 'the

Peace' of Constantine. There is no evidence of the existence of Christianity, either here, or in other parts of Gaul, before the arrival of Irenæus and his companions at Lyons. Cardinal Pitra, indeed, assumes (as Roman traditions, I believe, make it proper for him to assume) that the Gospel was preached there by Roman missionaries before 'Greek Christianity' (as they speak of it) was introduced by Irenæus and others from Asia Minor. But he gives not a particle of evidence in support of his assertion. And I believe that in point of fact there is no such evidence to be produced. M. Lenormant, who alone has given any special notice of the town and its history, says decidedly, that the Church was established *for the first time* in the city of Autun subsequently to the preaching of St. Irenæus and his followers. After the Martyrdom of St. Irenæus, terrible persecutions were directed against the churches of Gaul, during which Christianity was almost extirpated in Gallia Æduensis. In the middle of the third century, however, there was a brief period of peace, during which SS. Saturninus and Dionysius (the St. Denis of the French), and five other Bishops, restored the faith in Gaul. And it was then that Autun received her first Bishop, St. Amator. But this peace was not of long duration. Heathens and Christians alike suffered terribly at Autun in the latter half of the third century, during the peasant wars of the Bagaudæ. Tetricus besieged the town, took it after a prolonged resistance, destroyed many of the public buildings, and inflicted injuries upon the place from which it did not recover for many years.

With the accession of Constantius Chlorus, in the year 292 A.D., to the rank of Cæsar, and to the government of the provinces of Spain, Gaul, and Britain, a happier era dawned. Autun, the ancient capital of Gallia Æduensis, became a royal residence, and received many and substantial marks of Imperial favour. The wise and merciful policy of Constantius Chlorus averted from Gaul the horrors of the Diocletian Persecution. But up to the very time of the Peace of Constantine, we find conclusive evidence of the public maintenance, at Autun, of the old Pagan worship.

At this period, just before the conversion of Constantine, while Christianity was protected at Autun, but not formally recognised, M. Lenormant,[*] an eminent French critic, believes that this monument was erected.

When you have heard the further evidence yet to be adduced, you will, I think, be of opinion that yet a hundred years more, at the least, should be subducted from the age which he assigns to this Inscription, before we shall arrive at what is probably its true date.

2. *Palæographical Data.*

In saying this, I refer more particularly to the evidence of date afforded by the palæography of the Inscription itself, – the conclusions to be drawn from the form, the size, the arrangement, of the letters.

---

[*] Mélanges, &c., p. 21. He names the year 350 A.D. *as the latest* to which it can be probably assigned, and evidently inclines to the very beginning of the fourth century as its true date (compare p. 24): his chief reason apparently being this— that the '*disciplina arcani*' était encore en vigueur et encore nécessaire.' For a refutation of this argument see Rossignol, 'Explication,' &c., p. 101; and compare what is said in the appendix, in the notes on this paper.

The question now mooted is one upon which no one should venture to pronounce an opinion, who has not made Greek epigraphy a special subject of study. For this reason I shall appeal here exclusively to the opinion of experts; and these I will state in the order in which they became known to myself.

i. Cardinal Pitra, who with a pardonable enthusiasm for a monument which he may claim as specially his own discovery, has from the first contended* for a very early date, between the years 160 and 202 A.D. And in support of his opinion he alleges Franz, one of the editors of the 'Corpus Inscriptionum Græcarum.' He quotes him as saying (what in point of fact he really does say) that the monument dates from the close of the second century, or the beginning of the third. Till I had an opportunity of referring to Franz's own treatise, I attributed great weight to this opinion. But on reading this, I found that Franz expressly says he had not the means of forming any judgment upon the question of date on palæographical grounds (the very questions on which he, as presumably an expert

---

* 'Tria sunt in primordiis ecclesiæ Augustodunensis intervalla satis distincta; primum enim illac, uti et per cæteras Gallias *ignoti quidam apostoli romani* fidei semina jecerunt. Deinde græcorum Patrum Pothini et Irenæi asseclæ, præeuntibus tantis ducibus. Divi Johannis disciplinas ex Asia secum in Galliam attulere; postremo, ineunte sæculo III., truculenta cæde Irenæi et suorum cum immenso jacentis ecclesiæ Lugdunensis luctu patrata, tandem missi a Romano pontifice novi apostoli, tertia quasi vice, Christum in Galliis disseminarunt. Inde liquet medium tempus totum esse nostrum, neque aliud quærendum; quod scilicet inter annos CLX. et CCII. continetur. Qua quidem tempestate vix dubium vixisse auctorem inscriptionis nostræ, quem Græcum fuisse, vel ab Asia oriundum ex sermonis elegantia et quodam Asiaticæ scripturæ charactere, conjicere par est.'

in such matters, would have spoken with authority), and that he judged solely from the character of 'the little poem,' which, as he truly says, is a remarkable example of the language proper to the '*disciplina arcani*.' In short, Franz has simply taken for granted the historical data put forward by Cardinal Pitra ; and his opinion has nothing whatever to do with palæographical evidence, as he himself is careful to state.*

ii. Wishing to obtain the best opinion upon this question, I sent a photographed copy of the Inscription to Mr. C. T. Newton, the keeper of Greek and Roman antiquities at the British Museum, whose authority in questions of classical epigraphy, at least, no one would dispute. I knew that if he were not as much at home amid these comparatively late Inscriptions of Christian Gaul as he has shown himself to be with those of Cnidus and Halicarnassus, and other Greek cities, he would have at hand in Mr. Franks one whose knowledge of all questions of archæology is second to none that, in this country at least, could be named. And I asked him to give me his opinion of the date of the Inscription I enclosed, *having regard solely to palæographical data*. Not long after I received his answer. He told me that he had examined the Inscription very carefully with Mr. Franks, and they believed it to be of the fourth century, or perhaps of the fifth. He added, that after they had formed their own opinion on the question I had put to them, they turned to the fourth volume of the 'Corpus Inscriptionum Græcarum,' in which this Autun Inscription is edited (No.

---

* Christliches Denkmal von Autun. Berlin, 1841.

9890), and found that an almost exactly similar opinion * was there expressed by Kirchoff, the editor of that volume.

iii. M. Fr. Lenormant, a well-known French antiquary, was the first, as far as I am aware, who entered carefully upon the investigation of the palæographical evidence. And upon this particular question he expresses † himself as follows : ' L'allongement des caractères onciaux que nous remarquons dans l'inscription de Pectorius, règne partout dans l'écriture grecque soignée du vi^e siècle ; moins abondant au ve il est très rare au ive, et reste complétement étranger au iiie excepté dans le dernier quart, et cette seule observation suffirait pour ne pas faire monter plus haut le *titulus* d'Autun.' Writing in the year 1855, M. Lenormant speaks of his having put forth this expression of his opinion some time previously, adding that his judgment had been endorsed by the most eminent French authorities on ques-

---

* ' Ætatem tituli finibus satis certis circumscribere licet. Neque enim aut Irenæi temporibus haberi potest antiquior, quibus Græca Christianorum sacra primum ex Asia illata sunt Galliæ, neque recentior barbarorum incursionibus, quæ factæ sunt sæculo post Christum quinto medio. [*He refers here, no doubt, to the invasion of Gaul by the Huns under Attila, in 451 A.D., when Autun is said to have been sacked. But the victory at Chalons drove back that invading swarm very shortly afterwards.*] Jam quum litteratura lapidis nullum prorsus servet veteris consuetudinis vestigium, verum tota sit recentis notæ et noviciæ [*Kirchoff had an accurate photograph before him*] certum mihi quidem videtur, et extra omnem positum dubitationis aleam, titulum referendum esse ad seculorum post Christum quarti vel etiam quinti tempora.'

† Mélanges d'Archéologie, t. iv. Paris, 1855. The earliest treatise to which he refers is a ' Note sur un Amulette Chrétien conservé au Cabinet de Médailles,' in tom. iii. of the ' Mélanges d'Archéologie,' p. 156. The palæographical data on which he relies are stated partly in the one volume, partly in the other.

tions of epigraphy and palæography. What Kirchoff's opinion was ('*tota recentis notæ et noviciæ—nullum prorsus servat veteris consuetudinis vestigium*') we have already seen (note *, p. 134).

iv. M. Le Blant, who agrees with M. Lenormant on the question of the date to be assigned to this Inscription, is obliged to admit that it contains the germs of all the deviations from older usage, in point of epigraphy, which characterise the monuments of the fifth and sixth century.

v. M. Rossignol* is the last writer whom I will cite. He sums up a very able (yet unduly severe) critique on this Inscription, in the following terms : ' Les fautes de tout genre, que nous y avons relevées, et qui accusent à la fois l'ignorance de l'orthographe, de la syntaxe, de la propriété des mots, de la métrique et de la prosodie, obligent sans contredit à le refouler vers un âge d'extrême décadence. Nous n'hésiterons donc pas, et cela sans craindre qu'on nous oppose le moindre des signes qui se tirent de la paléographie, nous n'hésiterons pas à descendre l'inscription chrétienne d'Autun, quatre siècles environ plus bas que ne l'a fait Franz, c'est à dire jusqu'à la seconde moitié du vi^e siècle ; et nous ajouterons qu'après êtra arrivé là, si nous

---

* Revue Archéologique, 13e année, 1856, p. 65 *sqq*. Explication et Restitution, &c., par M. Rossignol, Membre de l'Institut. Compare his letter to Padre Garrucci, in the same volume, p. 491 ; and Garrucci's answer, in his ' Mélanges d'Epigraphie,' already quoted. I think it but right to quote this opinion, although it differs greatly from my own estimate of the literary and poetical merit of the lines before us. Those who wish to study this particular question more fully, cannot do better than refer to the discussion (a very bitter one, unfortunately, but of great literary merit) between M. Rossignol and Padre Garrucci, in the treatises already named.

pouvions éprouver un scrupule, ce serait d'avoir fait tort à l'époque plutôt qu'à l'inscription.'

3. *Internal Evidence of Date.*

Assuming now on the concurrent authority of the eminent archæologists I have quoted, confirmed as their opinion is by historical probabilities, that the true date of this Inscription is about the year 400 A.D., or, at any rate, not earlier than this time, a question will occur to most antiquaries, the answer to which will lead us to a field of most interesting inquiry, which I believe to present an almost virgin soil for archæological investigation.

The question of which I speak is this. On examining closely the language of this Inscription, and regarding it merely as a specimen of Greek composition, there are three salient facts which at once attract our attention. Two of these we might well expect, but the third is one very difficult to account for at first thought. That the doctrines implied in this Inscription should be identical with those implied in the teaching of our Lord and of His Apostles, this will not surprise the student of Christian antiquity. That those doctrines should be expressed in a form which bears a strong impress of the influence of Irenæus upon the Christian terminology of the early Gallican Church, this again will excite no surprise to any who have made a study of his great work, the 'Treatise against Heresies,' and who knows with what honour his name was cherished, not in Gaul only, but very widely throughout Christendom, even as early as the fourth century of our era. But what might well excite great surprise is this further remarkable fact, that while the *thought* of this Inscription is Scriptural and Patristic, yet that which is most prominent in its *language* throughout is its thoroughly Homeric character. One half line (the close of the ninth, τῷ'μῷ κεχαρισμένε θυμῷ) is taken straight from Homer, who uses it in the 'Odyssey' certainly (δ. 71), and, if my memory does not mislead me, in the 'Iliad'* also, not unfrequently. Such words, again, as θεσπέσιος (for the Scriptural θεῖος or οὐράνιος), ἄμβροτος for ἀθάνατος, μελιηδής, λιλαίομαι, take us at once to Homer. The word μνήσεο too, in the last line, for which there is no grammatical authority whatever, is formed, evidently, upon the analogy of characteristic forms in Homer, such as ὄρσεο, βήσεο, δύσεο. But the most interesting proof of familiarity with Homeric diction has yet to be noticed. The happiest conjectural emandation of the text of the Inscription was one to which M. Rossignol was led by his recollection of a very peculiar, and wholly exceptional, use of the word λιλαίομαι in the Eleventh Book of the 'Odyssey.' Many who hear me will recollect the passage. It is one in which Ulysses holds converse with the shade of his mother in Hades, and she bids him return to the light of day, φόωςδε τάχιστα λιλαίεο, literally '*long thyself* to light.' In thought of this, M. Rossignol conjectured that for the form ΛΙΛΑΙѠ (a mere solœcism) which had been given by all the former Editors, we should read ΛΙΛΑΙΕΟ, after the example of that φόωςδε λιλαίεο ('*long thyself* to light') of Homer. He had not a photographic copy of the Inscription to refer to at the time, nor had he seen the original; but on subsequent comparison with Garrucci's photograph he found this conjecture

---

* E. 243, 826; K. 234; A. 607; T. 287.

strongly confirmed. I will not now dwell upon this point in further detail; but experienced epigraphists will see at once, that the stone (as represented in the photograph before you) presents peculiar indications which strongly confirm this conjecture. What I would rather point to now is the beautiful application thus made of an exceptional Homeric form, for the expression of a wonderfully deep thought. Pectorius, in the Inscription before us, uses this term in addressing our Lord, praying to Him, as in the moment of death, or rather as in the confidence of death already passed. And he invokes His presence beside him with a word which, more beautifully than any that could be named, suggests that *drawing nigh* of Christ, which is but another term for the *yearning* of His love, and the saving presence of His power, to them that seek for Him in the hour of their need.

Time will not allow of my dwelling now in detail upon other evidence. The writer of this Inscription, be he who he may, must have had a command of the Greek language far beyond what we should have had reason to expect at a period so late as the beginning, or the middle, of the fifth century. There is an intuitive refinement, for example, in his choice of tenses (as *e.g.* between the present imperative and the aorist imperative, the present and the aorist participle), such as could only be expected in one who had either mastered the Greek language by very careful study, or had inherited a knowledge of it, as it were, by birthright. One fault of prosody there is in the third line, which would not pass uncorrected at Eton in our own day, though it did so at Autun some 1500 years ago. But for two other peculiarities which would strike most modern scholars as utterly strange and wholly indefensible, there is more to be said (in palliation, at least, if nothing more) than would at first thought be supposed. The writing λιτάζομε for λιτάζομαι, and making the final syllable short before φῶς, would have entailed upon some of us in our boyhood very disagreeable consequences. But those who have made a study of epigraphic Greek, know that no irregularity is more common than this substitution of a short final ε for a short final αι— the fact being that in monumental epigraphs, both Greek and Latin, *the spelling of words was determined by their actual sound when pronounced*, more than by conventional rule, or grammatical precept. In this way the mistakes in spelling (mistakes, when judged by the practice of the professional grammarians, whether of ancient or of modern times) are full of interest to the philologist. And I venture to think that a fault so glaring (from a scholar's point of view) as λιτάζομε φῶς τὸ θανόντων, at the end of an hexameter line, is to be taken as an indication that the Greek of the writer of this Inscription came to him through the ear, and not through the eye only; that he was familiar with Greek as an actually spoken language, as well as with the Greek of the 'Tale of Troy Divine,' and the story of him who 'looked upon the cities of many men, and came to know their mind.'

But this I will not insist on. The only question to which I am really concerned to furnish an answer is this: How are we to account for Greek so good as this (make what deductions you will from its merit on account of faults) in the centre of Gaul, as late as the fifth century, or even the fourth, of our era? The answer is a very curious and interesting one, specially interesting to me as an Eton master, and to others present (as I think) who are Eton or public-school men.

In saying this I allude to the fact that Autun was, in the earlier centuries of our era, a 'French Eton,' to use a phrase which we have lately heard—a place of education for the 'golden youth' of Gallia Æduensis. The topic is a tempting one, but I must not enlarge upon it here. For my present purpose it is enough to say, that we have distinct evidence of the existence of this school, and of its restoration to new vigour under Imperial auspices, at the beginning of the fourth century. And as from that time the country was at peace till the year 451 A.D., when this part of Gaul (and Autun itself) was overwhelmed, for a while at least, by the invading hordes of Attila, we cannot doubt that throughout that period, if not afterwards, this school was still maintained. It had been famous in old times as a school of Greek learning; and this monument is of itself, I think, a sufficient proof of the continuance of the old studies—of Homer more especially—and of the up-building, upon that basis, of those great truths of the Christian life, which find expression in the monument before us.

CHAPTER IV.

EXTERNAL APPEARANCE OF THE MONUMENT.

THERE is yet one more particular to be noticed in the monument before us, and this will complete its archæological history, with which alone we are now concerned. I will ask you to observe for a moment the outward appearance presented by the marble, as far as you can judge of it from the photograph before you.

One thing will, I think, at once be noticed as worthy of special attention, viz., that at the lower portion of the marble, on the *spectator's right*, and, to a smaller extent, on the left also, a blank space has been left, and that with evident design, many of the letters being greatly crowded in consequence. For what purpose this space was left, I do not think any one will have much doubt, who has studied the monuments of the first four centuries, and has observed how frequently inscriptions have beside them either an Orante figure, or a 'Good Shepherd,' a bird, a fish, or other symbolical representation. The letters of Paulinus of Nola, written about the close of the fourth, or the beginning of the fifth century, show us, that, both in baptisteries and in churches, in his time, the practice obtained, *of combining pictures in fresco or mosaic, with descriptive verses immediately adjoining them* (see, for an example, the lines quoted above,

p. 83). And the Roman catacombs furnish us with more than one example of a combination of the ΙΧΘΥC symbol with a sepulchral inscription, much such as that which I believe to have been exhibited on this monument when first put up in memory of the young Pectorius. Take, for example, the following, found in the cemetery of St. Priscilla.*

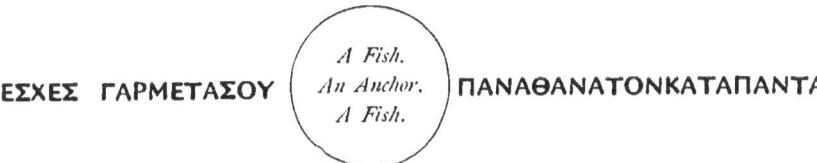

ΜΑΡΙΤΙΜΑ CΕΜΝΗ ΓΛΥΚΕΡΟΝΦΑΟCΟΥΚΑΤΕ ΑΕΨΑC †

ΕCΧΕC ΓΑΡΜΕΤΑCΟΥ *A Fish. An Anchor. A Fish.* ΠΑΝΑΘΑΝΑΤΟΝΚΑΤΑΠΑΝΤ/

ΕΥCΕΒΕΙΑΓΑΡCΗ ΠΑΝΤΟΤΕ CΕΠΡΟΑΤΕΙ

Μαριτίμα σεμνὴ γλυκερὸν φάος οὐ κατελείψας
ἔσχες γὰρ μετὰ σοῦ παναθάνατον κατὰ πάντα
εὐσέβεια γὰρ σὴ πάντοτέ σε προάγει.

Holy Maritima, thou didst no[t] leave the day's sweet light; for thou hadst with thee Him who knows n[o] death : for thine own godliness eve[r] leads thee on.

In the midst of these words, in the place indicated above, there is an anchor, with a fish on either side, significant, perhaps, of the presence of Christ, on the right hand and on the left, as our sure and certain hope (anchor) in death as in life.

But *what was the symbol represented on this Autun marble?* Not a fish only, if I mistake not; but a mystical

---

* Corpus Inscr. t. iv. No. 9687.
† So on the stone. Κατελείψας is. of course, the word intended. In the third line, ΠΡΟΑΤΕΙ is written in like manner, by mistake, for ΠΡΟΑΓΕΙ.

representation, we may at least reasonably conjecture, such as may be seen on this woodcut. For the existence of later monuments, such as those here figured, containing a modification of the ordinary Ichthyography so very peculiar as this is, can hardly be accounted for, except on the supposition of their being reproductions of still older

monuments, executed at a time when Christian art was still inventive, was adopting and modifying, for the expression of her own ideas, the older types of art which she found ready to her hand. As at Rome the 'Shepherd' and the Orpheus of earlier Greek art, had been adopted, and with slight modifications made available to Christian symbolism, so what more natural than that in these half Greek cities of 'Rhodanusia' (Rhone land, or the Valley of the Rhone),* connected as these were, through Marseilles, with the commerce of the East, an Eastern symbol should be adapted in like manner, and the Fish-god of the  Phœnician and the Syrian coast, such as he is here represented, be modified into a type such as we see exhibited on the columns of St. Germain des Prés, the exact reproduction in art† of the poetical description, and verbal symbolism, of the Inscription with which we are at this moment occupied?

Thus far I had written, a week ago, when preparing the present paper. But as I wrote it, and compared the Fish-god, such as you see him in the woodcut (No. 1) before you, with the descriptive lines of the monument itself, and with the remarkable embodiment of them which you see in yet another (No. 2) of those in your hands, I could not help feeling that a link was still wanting for the completion of the chain of presumptive evidence (I could not then claim more for it) for the existence, in the fourth or fifth century of our era, of precisely such a type as that exhibited on those St. Germain pillars. I had a strong conviction that a variation on the ordinary Ichthus type, so absolutely unique as that before

---

* So I venture to interpret the Ῥοἴονουσία (? Ῥοἴανουσία) of St. Irenæus, adv. Hær. lib. i. c. xi.). Compare the article on this word in Smith's 'Dict. of G. and R. Geography,' in which this reference is wanting.

† Woodcut No. 2 (p. 143) is here given on the authority of Cardinal Pitra, 'Spicil. Solesm.' tom. iii. Tab. iii. No. 6 A.

you, could not have been an *invention* of Christian art in the interval between the fourth century and the thirteenth, or indeed an invention of Christian art at all. For, in going back even to the very earliest period to which this can be traced, we find that Christian art was not *inventive*, but *adaptive*; selecting, among the older types of Pagan art, those which were in any way fitted to the expression of Christian ideas, and giving them, if I may be allowed the expression, a baptism of regeneration, in transferring them from their service to the kingdom of this world to a new service in the kingdom of Christ. Thus it was with the Orpheus of the earliest Christian catacombs, gathering around him even the wild beasts of the forest by the constraining attraction of his heaven-taught strains, and so not an unfit representation of Him who spake as never man spake, and whose voice has power, such as sweet music has, to touch even the hardest hearts. And so, again, the Hermes Criophoros, such as Pausanias[*] describes him at Tanagra, whether personified, as he was, in the yearly festival, by some tall youth, the choicest among many, who bore upon his shoulders the firstling of the year's flock; or in the marble of Calamis, in which the same type was embodied, never again to be forgotten—the one and the other were regenerated, nay, endowed with immortality, when adopted as the expression of that tenderest word of our Lord,—' I am the Good Shepherd' (John, x. 14); and of that parable which tells of him who, losing one out of a hundred sheep, leaveth the ninety and nine, and goeth after that lost one, until he find it; and when he hath found it, *layeth it on his shoulders rejoicing* (Luke, xv. 3–6).

---

[*] Pausaniæ Hist. lib. ix. c. 22.

With facts such as these in mind, I suppose there are few archæologists who would not agree with me in thinking, that one might count with some certainty on finding, among the older Pagan types, the counterpart of that, which is implied, indeed, by the Inscription now in your hands; but which survives to our own time in one monument only (I believe) of the whole Christian world, viz., in those pillars from the Baptistery of St. Germain des Prés, one of which is engraved in the woodcut now before us. (See No. 2 above.)

Where then, or in what direction, was one to make search for the symbol in question? It is unlike anything in the later Greek or Roman art, and at the first glance is suggestive of an Eastern origin—ultimately at least, if not immediately, of the East. But what in common between any cities of the East, and Autun in the centre of Gaul? A double connexion there was, though, antecedently, one might little have anticipated it. Connexion first, and a direct connexion, with the old course of Phœnician trade. But this is too remote in time to be relied upon with any certainty in relation to our present inquiry. But that line of trade, following the course which the nature of the country had prescribed, was in the fourth century, and is now, what it was in the days when the tin of the Cassiterides Insulæ was carried on the backs of mules down from the Sequana to the Rhone, and thence floated down to Massalia. Remembering this, it was natural to make a step further, and to anticipate, that, upon the coins either of Massalia itself, or of the Greek cities of Asia Minor, with which the Massaliotes traded, would be found the peculiar Ichthus-type of which I was in search. The question was easily to be answered, or rather an answer was easily to be obtained. I made application at the Coin Room of the British Museum; and though neither the coins of Marseilles, nor those of Phocæa, the mother-city of Marseilles, gave me what I was in search of, yet among those of Cyzicus, which was the great trading-city of Asia Minor in early Christian times, I found the exact type, dating from five hundred years at the least before the Christian era, which we have already seen reproduced, in Christian symbolism, in the word-painting of our Autun Inscription, and in the pillars of St. Germain, one of which (p. 143) is also before you.

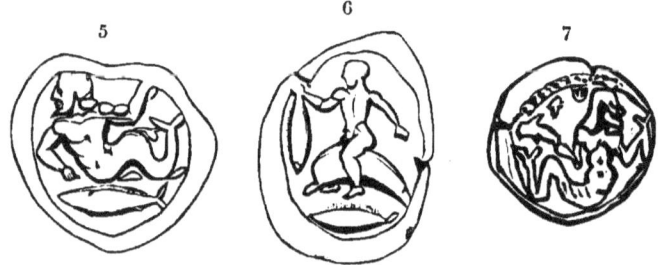

I said '*the exact type*,' but spoke somewhat inaccurately in so describing it. For in one very suggestive particular a slight change was made, when the old Pagan type was adapted to Christian use. That type, in its earliest form, was of the East, and an embodiment probably of some form of the ' Dagon ' or ' Fish-God ' worship. Possibly, however, it may have been, even in Phœnician hands, what it afterwards became when adopted by the Greek trading cities on the coast of Asia Minor—a symbol (and a very natural one in this last case) of a seafaring people engaged in commercial pursuits, and for whom the fish, which the Greeks exported to all parts of the Mediterranean coast, formed an important article of their trade. With this agrees the comment of an ancient writer* as to the virtues and the significance of gems, who says that 'a figure of a woman holding (a bird and) a fish is significant of trading business.' But the fish so held was a *dead* fish, as you may see by the Cyzican coins I have engraved (above, p. 147). But the Fish of the Christian monument before you, even as the 'Ιχθύς of the lines we have been interpreting, is the living Ichthus, in clinging to Whom we are uplifted (see No. 2, p. 143) to light and to new life, when the dark waters have, in all semblance, closed for ever over our heads.

In view of all these facts I think you will be of opinion, that the monument before us, if we could see it now as once it was, would be found to present a combination of symbolic representations, and of verses having reference to that symbolism. We should see probably, what on the columns of St. Germain, and on those old coins before you, we actually see, a figure represented as *combining two natures*, half Ichthus and half man, and him, τὰς χεῖρας

---

* 'Cethel, aut Veterum Judæorum Physiologorum de Lapidibus sententiæ.' (Apud 'Spicil. Solesm.' t. iii. p. 335.) This treatise, though a manifest imposture, is of ancient date, and has preserved, apparently, some floating traditions which might otherwise not have reached us. [It *professes* to have been written by a contemporary of Moses and Joshua, who, however, finds no difficulty in describing gems that belonged to Alexander the Great and Galen, and who derives his own Hebrew name from a Latin word!] The words to which I refer in the text are, 'Quando invenitur in Chrysolitho femina habens in una manu avem, in altera piscem, valet ad negotiandum.'

ἀραρότα, 'with hands close clinging' to a living Ichthus; while on the other side, if I mistake not, we should see a figure, some such as that in this woodcut* (No. 4), in which the combination of an Ichthus and a chalice are at once suggestive of yet another of those primitive symbolisms which I enumerated at the beginning of this paper, and to which there is a manifest allusion in the sixth line of the Inscription. And if we translate the Inscription before us, not only out of Greek into English, but out of the language of a now almost forgotten symbolism into that of Scripture, to which our own ears are more accustomed, this, I think, will in some sort give expression to the mind of him who wrote them—wrote them, there is strong reason for believing, on the tomb of a youth nurtured in that great Christian school already alluded to, and speaking, as in the name of the departed, to those whom he had left on earth.

4

'Ye that have received new birth from Christ, and mortal yet yourselves have now, from heavenly waters, a spring of life that is to immortality, see that a heart of holy reverence be yours. Refresh thy soul, beloved

---

* A small figure, in metal, preserved at Autun, and dating, Cardinal Pitra says, from the eleventh century. See 'Spicil. Solesm.' t. iii. Tab. iii. n. 5.

one, with ever-flowing waters of enriching wisdom, and receive the honey-sweet food of the Saviour of the saints. Eat, with a longing hunger in thine heart, holding in thine hands that Food which was given for the life of the world.

'On Christ I have laid hold, to Christ I cling. Let the yearning of Thy love bring Thee nigh unto me, my Saviour and my Lord. Haste Thee unto me, and be my Guide, I beseech Thee, Thou that art the Light of them for whom the hour of death is passed (θανόντων).

'And thou, my Father Aschandeius, endeared to my heart (thou, too, sweet mother, and all I love on earth), oft as you look upon yon holy sign of Christ, so often think of me, Pectorius your son.'

ΙΧΘΥΟC οὐρανίου ἅγιον γένος, ἤτορι σεμνῷ
Χρῆσε, λαβὼν ζωὴν ἄμβροτον ἐν βροτέοις
Θεσπεσίων ὑδάτων· τὴν σήν, φίλε, θάλπεο ψυχὴν
Ὕδασιν ἀενάοις πλουτοδότου* Σοφίης,
Σωτῆρος δ' ἁγίων μελιηδέα λάμβανε βρῶσιν.
Ἔσθιε πεινάων ΙΧΘΥΝ ἔχων παλάμαις.

---

* Another rare word occurring in this inscription (viz. πλουτοδότης) takes us to the Ἔργα καὶ Ἡμέραι of Hesiod (ver. 125), who employs it in a remarkable passage, to which I can well imagine the ἀρχιδιδάσκαλος of the Autun school directing the special attention of his boys. The heroes of the golden age, he says, when death, like a sweet sleep, had come upon them, became, so Zeus had willed, δαίμονες ἐσθλοί—ἐπιχθόνιοι, φύλακες θνητῶν ἀνθρώπων· οἵ ῥα φυλάσσουσίν τε δίκας καὶ σχέτλια ἔργα, ἠέρα ἐσσάμενοι, πάντῃ φοιτῶντες ἐπ' αἶαν, πλουτοδόται· καὶ τοῦτο γέρας βασιλήϊον ἔσχον. See the suggestive Scholia on this word in Gaisford's 'Poetæ Min. Græci,' t. ii. p. 121.

ΙΧΘΥΙ χεῖρας ἄραρα· λιλαίεο δέσποτα Σῶτερ
Εὐθύ* μοι ἡγητήρ, σε λιτάζομε, φῶς τὸ θανόντων.
Ἀσχανδῆ πάτερ, τῷ ᾽μῷ κεχαρισμένε θυμῷ,
Σὺν μητρὶ γλυκερῇ καὶ πᾶσιν τοῖσιν ἐμοῖσιν,
ΙΧΘΥΝ ἰδὼν υἷου μνήσεο Πεκτορίου.

CHAPTER V.

THE DOCTRINAL IMPORT OF THE INSCRIPTION.

I HAVE devoted the main part of this inquiry to the archæology of this Inscription, because it is only when this is determined, and the true text (or what remains of it) ascertained, that we can proceed with any certainty to draw conclusions from the evidence before us in reference to disputed questions of theology.

It is with pain and repugnance that I deal with such a monument in its bearing upon matter of modern controversy. It seems to me, I confess, something like desecration to put side by side in the same page the beautiful

---

* A comparison of my own photograph with that of Garrucci, which was taken (from a cast) fifteen years ago, leads me to think that EY CY (εὖ σὺ) must have been originally inscribed on the marble. But εὐθύ is better suited to the context, and recalls the λιλαίεο τάχιστα of the Odyssey (see p. 137). Other critics have fancied the third letter of this line to be a mutilated Ο, and I have therefore adopted (though with some hesitation) the reading above given.

expressions of primitive belief to which we have just been listening, and the comments upon that language (not to say the utter perversions of it) to which some modern theologians have had recourse. But it may be well to show, by a striking example, such as the comments upon this monument will afford, how easy it is for men to import into ancient monuments exactly what they wish to find there. We may thus enforce what is in these days a greatly needed lesson, that of profound distrust of mere assertions made by theological partisans as to what the evidence of antiquity is. For, as you will see, even men of considerable learning begin by deceiving themselves as to the nature of that evidence, and, having done so, it is but natural that they should go on to deceive others, who are content to accept the witness of antiquity on the authority of others, instead of requiring it to be set out in full before their own eyes.

You have the means of judging what that evidence is as regards the monument now in your hands; and you will probably be somewhat surprised to hear the enumeration of the following points of doctrine, or of ritual observance involving doctrine, for which it is supposed to give the strongest evidence, and that dating from the 'second century' of our era. M. Le Blant, an eminent French antiquary, quotes Padre Secchi (a Roman Jesuit) as finding here, amongst other things, '*la mention du cœur* sacré de Jésus Christ . . . . la présence réelle . . . . la communion*

---

* It is painful to write in detail upon such subjects. Those, however, who may be inclined to wonder why *this* should be brought into question by controversialists, may be referred to Cardinal Perrone, 'Prælect. Theolog.' tom. v. p. 301.

sous une seule espèce . . . . la prière des morts retenus au purgatoire.' And to this I may add, that Padre Garrucci finds in the same monument conclusive evidence of prayer offered to the Virgin Mary, and of belief in Transubstantiation.

I refer to this last writer the rather because he is a well-known antiquary of great repute, and a man of very great erudition. That he is well able to defend himself, if in any respect I shall do him wrong, his correspondence with M. Rossignol gives good proof. And if I seem now to invite controversy with him as to the true interpretation of this monument, it is because I will not doubt that he really desires that the truth, and nothing but the truth, should be established; and because I know that he is capable of conducting even theological controversy without forgetting, as too many do, the respect that is due to the cause of truth in which he is engaged.

In the eighth line then of this Inscription he reads as follows :—

Εὖ εἴλω (*or* εἴδω), Μῆτηρ, σε λιτάζομαι, φῶς τὸ θανόντων,

and this line he interprets (*ut devota mente accipiam, Mater, oro te, lucem mortuorum*) : ' I pray thee, Mother, that with devout mind I may receive the light of the dead,' *i.e.* (as appears from his previous[*] comment), ' That I may devoutly receive Him [viz. Jesus Christ] who is the Light of the dead.'

I need hardly be at pains to point out the repeated

---

[*] 'Pectorius prend la parole et prononce des actes fort tendres dans le désir de recevoir Jésus Christ dans ses mains; il prie la Mère du Sauveur.'

mistakes of grammar in which the writer has here involved himself, simply because, writing as he does from the point of view of modern Romanism, he expects antecedently to find Mary-worship in every ancient monument. In order to find evidence of this here, he writes εἴλω (*or* εἴδω) as a form of the subjunctive, apparently in entire forgetfulness that if the subjunctive were to be employed here at all it would be ἴδω, or ἕλω, without the augment. And so by assuming, without the slightest authority whatever, that Μῆτηρ, 'Mother,' would mean in the second century (to which he refers the monument) *the Virgin Mary*, addressed simply as 'Mother' in prayer, he contrives to import into this monument what no one but himself has ever been able to see there; proposing, with this view, a reading of the text, which no one with the slightest pretence to a knowledge of Greek ever has endorsed, or ever will.

What is really instructive in this matter, is the notable instance here before us of the way in which the defence of modern Romanism rests upon inexact scholarship in one, upon defective archæological knowledge in another. Padre Garrucci's forced introduction of prayers to the Virgin Mary into this monument, at the cost of all exactness of grammatical expression, and in direct contradiction to the evidence of antiquity, as to the feeling of the first four centuries in reference to the blessed mother of our Lord, is a fitting pendant to Dr. Northcote's discovery of 'the Virgin Mary' side by side with 'the Good Shepherd' in the cemetery of Priscilla,* or Mr. Brownlow's demonstra-

---

* As to this see above, p. 17; and for Mr. Brownlow's Latin, footnote, p. 92.

tion of the Petrine succession of the Roman Bishops by an utter perversion of the Latin lines which he quotes. All the three write in perfect good faith; but one in forgetfulness of Greek grammar, another of the most elementary rules of Latin construction, and yet another (Dr. Northcote) under an entire ignorance as to the real appearance of the monument which he edits, and which in editing he unwittingly misrepresents.

It would be a waste of time to deal seriously with anything so absurd as the attempt to prove a belief in Transubstantiation from the symbolical language of this Inscription.

But there will be some real advantage, perhaps, in well weighing another assertion, which is made not only by Roman Catholic writers of all kinds, but by some among ourselves, that this monument presents the most conclusive evidence of the doctrine of the Real Presence, as being held either in the second century (according to the date they assign) or in the fourth or fifth, which, for reasons already given, I myself believe to be its true date.

If for '*the* doctrine of the Real Presence' we would be content to say '*a* doctrine of Real Presence,' we should be so far nearer the truth, that we should recognise a fact, which is plain to all accurate students of theology, that there is more than one doctrine of the Real Presence. But if we would avoid the anachronism of importing into antiquity controversial phrases of comparatively modern theology, utterly unknown to the early Church, what we should rather say would be this, that the monument before us gives expression throughout to those ideas of the Spiritual Presence of Christ, as distinct from a Corporal

Presence, upon which the great contemporary teachers of the Church, both in East and West, most strongly insisted at the time from which this monument dates.

Let me not be misunderstood in saying this. I freely admit that one expression of the text, 'Eat, hungering, holding Ichthus in thy hands,' is in itself not inconsistent with any doctrine of the Real Presence whatever, even the most carnal and Capernaitic that can be imagined. But I maintain no less strongly, that the evidence already alleged of the very wide application of the symbolism of the word Ichthus, makes it clear that the language of this Inscription is also perfectly consistent with the most spiritual view of the Presence of Christ in this Holy Sacrament that any can hold. And the real question suggested by this monument is not one to be determined by reference to the controversial terms of modern divinity, but by reference to the language of the great teachers of the Church in the first four centuries of our era.

And it is a strange assertion to make, but yet it is a perfectly true one, as far as my own reading enables me to judge, that while bulky volumes have been written of late years professing to set forth the teaching of the Fathers concerning the Real Presence of Christ in the Holy Sacrament of His Body and Blood, *all that the Fathers really teach concerning the nature of Christ's Presence is passed over in the most absolute silence.* Pages after pages of quotations from the Fathers (and even these often gravely, though of course unintentionally, misrepresented) are brought forward, in which not one word is said about Presence, still less about 'Real Presence,' or 'Real Objective Presence' (a coinage of the last fifty years); and the very fact that many of the Fathers, both in East and West, have treated *ex professo* on the subject of Christ's Presence is in no way whatever so much as noticed. And this being so, I think that I may make a real contribution to the Patristic evidence hitherto alleged on this disputed question, if I take this opportunity shortly to state what their doctrine on this particular question of Christ's Presence really is.

CHAPTER VI.

TEACHING OF THE FATHERS BEFORE THE YEAR 450 A.D. CONCERNING THE NATURE OF CHRIST'S PRESENCE.

BEFORE quoting in detail the language of the Fathers, it may be well to say a few words as to the earlier use of terms of Presence, both in classical writers and in Holy Scripture.

For classical usage it will be enough to say, that words importing Presence were used with every variety of meaning, whether of physical and material, or of figurative and spiritual Presence (in this including the Presence of Power). Thus, on the one hand, Horace speaks of a Roman Emperor being regarded as a *present* God (*i. e.* as the context shows, *present upon earth*), in contradistinction to the Father of the Gods spoken of as reigning *in heaven;* while, on the other hand, we hear Cicero speaking of always having been *present* to Deiotarus *when himself absent* (*absenti Deiotaro* *semper adfui*), *i. e.* of his always having *supported his interests* (been to him a *present help*) in the Senate and Forum, when he was not on the spot to support his own cause. And the use of *præsentia* in the sense of *power* * is familiar to scholars; as, for example, in that expression of Ovid's, '*tanta est præsentia veri,*' 'such is the *power* of truth.' †

Passing on to the usage of Holy Scripture, we find in an expression employed by St. Paul a remarkable anticipation of the Patristic language which I am about to allege. Writing to the Corinthians (1 Cor. v. 1 *sqq.*) concerning a notorious offender, he speaks of himself as being *absent in body* from those Corinthians, but *present in spirit* with them (ἄπων τῷ σώματι—πάρων τῷ πνεύματι); and again adds, 'When ye are gathered together, *with my spirit*, together with the *power* (σὺν τῇ δυνάμει) of the Lord Jesus Christ, [I have already determined] to deliver such an one unto Satan,' &c. &c. Presence in spirit is, in St. Paul's mind, not inconsistent with absence in body.

With thus much premised as to the use of terms of Presence in classical writers and in Scripture, I proceed to the question now more immediately before us, viz. the teaching of the early Fathers, in East and West, concerning the Presence of our blessed Lord.

And I will begin with the Greek Fathers, seeing that in their language we find most faithfully reflected not only the

---

* Comp. Cyril. Hieros. Catech. xv. p. 165: ὁ εἷς ἐνιαυτὸς ἐν ᾧ αὔξει ἡ παρουσία αὐτοῦ (augebitur ipsius *potentia:* Interpres Lat.).

† Comp. Georg. ii. 127, 'Saporem Felicis mali, quo non præsentius (*more effectual*) ullum . . . auxilium venit.' And Pliny, H. N. xxi. 20, § 86, ' Idem (melissophyllon) præsentissimum est contra ictus earum (*sc.* apum) vesparumque.'

general doctrine, but the actual terminology, of primitive Christian revelation, as it had originally been taught by the Apostles and Prophets of the New Covenant.

And this first we may note, that the phrase ἡ παρουσία τοῦ Χριστοῦ, 'the Presence of Christ,' had in the early Fathers a distinct technical meaning when used without further limitation. It was used of the Presence of Christ upon earth —that Presence being either in the period which intervened between the Nativity and the Ascension, *a Presence which is past;* or of that Presence *which shall be hereafter,* when He who ascended into heaven shall come again in like manner.

Hence, in the language of the Greek Fathers, there are two 'Presences'[*] of our blessed Lord, and two 'comings down'[†] from heaven : one at the time of His Incarnation ; the other, yet future, when He shall come in glory. One of these is the former[‡] Presence (ἡ προτέρα παρουσία, Cyr.

---

[*] For illustrations of what is above stated see Justin Mart. 'Dial. cum Tryph.' p. 208, 9, δύο παρουσίαι τοῦ Χριστοῦ προεφητεύοντο γενησόμεναι, μία μὲν ἐν ᾗ παθητὸς καὶ ἄτιμος καὶ ἀειδὴς φανήσεται, ἡ δὲ ἑτέρα ἐν ᾗ ἔνδοξος καὶ κριτὴς πάντων ἐλεύσεται. And Cyril. Hieros. Catech. xv. (ad init.), Χριστοῦ παρουσίαν καταγγέλλομεν, οὐ μίαν μόνον, ἀλλὰ καὶ δευτέραν τῆς προτέρας πολὺ καλλίονα. Ἡ μὲν γὰρ ὑπομονῆς εἶχεν ὑπόδειξιν, ἡ δὲ θείας βασιλείας φέρει τὸ διάδημα. The term παρουσία is frequently used by Irenæus, and, with one exception, in one or other of the senses indicated in the text above. The exception (possibly such) is in lib. i. c. i., where he speaks of the αἱμορροοῦσα as being healed ὑπὸ τῆς παρουσίας τοῦ Σωτῆρος. This, however, is but a slight modification of the ordinary meaning. For further illustrations of the word see Origen in Joan. t. i. p. 8. Constitt. Apost. lib. viii. § 12 (τῆς μελλούσης αὐτοῦ δευτέρας παρουσίας).

[†] Διπλαῖ αἱ κάθοδοι, μία ἡ ἀσυμφανὴς ἡ ὡς ἐπὶ πόκον· καὶ δευτέρα ἡ ἐπιφανής, ἡ μέλλουσα. Cyril. Catech. xv.

[‡] Comp. S. Irenæus adv. Hær. iii. c. xii. He says that the Ethiopian eunuch was brought to his

Catech. xv. ad init.), the other, the second Presence* (ἡ δευτέρα ..... ἥν προσδοκῶμεν), for which we are still looking, at His coming to judgment. (ἡ παρουσία τοῦ Κυρίου ἡ τοῦ κόσμου συντέλεια. Ibid. in fin.)

This mere use of terms constitutes in itself a strong presumption that the doctrine of the Greek Fathers in early times concerning the Presence of our Lord in the Holy Eucharist must have been a very different one from that now taught in the Church of Rome, and by some among ourselves. But let us proceed now to consider something much more definite; their express teaching concerning the nature of Christ's Presence.

And here we shall find the Fathers, both of East and West, in full accord in teaching, that in the interval between the first and the second Advent (or Presence, παρουσία) of our Lord, there is a manner in which He is *present* upon earth, and a manner in which He is *absent*. He is absent, so they expressly teach, in respect of His human nature; He is present in respect of His divine nature. He is absent in respect of that which *is in one place only*, viz. in respect of His human Body present now in heaven; He is present in respect of that which is ubiquitous, viz. His divine nature, wherein He is one with the Father and the Holy Ghost.

None can speak more clearly upon this point than

---

own country to preach there what he had himself believed, the One God who had been proclaimed by the Prophets, and that τούτου τὸν υἱὸν τὴν κατὰ ἄνθρωπον ἤδη πεποιῆσθαι παρουσίαν.

* Comp. S. Irenæus adv. Hæres.

i. c. ii. : Τὴν ἐκ τῶν οὐρανῶν ἐν τῇ δόξῃ τοῦ Πατρὸς παρουσίαν αὐτοῦ, κ. τ. λ. In this use of παρουσία the Greek Fathers follow the language of Holy Scripture, as in 2 Thess. ii. 8; Jam. v. 7 (and 8); 2 Pet. iii. 4, &c.

St. Augustine. Commenting* on those words of our Lord, 'The poor ye have always with you, but Me ye have not alway' (John, xi.); or, as he renders them, 'Me ye *will not have* alway' (*non semper habebitis*), he writes as follows:—

'Let good men give ear unto that He saith, but let them not thereby be troubled. *For it is of bodily Presence that He spake this* ("Me ye will not have alway"). For in respect of His majesty, in respect of His providential care, in respect of His unspeakable and invisible grace, in respect of all these is that fulfilled which He spake, saying, "Behold, I am with with you alway, unto the end of the world." But in respect of the Flesh which the Word took on Him, in respect of that (Humanity) whereby He was born of a Virgin, seized by the hands of Jews, fastened to a tree, taken down from a cross, wrapped in linen cloths, laid in a tomb, and manifested in His rising therefrom,—in respect of all these, "Me ye shall not have alway." And wherefore this? Because, in respect of bodily Presence (*secundum præsentiam corporis*), He went in and out with His Disciples during the space of forty days, and then, while they followed Him in sight, though not in person, He ascended into heaven. And *He is not here*, for He is there: He sitteth

---

* Tractat. in Joan. L. With this compare Tractat. lxviii.: 'A quibus Homo abcedebat, Deus non derelinquebat : et idem ipse Homo ac Deus. Ergo et ibat per id quod Homo erat, et manebat per id quod Deus erat : *ibat per id quod uno loco erat*, manebat per id quod ubique erat.' And with a further distinction still, Sermo ccclxi. cap. vii.: 'Secundum præsentiam pulchritudinis et divinitatis suæ semper cum Patre est : secundum præsentiam corporalem jam supra cælos ad dexteram Patris est: *secundum præsentiam vero fidei in omnibus Christianis est.*'

at the right hand of God,—and *He is here*, for by the *Presence of Divine majesty* He hath not departed from us. Or, again, we may give answer thus :—In regard of the Presence of Divine majesty we have Christ alway with us; in respect of the Presence of the Flesh (*secundum p. carnis*) rightly was it said unto His Disciples, "*But me ye will not have alway.*" For the Church possessed Him but a few days in respect of the Presence of (His) Flesh; now by Faith she holdeth Him, with the eyes she seeth Him not.'

Precisely to the same effect are his comments* upon yet another passage of the same Gospel, on the words (John, xiv. 28), 'I go away, *and* I come again unto you.'

'As God He was not to leave those whom, as Man, He was to leave; and in Him, the one Christ, God and Man are united. Therefore was He to go away in regard that He was Man, and abide in regard that He was God. *He was to go away by that [nature] which was in one place [only]; He was to remain by that which was in every place.*'

It may be objected, that in this that he here says there is no special reference to the Holy Eucharist, and that he is speaking only in general terms of the laws of Christ's Presence generally, and that he would have used very different language had *this* subject been in question. To this I would reply (to the first objection), that His language, even if it proved nothing more, would at least suffice to show this, that St. Augustine's dogmatic language concerning the general law of Christ's Presence is the very

---

* Tractat. in Joan. lxviii. See note in preceding page.

reverse of that which a Roman Divine would naturally use now, and which certain among ourselves actually do use. That any such, when confronted with the language I have quoted, would be able to explain it away, and to say that in a sense they could adopt it as their own, I do not of course doubt. But that is a very different matter. What I maintain is, that language such as this is perfectly consistent and natural in the mouth of an English Churchman; and that it would be neither natural nor consistent in the mouth of one who holds the 'Real Presence' in the sense in which it has been taught for some centuries past in the Roman Church, and by some, of quite late years, among ourselves.

But I can say more than this. To the second of the two objections above supposed (viz. that St. Augustine would speak very differently if the doctrine of the Holy Eucharist had been prominently before him) I would reply, that we have distinct evidence leading to a directly opposite conclusion. For in another passage,* in immediate connection with the thought of the last Supper of our Lord, and of the Institution of the Holy Sacrament, he draws the very same distinction which to our own Divines has long been habitual, between a corporal (or bodily) and a spiritual Presence. 'After the Supper, being close now to His Passion, He spake unto His disciples as about to go away and to leave them in regard of bodily (or "corporal") Presence, *but with a spiritual Presence* to be

---

* Tractat. in Joan. xcii. : 'Dominus Jesus in sermone quem locutus est discipulis suis post cœnam, proximus Passioni, tanquam iturus et relicturus eos præsentia corporali cum omnibus autem suis usque in consummationem sæculi futurus præsentia spirituali.'

with all them that are His, even to the end of the world.'

And as showing further what was the mind of St. Augustine on this matter, I will refer to yet another passage, in the treatise against Faustus. (Lib. xx. cap. 21.) He is there indignantly rejecting the calumny of certain Manichæans who spoke of Christians as offering sacrifices to martyrs. He says that they offer sacrifice, it is true; but it is to God, and after that manner of sacrifice which in the manifestation of the New Testament God had prescribed. And after quoting Ps. xlix. 23, 'Sacrificium laudis glorificabit me, et illic via est ubi ostendam illi salutare meum,' he adds : ' The Flesh and Blood of this Sacrifice before the coming of Christ was set forth in anticipation by means of victims of resemblance; in the Passion of Christ it was rendered (unto God) in very reality; now, after the Ascension of Christ, it is celebrated by a Sacrament of Memorial.' 'Hujus sacrificii caro ac sanguis ante adventum Christi per victimas similitudinum promittebatur; *in passione Christi per ipsam veritatem reddebatur;* post ascensum Christi per sacramentum memoriæ celebratur.'* The *reality*, or truth (*veritas*) of that

---

* This, like other passages already alleged, is passed over altogether in the 'Catenæ' of Patristic authorities which have appeared of late years. With it compare St. Ambrose, ' De Cain et Abel,' i. 5, § 19 : ''Those things we must desire wherein is perfection, wherein is the truth (*veritas*). Here is the shadow, here the image, *there* the truth (*veritas*). The shadow in the Law, the image in the Gospel, the truth in the heavens.' [' *Umbra in lege, imago in evangelio, veritas in cælestibus.*'] And see the rest of the passage concerning Christ's offering Himself, *here in image, there in the truth, where He intercedeth for us as an Advocate with the Father.* [I quote this last the rather because it is, as

Sacrifice is to be found in the Passion of our Lord; the memorial of it in the Holy Communion.

It will hardly be said, I think, that these dogmatic distinctions thus made by St. Augustine are such as to harmonise with Tridentine teaching concerning the Real Presence. But let us hear yet another great doctor of the Western Church, who takes up precisely the same thought concerning the laws of Christ's Presence as that to which St. Augustine gives such pointed expression.

Leo the Great, in his 'Sermo de Ascens. Domini,' c. ii., thus writes on this question :—' Son of Man, [and also] Son of God, He made Himself known after a more excellent and mystical manner (*excellentius et sacratius innotuit*) when He returned unto the glory of the Father; and after an ineffable mode began to be more present by His Divine nature, Who, in respect of His humanity, became more distant from us.' '*Ineffabili modo cœpit esse divinitate præsentior, qui factus est humanitate longinquior.*'

And when from the Western Doctors we turn once more to the Greek Fathers, we find precisely the same language used. Hear, for instance, St. Cyril of Alexandria. He is commenting, like St. Augustine, already quoted, on St. John's Gospel, and dwelling, as he had done, upon the difference between our Lord's local Presence, in respect of His humanity, a Presence which is now in heaven, and His

---

far as I know, the only passage in all the Fathers which speaks of our Lord as 'offering Himself' in heaven. The sense in which he uses the expression '*offert se*' is, however, indicated by the words that immediately follow; and his contrast between '*here in image*' (or likeness), '*there in the truth*,' is as unlike that of modern Roman theology as possible.

Presence of Divinity, or Presence of Power, whereby He is even now present with all them that are His. 'Though * He is absent from us in the flesh, seeing that He hath gone away from us and departed unto God the Father, yet by His divine power He compasseth the whole universe, and is closely present unto those that love Him.' Εἴ καὶ ἄπεστιν ἡμῶν τῇ σαρκὶ, τὴν πρὸς θεὸν στειλάμενος ἀποδημίαν, ἀλλ᾽ οὖν τῇ θείᾳ δυνάμει περιέπει τὰ σύμπαντα, καὶ συμπάρεστι τοῖς ἀγαπῶσιν αὐτόν.

If it be asked how language such as this can be reconciled with those many passages in which the Fathers speak, in the same way as Holy Scripture speaks, of the Bread which we break being the Body (or the Flesh) of Christ, and the Wine of which we drink being the Blood of Christ, the answer is not far to seek. They had learnt from the words of the Lord Himself that the Body there partaken of by the Faithful is the Body *offered upon the Cross* (τοῦτό ἐστι τὸ σῶμά μου τὸ διδόμενον ὑπὲρ ὑμῶν), and the Blood of the New Covenant that Blood which was shed for the forgiveness of our sins (τὸ αἷμά μου τὸ ἐκχυνόμενον). That the power of the Holy Spirit co-operates with the faith of believers to make the Bread of the Eucharist to be to us, after an ineffable manner, the crucified Body, and the cup of the New Covenant to be, after the like manner, the Blood that for us was shed, this with an adoring faith they believed. But while believing this, they had thought also of yet other words of the same Lord in speaking (John, vi.) of the very same truth. The words that He had spoken concerning eating the Flesh, and drinking the Blood, of

* Comment. in Joan. c. xiii.

the Son of man, He had declared to be *spirit and life;* and the great teachers of the early Church echo their Master's words in terms such as those of St. Augustine : ' What is this that He saith, " Spirit and Life ?" Spiritually His words are to be understood. Hast thou understood them spiritually ? Then are they spirit and life. Hast thou understood them carnally ? Even then are they spirit and life : but they are not such to thee.' *

Such passages as these might be largely added to if need were. But enough has been already said for my present purpose. I do not for a moment maintain that a few passages such as these are sufficient to determine the question of what was the mind of the Fathers upon that mysterious question, which is involved in the Eucharistic controversies of our own day. But thus much I may say. The phrases, ' the Real Presence,' or ' the Real Objective Presence' (phrases which, whether good or bad in themselves, are neither Scriptural nor Patristic), are now being made a Shibboleth whereby to divide into two hostile camps those whom God would have to dwell as brethren in mutual love and peace. Those who so use them must surely have forgotten that even the declaration, '*I am of Christ,*' is condemned by the voice of an Apostle, when it is used as a symbol of party divisions within the Church.

And this further I cannot but add. The number of those in our own country who have at once leisure, and power, and opportunity, for original research into the records of

---

* In Joan. Evang. Tract. xxvii. n. 6 : 'Quid est, *Spiritus et vita sunt ?* Spiritualiter intelligenda sunt. Intellexisti spiritualiter? *Spiritus et vita* sunt. Intellexisti carnaliter? Etiam sic illa *Spiritus et vita sunt,* sed tibi non sunt.'

the Church, is very limited. And the greater the personal influence that any such have, the higher their claim to the respect and veneration of others, the greater is their responsibility for perfect '*faithfulness of stewardship*,' when dealing out for the instruction of others that which is laid up in the treasure-house of antiquity. If those to whom, and to whose writings, I now refer, had really laid before the Church in our own days, with perfect accuracy of statement, the *whole* teaching of Holy Scripture, and of the ancient Fathers, in reference to points now disputed, instead of selecting, and oftentimes, though unconsciously, manipulating their authorities, so as to make them accord with predetermined conclusions, in how different a spirit might the controversy of our own days have been conducted; how different might now have been the spiritual condition of our Church! How might men, now sundered in two hostile camps, and turning one against the other all the resources of human law, have still continued in the same path which, till quite late years, so many had followed, and still have been drawing nearer the one to the other, as they made onward progress in ever higher knowledge of the truth as it is in Christ.

And now from these thoughts of the controversies of our own day, I return, and with a very different feeling, to the beautiful expressions of Christian truth which have already been before us in the Inscription itself.

CHAPTER VII.

THE DOCTRINES IMPLIED IN THE INSCRIPTION.

ON looking once more to the Inscription itself, it will be seen that it has reference to two main subjects,—the life, and the death, of the Christian man. Of these we will speak in their order.

1. *The New Birth, and Growth in Grace and in Knowledge thereupon following.*

Offspring* of the heavenly Ichthus, put forth a heart of holy reverence, now that from divine waters thou hast received, while yet among mortals, a spring of life that is to immortality.

'Ιχθύος οὐρανίου θεῖον γένος, ἦτορι σεμνῷ
Χρῆσε, λαβὼν ζωὴν ἀμβροτον ἐν βροτέοις
Θεσπεσίων ὑδάτων.

---

* 'Ιχθύος οὐρανίου [ἅγιον or θεῖον] γένος. In speaking here of our Lord as the Author of the regenerate life, the writer of this Inscription follows (as elsewhere) St. Irenæus. Thus, in lib. iii. cap. xx. the latter says, '*Primogenitus enim mortuorum natus Dominus et in sinum* suum recipiens pristinos patres, regeneravit eos in vitam Dei.' Compare the fuller statement quoted below (p. 170), where he describes the co-operation of the Father, the Son, and the Holy Ghost, in the work of the new creation. And again, in lib. i. c. xi., he says that the last

In the thought here expressed, as in the language of Holy Scripture, the doctrine of our New Birth is regarded as a foundation on which to build up precepts of holy life, and of onward growth at once in grace and in knowledge. As St. Peter (2 Pet. i. 3 *sqq.*), to take but a single example, combines* the two thoughts of the grace of God enabling us to spiritual life (ζωή) and godliness, with that of the need of all diligence and earnestness (πᾶσα σπουδή) on our part in putting forth those powers in onward progress towards 'perfection,' or fulness of growth, so do the great teachers of the early Church—the Greek Fathers more particularly. And among these none with more earnest insistence, or in more exact conformity with the teaching of Holy Scripture, than St. Irenæus, whose influence, as already remarked, may be clearly traced in the language of this monument. Take, for example, the passage that follows (Adv. Hær. iv. cc. 38, 39) :—

Man (*i. e.* the 'second Adam' of St. Paul) was manifested for the regeneration of the first man (*i. e.* of the natural man, the παλαιὸς ἄνθρωπος of St. Paul) : τὸν ἔσχατον ἄνθρωπον εἰς ἀναγέννησιν τοῦ πρώτου ἀνθρώπου πεφηνέναι. It is with the same thought, again, that he speaks of *eam quæ est ex Virgine per fidem regenerationem* [no doubt τὴν ἐκ τῆς παρθένου διὰ πίστεως παλιγγενεσίαν]. Lib. iv. Potter, p. 358. With the above agree occasional expressions of other Fathers, as that of Clemens Alexand. (Pædag. i. vi.) : 'The Word is all things to the infant (*i. e.* to the infant by new birth), both

Father, and Mother, and Teacher (παιδαγωγὸς), and Foster-father (τροφεύς). And the same writer speaks of Christians as Χριστόγονοι, 'Christborn.' (Pæd. iii. c. 12.)

* 2 Pet. i. 3, *sqq.* 'Seeing that the Divine power *hath already bestowed upon us all things that are needed for life and godliness* . . . . *bring ye in* (παρεισενέγκαντες, a word implying *contribution*, as to an united work) *all diligence*, and furnish forth abundantly (ἐπιχορηγήσατε) in your faith virtue, in your virtue knowledge, in your knowledge temperance' (ἐγκράτειαν, self-mastery), and so the rest that follows.

'God in all things hath first place, Who alone is unbegotten, and first of all, and the cause of being to all. But all things else abide in subjection to God; and subjection to God is incorruption; and to abide in incorruption is the glory of Him who is unbegotten. This, then, is the order, and such the harmonious action, and such the onward guidance, by which man, begotten and fashioned by the Creator's hand, cometh to be (γίνεται) after the image and likeness of God the Unbegotten; the Father so willing and giving command, and the Son acting and fashioning as with a workman's hand (πράσσοντος καὶ δημιουργοῦντος), and the Spirit ministering food and increase (τρέφοντος καὶ αὔξοντος), and the man the while making onward advance as with a silent, unobserved growth, and reaching up unto perfection, coming nigh that is, to the Unbegotten; for perfect is He who is Unbegotten, that is God. For need there was that man should first come into being; and having come into being that he should make growth; and having made growth attain matured manhood; and from matured manhood that he should be multiplied;* and being multiplied that he should become strong; and becoming strong that he be glorified; and being glorified that he see Him who is his Lord (τὸν ἑαυτοῦ δεσπότην). For it is God that shall be seen of us; and the vision of God produceth incorruption; and incorruption maketh nigh unto God.'

[Then, after speaking of man as having knowledge both of good and evil, and the power (and therefore the responsibility) of choice between the two, he proceeds:]

---

* Πληθυνθῆναι. Probably his thought is of grace being 'multiplied' to the Christian man of whom he speaks, according to that of St. Peter, χάρις ὑμῖν πληθυνθείη. (1 Pet. i. 2; 2 Pet. i. 2.)

'How then shall he become [as] God, who hath not yet become man? Or how attain to fulness of growth, who hath but as now come into being? Or how shall he become immortal, who while yet in a mortal nature hath not been obedient to his Maker? For first must thou keep thyself after the order of humanity, that so afterward thou mayest be partaker of the glory of God. For it is not thou that makest God, but God that maketh thee. If therefore thou art God's work, await thou the hand of thy Maker, who doeth all things in fit time; in fit time as regards thee, who art being formed by Him. *But do thou so present thine heart unto Him that it shall be soft and responsive to His touch, and keep that likeness whereunto He hath fashioned thee, having moisture in thyself, lest being hardened thou lose the mark which His fingers have impressed.** But if thou keep that likeness whereunto He hath fashioned thee, thou shalt mount upward to perfection; for by God's handiwork that clay which is in thine own self is put away out of sight. His hand hath fashioned the substance that is in thee; He will cover thee, within and without, with a covering of pure gold and silver; yea, He will so adorn thee that the King Himself shall have pleasure in thy beauty. But if, being straightway hardened, thou wilt none of His fashioning;† if thou show thyself unthankful unto Him, being ungrateful unto God because

---

* 'Præsta autem ei cor tuum molle et tractabile, et custodi figuram qua te figuravit artifex, habens in temetipso humorem, ne induratus amittas vestigia digitorum ejus.' [The Greek original is lost.] This '*præsta cor tuum molle et tractabile*' is a close approach to the χρῆσε = χρῆσαι) ἤτορι σεμνῷ of the Inscription.

† *Artem* is the word of the translator, but evidently = δημιουργίαν.

thyself made man, then wilt thou in the same moment lose both His forming* hand and thine own true life. For it is proper to the goodness of God that He should thus make, and proper to the nature of man that he thus be made. If therefore thou render unto Him that is thine, even faith in Him and subjection, then shalt thou receive His fashioning* power, and shalt be God's perfected work.'

More briefly, but with thought and expression closely in accord with this, St. Augustine writes as follows:—

'Man, to attain to any true being, must turn himself toward Him by whom he was created. For in drawing back he waxeth cold; in drawing nigh he waxeth warm. Drawing back he gathereth darkness; drawing nigh he gathereth light. Wherefore, whosoever would be like unto God, that so he may stand in His presence, and, as it is written, "preserve his strength before Him," let him not draw back from Him; to Him clinging (*cohærendo*) let him take His impress, as wax taketh impress from a seal; to Him closely joined let him keep His likeness, doing that of which it is written, "It is good for me to hold me fast by God!" let him retain in deed and truth that similitude and likeness after which he hath been made.' (Enarr. in Ps. lxx. 6.)

It can hardly be necessary for me to point out to you in detail the close resemblance in thought, and occasionally even in expression, between the language I have now quoted and that of the Inscription now in your hands.

---

* See note † in preceding page.

2. *Of Man's part of Duty in feeding his Soul with Spiritual Food.*

Quicken thy soul, beloved one, to ever fuller life,* with the unfailing waters of wealth-giving wisdom; and receive the honey-sweet food of the Saviour of the Saints. Eat, with a longing hunger, holding Ichthus in thine hands.

τὴν σὴν φίλε θάλπεο ψυχὴν
"Ὕδασιν ἀενάοις πλουτοδότου σοφίης,
Σωτῆρος δ' ἁγίων μελιηδέα λάμβανε βρῶσιν.
"Ἔσθιε πεινάων, Ἰχθὺν ἔχων παλάμαις.

That there is a direct reference in the last line to that feeding upon heavenly food which is vouchsafed to us at

---

° ' *Quicken . . to ever fuller life.*' Only by periphrasis can the pregnant meaning of such an expression as θάλπεο be brought out. The word itself, and the tense employed (present instead of the more usual aorist), are both significant. Θάλπειν is, as nearly as may be, the Latin *fovere*. And as it is nowhere found in classical usage in the middle voice, its use here has been exclaimed against (by M. Rossignol) as a solœcism. But such criticism appears to me to lose sight of an important distinction. Modern scholars, when writing Greek, are bound to adhere to the usage sanctioned by those ancient masters whom they professedly imitate. But to the educated inhabitants of some parts of Gaul in early times, Greek was, it is hardly too much to say, a native language. And they had the power, and with the power the right, to modify the language of Homer and of Hesiod (the former of whom, more particularly, was as familiar to them as Shakespeare is to us), and to adapt it, even with slight changes from ordinary usage, to the expression of specially Christian ideas, such as that in the line now under consideration.

the table of our Lord, none can fail to see. But I venture to think that those commentators are mistaken who so interpret the line immediately preceding. Nor has any of these, as far as I have observed, brought out the meaning, which, if I do not mistake, is veiled under the figurative expressions with which the passage last quoted opens.

In order to understand the thought of the writer of this Inscription in the three first of the four lines just quoted, we should bear in mind the figurative language, both of Scripture and of early Fathers, in reference to gifts of God's Holy Spirit following upon, and in some sense distinct from, the gift of New Birth in Baptism.

These are plainly distinguished, first, in Holy Scripture: ' Then the Apostles laid their hands on them (Disciples in Samaria), and they received the Holy Ghost. *For as yet He had fallen upon none of them, only they had been baptized in the Name of the Lord.*' And so our Lord in one passage (John, iii. 3, 5) speaks of New Birth—Birth of (ἐκ) water and the Spirit—as necessary to our first entrance into the Kingdom of Heaven; and in yet another (John, vii. 37–39) He compares those *gifts of the Spirit*, which were to be bestowed upon believers after His own Ascension, to *rivers of living water*, springing (or welling) up, as to another He said, unto everlasting life. And He compares the gifts of the Holy Spirit bestowed upon us by our heavenly Father to the daily giving of food (both bread and fish are named) by parents to their children.

Such language occurs again and again, under various modifications, in Holy Scripture. And this we find re-echoed by that of early Fathers, both in East and West.

Thus, for example, St. Irenæus speaks, in more than one place, of the Holy Spirit, imparted to man, as being *the Food of Life* (βρῶμα ζωῆς), or *the Bread of Immortality* [adv. Hær. lib. iv. cap. 38], and that with express reference to the Holy Spirit as imparted through the laying on of the Apostles' hands. Ὡς οὖν ὁ Ἀπόστολος δυνατὸς ἦν διδόναι τὸ βρῶμα· οἷς γὰρ ἂν ἐπετίθουν τὰς χεῖρας ἐλάμβανον Πνεῦμα Ἅγιον, ὅ ἐστι βρῶμα ζωῆς. And so in a passage already quoted, while the Father willeth, and the Son worketh, it is the Spirit who feedeth (τρέφοντος) the new life that is God's gift, and giveth it due increase. To the same effect writes St. Clement of Alexandria, in a very remarkable passage. (Pædag. lib. i. cap. vi.) Referring to the words, 'I fed you with milk' (1 Cor. iii. 2), he says, 'The Holy Spirit which was in the Apostle, speaking as with the voice of the Lord (τῇ τοῦ Κυρίου ἀποχρωμένου φωνῇ), saith, "I gave you milk to drink." For if we have been regenerated unto Christ, then He that regenerated us feedeth us with His own milk, even the Word : for whatsoever it be that generateth, that same doth provide food for that which is begotten. *And as with the Regeneration, so with the food, by analogy therewith—one and the other are alike spiritual.* Καθάπερ δὲ ἡ ἀναγέννησις ἀναλόγως, οὕτω καὶ ἡ τροφὴ γέγονε τῷ ἀνθρώπῳ πνευματική.'

The 'ever-flowing waters,' then, wherewith the Divine life is to be cherished in the heart, are to be interpreted, so all I think will allow, of those confirming and strengthening gifts of the Holy Spirit, which, according to the teaching of the Divine Word, follow upon the communication of the first gift of New Life.

But what is the thought involved in the line that

follows ? 'Receive (from day to day)* the honey-sweet Food of the Saviour of the Saints :'—

Σωτῆρος δ' ἁγίων μελρηδέα λάμβανε βρῶσιν.

Without excluding that thought which to most ears will at once be suggested by these words, I cannot but think that the language of Scripture, and the comments of early Fathers, will lead us to see another meaning as at least suggested by the words before us.

The very word βρῶσις takes us at once (as some earlier commentators on this monument have observed) to the Fourth Chapter of St. John : ' I have a meat (βρῶσις) to eat that ye know not of. My meat (ἡ ἐμὴ βρῶσις) is to do the will of my Father which is in heaven.'

These words we may in a sense apply to ourselves ; nor should we, I think, in so doing run counter at all to the mind of the writer of this Inscription. But yet the language of the earlier teachers of the Church, and the context of the present passage, would lead us to think that the food here spoken of is the food which the Saviour of the Saints ministers to them that are His. And that special food that in this line is spoken of I believe to be the Word of Truth, *the revealed Word*, spoken of both in Scripture, and in innumerable passages of early Fathers, as a food whereby the spiritual life is fed.

In Holy Scripture, first; as when our Lord says that ' man shall not live by bread alone,' bread for the support

---

* I add these words in order to bring out the special connotation (continued or repeated action) of the *present* imperative. See ' Eirenica,' part ii. note 50.

of his natural life; but for the nurturing of that new life, which is of the Spirit, 'by every word (ῥῆμα) that proceedeth out of the mouth of God.' And so St. Peter bids his Disciples, as newly-born babes (ἀρτιγέννητα βρέφη), '*to long for the unadulterated* milk of the Word, that they may grow thereby.*' Life they have already received, but they need food for the support of that life. That expression of St. Peter's, however, is not so manifestly limited as is that of St. Paul in another passage ; where, with evident reference to teaching in the revealed word, he speaks of this as being either milk suited for babes only, or as strong meat fitted only for those who have made some advance towards maturity of Christian life. (Heb. v. 12.)

With all this agrees the language of early Fathers, both in East and West, who speak either of Divine Revelation generally, or more particularly of the Books of the Old and the New Testament, the teaching of Apostles and Evangelists, as being a divine food, wherewith Christ feedeth them that are His.

To St. Clement of Alexandria, for instance, Christ, the personified † 'Wisdom' of the Book of Wisdom (the πλουτοδότης Σοφία of this Inscription), is a πηγὴ μαθημάτων, a Fountain from whose waters we may imbibe what most we need to learn. ('Strom.' lib. vi. p. 786, Potter.) And the same writer interprets the 'milk' of which St. Paul speaks

---

* *Unadulterated:* "Ἄδολον. The expression is well illustrated by a proverb quoted by St. Irenæus, in reference to heretical corruptions of the divine word: '*Lacte gypsum male miscetur.*'

† It is this personification of Σοφία which accounts, probably, for the use of the masculine form, πλουτοδότης (for which see note, p. 150), rather than, what by analogy we might have expected, πλουτοδότειρα.

as being τὴν γνῶσιν τὴν ἐκ κατηχήσεως ἀνατρέφουσαν εἰς ζωὴν ἀΐδιον, that true knowledge which, resulting from instruction in the faith, ministers food unto life eternal. ('Pædag.' lib. i. c. vi.) And in the same passage (p. 119, ed. Potter) he speaks of the teaching of St. Paul as being a spiritual food (πνευματικὴ τροφή), and of the Apostle himself as instilling such a food by that milk which is of Christ, that milk being the word: τοῦ Χριστοῦ τῷ γάλακτι λόγῳ πνευματικὴν ὑμῖν ἐνστάζων τροφήν.

And, in connexion with this Inscription, there is a special interest in noting how the 'fish' and the loaves, with which, on more than one occasion, our Lord fed His disciples, were interpreted by Fathers both of East and West. Passages have been already quoted (p. 122) which may serve as examples of many more that might be alleged. They show that, in the eyes of these earlier teachers of the Church, this food which, with a mystical significance, our Lord distributed, was typical of *the Word of God contained in Holy Scriptures of the Old and of the New Testament.*

And putting together now these two interpretations upon which we have been dwelling—one pointing to the Holy Spirit, or the grace of God, as man's spiritual food; the other to the word of God, or His revealed truth—we find that the language of this Inscription, in the lines now before us, is an exact reproduction of precepts of Holy Scripture. Such, for example, is that of St. Peter (2 Pet. iii. 18), bidding the young Christian not to fall away from his own 'stay' (στηριγμός), or source of steadfastness, but to *grow in grace and in knowledge* of the Lord Jesus Christ (αὐξάνετε ἐν χάριτι καὶ γνώσει τοῦ Κυρίου). And so St. Paul (Col. i. 10) speaks of his prayer for his own children in the faith being this, that they may . . . . *grow by ever higher knowledge of God* (αὐξανόμενοι τῇ ἐπιγνώσει τοῦ Θεοῦ· such, probably, is the true reading).

And, lastly, this thought of needful food wherewith to sustain that new life which is God's gift to the regenerated man, found expression in an usage which was of wide extent, though not of universal occurrence, in the early Church—that of giving honey and milk to the newly baptized. To this usage, and to the thought therein embodied, there may probably be an allusion in the 'honey-sweet' food spoken of in the text.

3. *The Feeding upon Christ crucified, which is in Holy Communion.*

The line which next follows carries on our thoughts to that feeding upon the Body given for us on the Cross, which is vouchsafed to faithful souls in the act of Communion at the Table of the Lord :

"Εσθιε, πεινάων, Ἰχθὺν ἔχων παλάμαις.

'*Eat, with a longing hunger, holding Ichthus in thine hands.*'

There is here exactly the combination of Scriptural thought, and of symbolical expression characteristic of the earlier Church, which, in view of the date assigned to the monument (*circ.* 400 A.D.), we might antecedently have expected to find. Of Scriptural thought, first; for that longing hunger of the heart, which is here beautifully expressed in a single word (πινάων = πεινάων), is that which, in Holy Scripture, is again and again set before us as the true preparation of the soul that would be filled with the 'good things' of the Lord. '*Blessed are they that hunger*' (οἱ πεινῶντες, the very same word) '*and thirst after righteousness, for they shall be filled.*' '*If any man thirst, let him come unto me and drink.*' And in close agreement with this is the language of early Fathers in all parts of the Church. '*The Lord feedeth to the full them that hunger for the word:*' such is the language of one.* '*We have been taught,*' says another,† and he one of the 'Apostles' of central Gaul, '*with hunger to receive that food which is bestowed on us of God.*' And again, the word 'Ἰχθύς, as we have already seen (p. 123), carried back the thought of the faithful in early times to Christ, and more especially to Christ crucified,‡ in respect that His Body offered for us to God, and His Blood outpoured on our behalf, are the spiritual food given to us of God, whereby believing souls may be fed unto life eternal.

I am unwilling to quit this portion of my subject without referring, though very briefly, to another Inscription,§ the date of which, however, is uncertain, and its true text, in many parts of it, hopelessly corrupt. But in the symbolical language therein employed in reference to the Holy Eucha-

---

* Clement. Alex. Pædag. lib. i. c. vi. 'Ο Κύριος ἐκθρέψει τοὺς πεινῶντας τὸν λόγον.

† S. Irenæi adv. Hæres. lib. v. c. xxii. : 'Nos docuit . . esurienter sustinere (? ὑποδέχεσθαι) eam quæ a Deo datur escam.'

‡ '*Piscis assus, Christus passus.*'

§ Edited by Halloixius, in his 'Collectio Orientalium Patrum;' and again by Cardinal Pitra ('Spicil. Solesm.' iii. p. 532), after comparison of seven manuscripts in the Imperial Library at Paris. Padre Garrucci gives an ingenious, but purely conjectural, restoration of it, the *Roman* authorship of which is, I need hardly say, sufficiently evident. ('Mélanges d'Epigraphie ancienne,' p. 1. Paris, 1856.)

rist, it presents a curious parallel to that now under our consideration. I refer to the Epitaph of Abercius, Bishop of Hierapolis, in Phrygia. He writes his own epitaph by anticipation; and after describing his travels in different parts of the world, he speaks of certain as 'gathering together with him,' and then proceeds as follows :—

...... Πίστις δὲ προςῆγε
Καὶ παρέθηκε τροφὴν, 'Ιχθὺν [? θείας or ἱερᾶς] ἀπὸ πηγῆς,
Παμμεγέθη, καθαρὸν, ὃν ἐδράξατο παρθένος ἁγνή·
Καὶ τοῦτον ἐπέδωκε φίλοις ἔσθειν διαπαντὸς,
Οἶνον χρηστὸν ἔχουσα, κέρασμα διδοῦσα μετ' ἄρτου.

'*Faith brought to us*, and set before us, Food, a Fish from a [? holy or divine] Fount, great and clean, which the holy Maiden* took in her hand, and gave it to her friends, that they should alway eat thereof, holding goodly wine, giving, with bread, a mingled drink.'

3. *Christ's Presence in the Hour of Death.*

The next two lines open up an entirely new subject, to which, however, those already quoted lead us up as by natural sequence :—

---

* The holy [virgin] Maiden is evidently, from the context, Faith, personified. The absence of the article with παρθένος cannot be pressed in regard of lines so barbarous as many in this epitaph are. But in the eyes of Padre Garrucci and Dr. Northcote, the παρθένος ἁγνή can be no other than the Virgin Mary; and 'Faith' to the former of the two is not Faith, but 'the Church.'

'On Ichthus my hands are clasped : in Thy love come nigh unto me, and be my guide, my Lord and Saviour : I intreat Thee, Thou Light of them for whom the hour of death is past :'

Ἰχθύι χεῖρε ἄραρα· λιλαίεο, δέσποτα σῶτερ,
Εὐθύ μοι ἡγητήρ, σε λιτάζομε, φῶς τὸ θανόντων.

The exact translation of the lines before us cannot be determined with certainty, till it can be ascertained* whether the true reading of the second of these two lines be εὐθύ or εὖ σύ. Whichever this be, the general sense is, I think, clear. From thought of that feeding upon the Bread of Life (John, vi. 51), which is the pledge to us of our not dying eternally, and of our being delivered, not, indeed, *from* death, but *out† of* death, by the present power of our Lord, the transition is natural to a passage such as this, in which a prayer

---

* While these sheets were passing through the press I have had an opportunity of examining the original Inscription, preserved in the Musée Lapidaire at Autun. Either **ΕΥΘΥ ΜΟΙ** or **ϹΥΘΙ ΜΟΙ** may be regarded as not improbably the words with which the line begins. But **ΕΥ ϹΥ ΜΟΙ** would agree still better with the marble itself. This expression appears a weak one, as compared with either of the two others. But the evidence of actual text is of far more importance than individual fancy as to what text ought to be. And I incline to think that λιλαίεο . . .

εὖ σύ μοι ἡγητήρ should be regarded as the actual wording of the original. [The correction of the *workman's* λιλαίω into λιλαίεο, *a secunda manu*, is quite clear on the marble.]

† Compare that which is said (Heb. v. 7) of our Lord praying, in the hour of His agony, to Him who was able σώζειν αὐτὸν ἐκ θανάτου, and of His prayer being *heard* (εἰσηκούσθη). The thought implied is that of death, followed by deliverance *out of* death. Compare that expression of the psalm, 'Great are the troubles of the righteous : but the Lord delivereth him *out of* all.'

is offered to Christ, as the Light of them that have died, for His guidance through the valley of Death to the bright Paradise of rest and peace which lies beyond.

The thought here implied, of an intermediate state of rest and peace for the godly, intervening between death and the general resurrection, as again in another somewhat similar inscription already quoted (see p. 142), is one which in Holy Scripture is in many ways suggested, though not drawn out (intentionally this, we may well believe) with any clearness of definition.

Our Lord says to the penitent robber, 'Thou shalt be with me *in Paradise*' (not in heaven), and that not 'hereafter,' not 'at the last day,' not 'at my coming' (ἐν τῇ παρουσίᾳ μου), but 'to-day :' ' *Verily I say unto thee, This day shalt thou be with me in Paradise.*' And this thought of a greater nearness to Christ (at least a more conscious nearness) being vouchsafed to His holy servants after their ' departure,' is plainly implied in more than one passage by St. Paul : as, for example, when he says, that ' in a strait between two,' between life and death, his own desire, in regard of himself, was that he might '*depart, and be with Christ*' (Phil. i. 23). And very beautifully is a similar thought expressed in another epistle, where he speaks of the quitting of our home (ἀποδημεῖν) in the body being an entering upon our true home with the Lord (ἐνδημῆσαι πρὸς τὸν Κύριον). 2 Cor. v. 8.

That the truths shadowed out in expressions such as these have been 'developed' in mediæval times into the doctrine of Purgatory, with all the gross abuses, both of belief and of practice, which have clustered about this doctrine ; this, surely, is no reason why we should shut our eyes to that which the Apostles of Christ taught from the beginning. But it is doubtless a reason why in this, as in other matters of revealed truth, we should not attempt to lift the veil from that which God, in His wisdom, hath not thought fit to reveal : it is a reason why in this, as in many other matters of doctrine wherein men presumptuously define what God, all-wise, hath left undefined, we should listen to the warnings of great teachers of the early Church,

Μὴ πολυπραγμονεῖν,

not curiously to pry into the secret things of God. For, as the same thought has elsewhere been well expressed (by whom first I know not) :

'*Nescire velle, quæ Magister Optimus
Docere non vult, erudita inscitia est.*'

4. *The Farewell, but not 'for ever,' to those beloved on earth.*

Thoughts such as those dwelt on in the last section, and which were familiar to Christian people in those early ages of the Church from which this monument dates, lead on, by natural sequence, to the simple but suggestive expressions of family affection with which this Inscription ends :—

'Ασχανδῖε πάτερ τῷ 'μῷ κεχαρισμένε θυμῷ
Σὺν μ[ητρὶ γλυκερῇ καὶ πᾶσιν τ]οῖσιν ἐμοῖσιν
Ι[ΧΘΥΝ ἰδὼν υἱοῦ] μνήσεο Πεκτορίου.

' My Father Aschandeius, dear unto mine heart,
And thou, sweet Mother, and all I love on earth,
Oft as you look upon yon holy Sign of Christ,
So often think of me, Pectorius your son.'

Though we cannot be sure of the exact wording of these concluding lines, enough remains of them to guide us, with all but certainty, to their general meaning. The consent (with scarce an exception) of interpreters of all schools, in all but minute points of expression, constitutes a strong presumption that we are not far from the truth, though we can hardly expect exactly to have divined it. Enough remains to enable us to see in this, as in so many other Christian monuments of early Christendom, an evidence of the marked contrast of feeling between Pagan and Christian thought in regard of death. In a Roman monument, which I had occasion to publish* not long since, a father (Caius Sestius by name) is represented bidding farewell to his daughter; and two words, 'VALE ÆTERNOM'—*Farewell, for ever*, give an expressive utterance to the feeling of blank and hopeless severance with which Greeks and Romans were burdened when the reality of death was before their eyes. But in the lines before us there breathes the assurance of Christian faith, that those we have loved on earth still live, and are still ours, after the hand of death has separated them from us for a while.

Recapitulation.

In conclusion, I may briefly sum up the truths, which, under the veil of a symbolism now well-nigh forgotten, come before us in the language of this Inscription.

Christ is here set forth as the cause of the regenerate life to man. This life, imparted at the first in heavenly

---

* Vest. Christ. Pl. i.

waters (ver. 2), is not a gift only, but a gift that entails responsibility—even this, that we cherish that life by drinking of the unfailing streams of God's Holy Spirit (ver. 3, 4); streams at once of grace and of knowledge. And yet further, Christ, the Healer and Deliverer of His saints (Σωτὴρ ἁγίων), is not only the Source of new life to them that are His, when first admitted into the kingdom of His grace, but the Food and Sustenance of their spiritual life from the beginning even unto the end—' *Christus passus*,' is in such sense '*Piscis assus*,' that His Body given for us on the cross is, in a mystery beyond our understanding, but not beyond our faith, the food whereof they eat and drink whom Christ hath made His own. And the same Saviour ceaseth not from His care for us when the short span of our life is at an end : He is our guiding Light through the dark valley to the Paradise of light and rest which lieth beyond, the Light of them that have died in the faith, as He is the Light of them that live therein. All these are truths which find expression in the touching memorial of primitive Christian belief, the representation of which is now in your hands. I, for one, cannot but feel, that in tracing, under a symbolism which belonged to an age now long since passed, the truths which are our common inheritance, we are dealing with antiquity more truly, and withal more reverently, than if our first, perhaps our only thought, were to seek support therefrom for some modern formula of controversial theology, unknown alike to Scripture and to the primitive Church. If new formulæ for the expression of sacramental truths be indeed a necessity, let us seek to make them, as was this ΙΧΘΥC symbol of old, a watchword of love and peace, and of unity with one and the same Saviour ; not a Shibboleth of division, which shall sunder in two hostile camps those whom God has bidden as brethren to dwell together in unity.

Yet one lesson more, however, and one much needed in these days, the contemplation of a monument such as this may well teach us. We may see herein an evidence that the same primitive truths, of divine revelation, may be held, in common with ourselves, by men who, from peculiarities of previous habit, or of outward circumstance, through the diverse influences of varying times and different countries, have learnt to express their belief under very different forms. We may thankfully believe this for our comfort, even in these days, when controversy is so bitter upon this Sacrament of Peace; believe, and thankfully, that men differ far less in the reality of their own belief, than they differ in respect of the diverse formulæ, Scriptural, Patristic, or mediæval and modern, under which they give expression to that belief.

APPENDIX.

A.

On the Terms of Worship, Λατρεία *and* Προσκύνησις, *employed in Scripture and in the early Fathers.*

IN the title given to the first paper in this series I have purposely avoided using the term Mariolatry, because, in doing so, I should have assumed as true, at first starting, what Roman writers would earnestly deny, viz. that the worship now paid to the Virgin Mary in the Roman Church is such as can only rightly be rendered unto God.

I need hardly remind any readers of this volume, that Roman theologians distinguish* carefully between the terms *Doulcia* and *Latria*, and *Cultus*, answering to our own 'Worship' in its older and more comprehensive use. This last is a generic term, embracing various kinds of worship, both that which is proper to God alone, and that which may be rendered to men (as, *e. g.*, to 'worshipful' magistrates and others in authority). And when they would distinguish accurately, and in technical terms, these two kinds of worship, they make use of the two words, Doulia (δουλεία) and Latria (λατρεία), which they have adopted from the Greek for the purpose.

Lastly, the word *Adoratio* (with *adorare*), and its equivalent, the Greek προσκύνησις, are terms which they regard as *properly* importing *Divine* worship, but which are not to be considered as absolutely limited to such use.

Latria.

As to Latria, then (as far as the *word* is concerned), there is no difference between the Roman Church and our own. Both are agreed that there is a kind of worship which should be offered to God, and to God alone. Both are agreed that the term λατρεία is in Holy Scripture, and in ecclesiastical use, used always with reference to such worship. As to this word, therefore, no detailed notice is necessary.

---

* See Petavius, 'De Theolog. Dogmat.' lib. xv. c. 11 *sqq.*

But the two words, προσκύνησις and *adoratio* (προσκυνεῖν and *adorare*), have an important history attaching to them, and in making this history clear we shall have advanced a long way towards the solution of some difficult theological problems.

It will be convenient to distinguish the uses of these terms in four periods.

§ 1. Προσκύνησις *and* Adoratio *in Classical Use.*

In order to understand the use of these words in the earlier writers, before the Christian era, we must bear in mind the strong contrast of feeling between the servile nations of the East, habitually under despotic government, and the free nations of the West, to whom an absolutely despotic government was wholly exceptional, and utterly repugnant.

That difference of feeling showed itself among other things in this, that Eastern peoples prostrated themselves with the same attitude of outward adoration (upon their knees, and even with their faces touching the ground) before their kings, as they did before their gods. But to the free Greek, and to the Roman, such abject deference was utterly contemptible, and held unworthy of any true man. They would bow themselves before their gods; they would not bow themselves, in the like attitude of prostrate supplication, before men.

This feeling is well illustrated by a story told by Herodotus (lib. vii. c. 136). He is speaking of the two Spartans who volunteered to give themselves up to Xerxes, in atonement for the violence done to the envoys from Darius. When they came into the king's presence, the guards in attendance tried to force them to prostrate themselves, in Eastern fashion, before the king : προσκυνέειν βασιλέα προσπίτνοντας. But they said that no force should compel them to do this, for they were not in the habit of prostrating themselves *before any mere man :* οὔτε γάρ σφι ἐν νόμῳ εἶναι ἄνθρωπον προσκυνέειν.* With this may be compared Xenophon. Anab. i. 6, § 10. To the same effect are the words of Q. Curtius ('De Rebus Gestis,' &c. lib. viii. c. 5, § 6). Speaking of a time when Alexander the Great claimed to be the son of Jupiter, and to be approached with *divine honours,* he says, that, in accordance with his wish, the Macedonians '*venerabundos ipsum salutare, more Persarum, prosternentes humi corpora.*'

---

* Compare Aristotle, 'Rhet.' i. 5, 9. After defining τιμή, 'honour,' as being σημεῖον εὐεργετικῆς δόξης, he enumerates a variety of ways in which honour is customarily shown, and then adds τὰ βαρβαρικά, ceremonies, *i. e. unknown to Greek usage,* and these are προσκυνήσεις καὶ ἐκστάσεις, *bodily prostrations,* and other such extravagancies.

But perhaps the most suggestive passage of all, referring to this subject, is that of Plutarch in the life of Themistocles, where he says, that on Themistocles coming to the Persian court he was instructed by Artabanus to prostrate himself, after the Persian fashion, before the king, if admitted into his presence. 'You Greeks,' added the Persian, 'are said to regard liberty and equality more than aught else; but we Persians have many good customs, and among them all none better than this of honouring the king, *and worshipping him as the image of God, who is the Saviour of all* .... For the customs of our country suffer not that the king should give ear to any who hath not first (worshipped) done him homage.' Βασιλεῖ γὰρ οὐ πάτριον ἀνέρος ἀκροᾶσθαι μὴ προσκυνήσαντος.

§ 2. *Use of these Terms in Holy Scripture.*

The passages above quoted will suffice to show the marked difference of feeling between East and West in this matter of prostration. And this difference it is important to bear in mind for the due understanding of Holy Scripture. A native of Syria, or of other Eastern lands, might (προσκυνεῖν) prostrate himself before another, without *necessarily* implying any greater homage than he would show to a king, or other great personage, far his own superior in rank. But when *a Roman centurion* προσκυνεῖ, prostrates himself before Peter, the latter raises him up, saying, 'Stand up; I myself also am *a man*' (not *a God*, as the action of Cornelius would import). And even in one brought up in Eastern habits, this προσκύνησις is an attitude which (except to a king or an absolute master) imports Divine honour. Hence that of the angel to St. John (Apocal. xix. 10), 'I fell at his feet,' says St. John, προσκυνῆσαι αὐτῷ, '*to worship him*. But he said unto me, *See thou do it not: I am thy fellow-servant* .. *Worship God*.' Τῷ Θεῷ προσκύνησον. The same words recur, almost *verbatim*, in ch. xxii. 8, 9.

From a review, then, of the New Testament usage of this word (which agrees with that of the LXX.), we should infer, that the proper connotation of the term is such a prostration as, even to Eastern idea, belonged primarily to God, or to kings, as being as gods upon earth; but which a slave might also on occasion use (Matt. xviii. 26) in earnest entreaty to his lord; or one in grievous need (Matt. xv. 25), or abject misery, towards one whose aid he would implore as being to him 'in the place of God.'

§ 3. *Use of* Προσκύνησις *in early Christian Writers.*

The use of the word προσκύνησις, as far as we have traced it hitherto, will be found to be preserved, in ecclesiastical writers, without any innovation, for 450 years; at the close of which time we find the first indication of any important change.

That use may best be illustrated, in reference to our present subject (that of the Cultus of the Virgin Mary), by the following remarkable passage of St. Epiphanius, the 'five-tongued' Bishop of Constantia in Cyprus, *circ.* 370 A.D.

He is referring to a sect of heretics in Arabia, known as Collyridians. Rebutting their blasphemous language and idolatrous rites he says, '*Honoured* let her [Mary] be: but let worship be paid to the Father, the Son, and the Holy Ghost:' Ἐν τιμῇ ἔστω· ἀλλὰ Πατὴρ καὶ Υἱὸς καὶ Ἅγιον Πνεῦμα προσκυνείσθω. 'Let none worship Mary:' Τὴν Μαρίαν μηδεὶς προσκυνείτω. Similar passages occur again and again throughout this section of his treatise. [Hæres. 79.]

It may be asked, how it should be that in Epiphanius alone assertions such as these are to be found? The reply is a very simple one: that in no part of the Church, whether in East or West, had the idea of worshipping the Virgin Mary (or showing her honours which could be regarded as importing Divine worship) anywhere been heard of till, in Epiphanius' time, two sects made their appearance in Arabia; one of which was known as that of the Antidicomariani, because of their denying the virginity of the Mother of our Lord, the other as Collyridians, because of the extravagant honours they paid her, and expressly their bringing offerings of cakes (*collyria*), possibly with a kind of parody upon the 'oblation' of bread and wine made in the Holy Eucharist.

These heresies having arisen (the one probably a reaction against the other), Epiphanius impartially condemns them both, saying again and again (for what concerns our present question) what I have quoted above, though with slight variations of expression.

But I may add further, that what St. Epiphanius says in direct terms, and unmistakably, is affirmed again and again, by implication, by other Fathers; as, for instance, by St. Athanasius and St. Cyril of Alexandria. They carefully define, not λατρεία, '*latria*,' only, but προσκύνησις, as due to God alone. So much so, that, even as regards our blessed Lord, they affirm that worship (προσκύνησις) is due to Him in respect of His divine nature, not in respect of His human nature, immediately and directly, and regarded as ideally (though not truly) separable from His Divinity. Thus, St. Athanasius, for example (quoted by Suicer), writes,[*] '*The creature worships not the creature;* but the servant worships his master, and the

---

[*] Orat. III. contr. Arianos, tom. i. p. 394.

creature worships God:' Κτίσμα κτίσμα ού προσκυνεῖ, ἀλλὰ ὁοῦλος δεσπότην, καὶ κτίσμα Θεόν. Then, after allusion to the 'worship' of the centurion rejected by St. Peter (Acts, x. 25), and that of St. John rejected by the angel, he adds, Οὐκοῦν Θεοῦ ἐστι μόνου τὸ προσκυνεῖσθαι· '*To God alone, therefore, is worship due.*'

§ 4. *Change in the Usage of* Προσκύνησις, *circ.* 450 A.D.

The very earliest writer (as far as I have observed) who innovates upon this older use of προσκύνησις, 'adoration,' is St. Proclus, Patriarch of Constantinople *circ.* 450 A.D., a highly rhetorical writer, who, in direct contradiction (as far as *words* are concerned) to St. Epiphanius, already quoted, asserts that προσκύνησις,* or 'adoration,' is rendered to the Virgin Mary. After enumerating the noble and saintly women of earlier times, and saying that praise is given to one, admiration to another, and the like, he ends by saying that 'to Mary also worship is given' (προσκυνεῖται καὶ ἡ Μαρία), because she has become Mother, and Handmaid, and Cloud, and Bridal Chamber (θάλαμος), and the Ark of Him who ruleth over all.

It is not difficult to account for this change, and Constantinople is the place of all others in which we might expect to find the first indications of it. For in the four hundred years, or more, which had already elapsed since the establishment of Imperialism at Rome (and later at Constantinople), a complete change had been effected in the habits of Western nations in that matter of outward prostrations before *men*.

The etiquette and ceremonial of the Imperial court, at Rome first, and afterward more fully at Constantinople, were modelled in great part upon the traditions of the despotic courts of the East. And that servile adulation of the Emperors, as gods upon earth, of which we find traces even in Horace, found expression, habitually, at a later time, in 'adoration' at Rome, and in προσκύνησις, or abject bodily prostration, at Byzantium, such as the free Greeks and Romans of earlier times would have regarded as fit only for slaves and barbarians.† These extravagant honours were paid not only to the Emperors themselves, when actually present, but to their images, and even to letters purporting to contain their 'celestial words,' or the expression of their 'sacred will.'

This outward homage, adopted first while the Empire was in open opposition to Christianity, was afterward continued in the case of Christian

---

* S. Procli Laudatio Deiparæ Virginis, iv. p. 343. Combefis Auctarium Bibl. Patt. Fol. Paris. 1648.   † See note above, p. 192.

Emperors. And thus the old notion common to classical antiquity, and to Holy Scripture, of προσκύνησις, or 'adoration,' being due to God alone, became more and more weakened; and abject servility towards earthly princes paved the way for a worship which, by degrees, became idolatrous (in practice, though not in theory), of angels, of saints, and among these more especially of the Virgin Mary.

And the lax use of words importing worship, and the breaking down of the older ecclesiastical distinctions, already traced, between τιμᾶν and προσκυνεῖν, between *colere* and *adorare*, which takes its first beginning from the close of the fifth century, or thereabouts, is the natural expression of this change in actual practice. In mediæval usage, as we have already seen, *adorare* is the word used of the homage paid to an Emperor by the Pope who had just crowned him (above, p. 101). And at a later period still (early in the fifteenth century), of which we have also had occasion to speak in connexion with the Council of Florence, we find the word προσκυνεῖν used by the Greeks from Constantinople (Syropylus and others) of every kind of formal salutation, from the most abject prostration to a simple inclination of the head, or kissing of the hand.

B.

The Teaching of the early Fathers concerning the Virgin Mary.

THE evidence of Christian art already summed up in the earlier pages (pp. 60, 61) of this volume is such as to show that, in the more public monuments expressive of the deliberate belief of the Church, no change was made for upwards of five hundred years in the representations of the Virgin Mary, such as would support, in any way, the later developments of doctrine concerning her, both in the Roman Church and, in a much less degree, in the various Churches of the East.

But towards the close of that period, as we have seen reason to think, traces may be found in less important works of Christian art, such as the Vetri Antichi, of a change having already begun, coincident in time with that utter decay of primitive learning which followed closely after the invasions of barbarians in all the countries of Europe, of Africa, and of the

TEACHING OF EARLY FATHERS.   197

East, which they successively overran. The conclusions to which these facts point are strongly confirmed by literary evidence.

For four hundred and fifty years, or more, the language of the greatest teachers of the Church, upon this subject, is directly contradictory to modern Roman doctrine.

Petavius himself* quotes, among others of less note, St. Basil of Cæsarea, St. John Chrysostom, and St. Cyril of Alexandria, as using language which he, by no means extreme among Roman theologians, on this subject, can only describe as '*infanda*,' not fit to be uttered.

The following are the passages which he quotes :—

1. St. Basil. (379 A.D.)

S. Basilii Cæs. Cappod. Archiepisc. [Opp. Omnia. Ed. Benedict. 3 foll. Fol. Paris, 1730], ep. cclx. *ad fin.* [tom. iii. p. 400 D]. Commenting on the words, '*A sword shall go through thine own soul also*,' he says, that these words have reference to the time of our Lord's Passion—that when Mary saw the things which were done, and heard the words from the cross —then, albeit she had heard the witness of Gabriel, and had learnt the secret things of the Lord as concerning the divine conception, and had seen Christ manifested in many miracles, *yet would her soul then be tossed upon waves of doubt:* γενήσεται φησί τις καὶ περὶ τὴν σὴν ψυχὴν σάλος. 'For need there was,' he proceeds, 'that the Lord should taste of death for every man, and having become a propitiation for the world, that He should justify all men in His own blood. Therefore shall something of doubt (that is, the sword) affect thee also, though thou hast been taught from above the things concerning the Lord, that so thoughts' (διαλογισμοί· literally, disputings, and so doubts) 'out of many hearts may be revealed. In this he intimateth to us, that *after the offence, both to the disciples and to Mary, that was caused by the cross of Christ, a speedy healing should follow from the Lord, confirming their hearts to faith in Him.*'

The language of St. Chrysostom, which follows, is much stronger.

2. St. Chrysostom. (407 A.D.)

Hom. in Matt. xliv. *al.* xlv. [Migne, t. vii. p. 525.] Referring to the words, '*Behold, thy mother and thy brethren stand without, seeking to speak unto thee*,' and to our Lord's reply, '*Who is my mother?*' &c., St. Chrysostom writes as follows :—'This He spake, not as one ashamed of his mother,

---

* Theolog. Dogm. de Incarnat. lib. xiv. cap. i.

nor as denying her that bare Him, for if He had felt such shame He would not have passed through that womb, but in order to show that from this fact [of her giving birth to the Saviour] she will have no benefit, unless in all things she doeth what is right. For what she then took in hand to do gave proof of excessive ambition (φιλοτιμία), for she was desirous of showing to the people how she bare rule, at her own will, over her Son; for as yet she had no exalted thoughts concerning Him. And for this reason her coming was unseasonable. See, for instance, the thoughtlessness (ἀπόνοια) both of her and them. For whereas they ought to have entered in with the multitude, and have listened, or, if they would not do this, to have waited till the Lord had closed His discourse, and then have approached Him, yet do they summon Him out; and they do this in the sight of all, therein showing great ambition, and wishing to prove that with great authority they lay their commands upon Him. And the Evangelist showeth that He chargeth this upon them' . . . And so on, more to the same effect. With this compare his Hom. xxi. on St. John [Migne, t. viii. p. 141], where he uses similar language, saying that she wished both to gratify His brethren and to make herself more distinguished by means of her Son. So again his Hom. iv. in Matt. i., where, speaking of the Annunciation, he mentions her asking, 'How shall these things, be?' &c., as a proof of human frailty [want of faith] on her part.

3. ST. CYRIL OF ALEXANDRIA. (444 A.D.)

This writer, who was regarded by his contemporaries in the fifth century as the great champion of the true faith, uses language concerning the Virgin Mary closely resembling that of St. Chrysostom, and which is, in some respects, even more disparaging; as when, for example, he says that none can wonder that she, as a mere woman, should have given proof of a want of faith, such as even Peter was not exempt from. (Opp. tom. iv. pp. 1064, 1065.)

Such is the language of the Fathers for the first five hundred years; and what can a writer so learned as Petavius allege in reply? First, that in his opinion the reasons are very weak on which these various Fathers ground their statements. It is strange that he, and that others who follow in his wake, should not see, that, whether those reasons be strong or weak, is a question which in no way invalidates the conclusion that *no such doctrine as the Roman Church now holds could have been ever dreamed of* at the time when St. Chrysostom, St. Basil, St. Cyril, and the rest whom he quotes, wrote and spoke in the terms they did.

Language of St. Augustine.

But he has another answer to make, which requires somewhat fuller consideration. He appeals (as writers of his school always do) to a well-known passage of St. Augustine, which he describes as a testimony in proof that the Virgin Mary was never guilty of any act of sin ('*nunquam actuale peccatum admisisse*'). How far this holds good my readers may best judge by examining the passage itself. Before doing so, however, it may be well to remind ourselves what was the teaching of St. Augustine in other passages concerning 'Christ alone without sin.'

The following passages will serve to show what this was:—

'De Peccatorum Meritis et Remissione,' lib. i. c. 29.—'*One only was born without sin*, whom a Virgin conceived.' 'Solus sine peccato natus est, quem sine virili complexu, non concupiscentia carnis, sed obedientia mentis, virgo concepit.'

Ibid. lib. xi. c. 1.—He states the subject of his present inquiry to be, whether any one was either then living, or had lived in time past, or ever would live, while the world lasted, without any sin whatsoever ('*sine ullo omnino peccato*'), 'with the exception of the one Mediator between God and men, the man Christ Jesus.'

Ibid. c. 20.—In this chapter he answers the question by saying, that, *with the one exception named*, it is most certain that no such person either had been or ever would be. ' Hunc [*i. e.* one free from all sin] prorsus nisi unum mediatorem . . . nullum vel esse, vel fuisse, vel futurum esse.'

Ibid. c. 24.—Like many other passages relating to the Virgin Mary, this, *for obvious reasons*, has been corrupted by the later copyists. In a very remarkable passage, St. Augustine is speaking of the points at once of likeness and of unlikeness between human nature as it is in *us*, and that same human nature as it is in Christ; between that divine nature which is inherent in Him, and that divine nature of which we are made 'partakers.' He was made *in the likeness of sinful flesh*, whereas we are born *in sinful flesh*. And he concludes, '*Solus ergo ille etiam homo factus, manens Deus, peccatum nullum habuit unquam, nec sumpsit carnem peccati quamvis de materna carne peccati.*' He, therefore, and He only, remaining God even when He became man, had never sin at any time; nor did He take upon Him a flesh that was of sin [sinful], albeit the flesh of His mother, whence He derived His, was of sin [sinful].

The reading '*materna carne peccati*' (which is that of the Benedictines) rests on the authority of the 'Vetustissimus Codex Corbeiensis,' and all the other Gallican MSS. (two only excepted), and of all that were examined by the Louvain editors. Two of the Sorbonne MSS. and one at Monte Casale read '*de materia carnis peccati*;' but printed editions earlier than the Benedictine commonly altered the text, and read '*de natura carnis peccati*.'

Ibid. c. 35.—He repeats his strong assertion in a yet stronger form:— 'Teneamus ergo indeclinabilem fidei confessionem. Solus unus est qui sine peccato natus est in similitudine carnis peccati, sine peccato vixit inter aliena peccata, sine peccato mortuus est propter nostra peccata.'

Such is the formal teaching of St. Augustine upon the question thus formally proposed, and dogmatically answered. We may now consider the only passage which Roman theologians, and those who think with them, can quote with satisfaction upon this particular question from the Fathers, whether in East or West, for upwards of four hundred years from the first beginning of the Church.

It occurs in the treatise 'De Natura et Gratia' [Migne, t. x. p. 267,] c. 36. Pelagius, while maintaining his own heretical opinions, had asserted that 'Abel, Enoch, Melchisedec, Abraham, Isaac .... Simeon, Joseph, John' (the Baptist)—and not man only but woman also—'Deborah, Anna, mother of Samuel, Judith, Esther, the other Anna, daughter of Phanuel, Elizabeth, and also Mary, the very mother of our Lord and Saviour;'—that these had not only not sinned, but had lived righteously: adding, as to the last of those enumerated above, that 'piety required us to allow that she was without sin' ('*quam sine peccato esse confiteri necesse esse pietati*'). Referring to this St. Augustine writes as follows:—'With the exception, then, of the holy Virgin Mary, *whom, out of honour to the Lord, I do not choose to have brought into question when we are speaking about acts of sin* .... with this exception, if we could gather together all those holy men and women (for holy when living here on earth they were), and ask them whether they were without sin, what do we suppose they would have answered? As Pelagius did, or as did John the Apostle [in saying, 'If we have no sin,' &c.]?'

Between the first and the second parts of the above there intervenes, as I have indicated, a parenthesis, which I have reserved for separate notice. The Benedictines read as follows:—

'*Unde enim scimus quid ei plus gratiæ collatum fuerit ad vincendum omni ex parte peccatum, quæ concipere ac parere meruit quem constat nullum habuisse peccatum?*' But out of sixteen manuscripts which they examined, two (two of the five in the Vatican Library) gave the reading adopted by Thomas Aquinas (p. 111, qu. 27, a. 4), '*Inde enim scimus quod ei plus gratiæ collatum fuerit ad vincendum o. e. p. p. quod concipere et parere*,' &c.

According to the first reading of the parenthesis (which is that of *all the*

Gallican MSS. consulted by the Benedictines, and of three out of five of those in the Vatican), the words literally translated mean, '*For how do we know what more of grace, for the overcoming of sin in every respect, was bestowed upon her, who was found worthy to conceive, and to give birth to, Him of whom we know that He had no sin?*' According to the other, '*For it is from this we know that more grace was bestowed upon her for the complete conquering of sin, because she was found worthy to conceive, and to bear, Him of whom it is certain that He was without sin.*'

Now let us consider what would result from this passage even if taken in this latter form, which a Roman controversialist would naturally prefer. We should have, first of all, the plainest possible condemnation from St. Augustine of the doctrine now taught on the authority of the Roman Church, viz. that the Virgin Mary was born free from all sin, *original* as well as *actual*. For if, by greater measures of grace she was enabled completely to *conquer* sin, it follows that 'sin' (not necessarily developed in act, but yet existing as a power) was in her (so the context implies) to be conquered. We should have, on the other hand, an assertion made by St. Augustine, that '*we know* that more grace was given her for the complete conquest of sin, *because* she was deemed worthy to give birth unto Him of whom it is certain that He was without sin.' That St. Augustine ever rested a dogmatic assertion so momentous upon an inference so illogical as this, it would require more than the authority of two Vatican MSS. to convince me. But assuming, for argument's sake, that he wrote it, the utmost result would be this,—that St. Augustine, in so saying, asserts, as an inference from our Lord's sinlessness, that the Virgin Mother completely conquered sin. But *if* St. Augustine really said this, it would follow further, first, that St. Augustine was, for once at least, an exceedingly illogical reasoner; and, secondly, that he was, in this special opinion of his, in direct opposition to the greatest authorities of the early Church, such as those already quoted.

All these grounds considered, there are few, I suppose, who would not agree with the Benedictines, and other editors, in rejecting the reading adopted by Aquinas, and found in two MSS. only. But if we fall back on the reading of the Benedictines, we have a sentence which (under the form of a question, '*Whence* do we know?' &c.) plainly implies that we have no knowledge whether the Virgin Mary did or did not completely conquer sin; and that, this being so, he will not have her brought into question in such a matter, out of regard to the honour of the Lord. This want of knowledge, in her case, is contrasted with the certainty that our Lord Himself was without sin.

Whichever reading* be the true one, there is clearly here a direct contradiction to those very dogmas of modern Rome in support of which the passage is alleged.

C.

Literary Evidence concerning the Bodily Assumption of the Virgin Mary.

UPON this subject, as upon so many others, one Roman writer has copied what he found asserted by others before him, apparently without ever verifying the references given, and rarely adding anything to the statements which they found ready to their hand.

I may refer, for an example of this, to Pelliccia ('De Christianæ Ecclesiæ Politia,' libri sex. Neapoli, 1777). His statements are copied, almost *verbatim*, by the Abbé Martigni, in his recent 'Dictionary of Christian Antiquities;' and certain writers among ourselves quote the book as if its authority were unimpeachable.

He states (tom. ii. p. 69 *sqq.*), by way of proof of the very early date of the Feast of the Assumption, that St. Gregory of Tours speaks of its being observed in Gaul; that Constantinus, Bishop of Constantia in Cyprus, refers to the same festival at the Seventh Œcumenical Council (*i.e.* Nicæa II. in the eighth century); and, lastly, he appeals to what Anastasius the Librarian records concerning Pope Sergius I., who lived in the seventh century.

He does not quote the words of either one of those three, but he affirms that they manifestly convict of error those who had pretended that the festival in honour of the Assumption was not instituted before the ninth century. [The Assumption itself being, as he had already stated, *the ascent of the Virgin Mary into heaven, body and soul together.* 'Ecclesia enim Mariam cælos petiisse anima pariter atque corpore docet.']

Thus we have, according to Pelliccia, St. Gregory of Tours, in the sixth

---

* Mere conjectural readings are of little worth in the absence of MS. evidence; otherwise I would suggest that *quin* in place of *quid* would make better Latin and better sense of the passage.

century, Pope Sergius in the seventh, Constantinus in the eighth, all testifying to the existence of this primitive belief, and of the festival by which the event was commemorated.

Nothing can be more utterly untrue (though I have no doubt the worthy Archbishop was not aware of his untruth) in respect of two out of three references: the third I have been unable to verify—that of Constantinus of Cyprus.

Gregory of Tours, to take him first, says not a word of the 'Festival of the Assumption' being held in Gaul. In the 'De Gloria Martyrum,' lib. i. c. 9, he refers to a festival (*festivitas*) in memory of the Virgin, celebrated 'mediante mense undecimo;' *i. e.* (probably) on the 18th of January.* Had he named the Feast, he would probably have called it the 'Dormitio,' or 'falling asleep;' *i. e.* the Death of the Virgin Mary. But even had he used the word 'Assumptio,' it would not the least follow that he meant what is *now* meant by 'the Assumption.'† For in those days, nay, even two centuries earlier, as the language of Paulinus of Nola shows, this word 'Assumptio' was used in speaking of God 'taking to Himself' any of His saints: so that the word, *as such*, would prove nothing at all, even if it had been used.

But from another passage we learn what particular form of the many stories current about the death of the Virgin St. Gregory had received. In the fourth chapter of the 'Gloria Martyrum,' lib. i., he repeats the story contained in the spurious 'Transitus Mariæ Virginis,' falsely ascribed to Melito of Sardis. He says, that when the Virgin was about to be taken from the world, the Apostles assembled from various countries, and came to her house, and watched with her. 'And lo! the Lord Jesus came with His angels, and receiving her soul, delivered it to the Archangel Michael, and so departed. At dawn the Apostles lifted up her body, with the couch on which it lay, and laid it in a tomb, and kept watch over it, expecting the coming of the Lord. And lo! a second time He stood by them, and receiving the holy body in a cloud, *bade that it should be conveyed to Paradise;* where now, her soul being reunited to the body, exulting, together with His elect, she enjoys the blessings of eternity, which shall never end.' Her soul is in Paradise (not in heaven) according to St. Gregory, as are the souls of God's elect departed this life. She differs from

---

* He generally speaks of the year as beginning with March.

† Thus he speaks of the 'Assumptio' of St. Andrew ('De G. M.' lib. i. c. 31) and of St. Martin ('De Mir. S. Martini,' c. 32). Bede, and other Latin writers, use the word in the same way in speaking of the 'departure' of the faithful.

them, as it would seem, in St. Gregory's belief, in this only, that her body is in Paradise as well as her soul.

But where is the '*cælos petiisse*,' the ascending into *heaven*, both body and soul, of which Pelliccia so confidently speaks? Not one word of this does St. Gregory say, from the beginning of his book to the end.

Failing this, what shall we say of Anastasius and Sergius I.? The passage referred to is this:—Sergius, anno Christi 687 (p. 164). 'Hic statuit . . . . ut diebus Annuntiationis Domini, Nativitatis, *et Dormitionis Sanctæ Dei Genitricis* . . . . *litania exeat a Sancto Adriano*,' &c. In other words, he alludes to a festival known as the 'Dormitio,' or 'Falling asleep,' of the Virgin Mary—the very same word which is constantly used in the Catacombs, and elsewhere, of the death of the faithful generally; and which, therefore, like the Greek title of this festival, the Κοίμησις, proves nothing at all as to any belief of her 'Assumption into Heaven.'

If the passage in the 'Actio Quarta' of the Seventh General Council could be found, I have little doubt that Constantinus would be found speaking in like manner of the 'κοίμησις of the holy Theotokos;' a phrase which simply proves nothing as to the acceptance *then* of a doctrine like that of modern Rome.

The above will serve as examples of what Roman writers *say*. The following will give some idea of *what they leave unsaid*.

One Adamanus (or Adamnanus) was abbot of a monastery '*in insula Hyensi*,' off the coast of Scotland, and died, when nearly eighty years old, in the year 704 A.D. He received in hospitality St. Arculfus, who had been a traveller in the Holy Land, and took down from his lips a description of the holy places his visitor had seen.*

Upon the subject of the supposed Tomb of the Virgin Mary in the Valley of Jehoshaphat he writes as follows:†—' Sanctorum locorum sedulus frequentator Sanctus Arculphus Sanctæ Mariæ ecclesiam‡ in valle Josaphat frequentabat cujus . . . . in orientali parte altarium habetur: ad dextram vero ejus partem Sanctæ Mariæ inest saxeum cavum sepulchrum, in quo aliquando sepulta pausavit. Sed de eodem sepulchro quomodo, vel quo tempore, vel a quibus personis, sanctum corpusculum ejus sit sublatum, *vel quo loco resurrectionem expectat nullus, ut fertur, pro certo scire potest.* . . . Ita nobis frater Arculphus pronuntiavit, sanctorum visitator locorum, qui hæc quæ nos describimus propriis conspexit oculis.'

---

* De Locis Sanctis. Migne, P. C. C. tom. lxxxviii. p. 722 *sqq*.
† Ibid. lib. i. c. xiii.

‡ For details as to this church see Quaresmius, ' Terræ Sanctæ Elucidatio,' Antwerp, fol. 1639, tom. ii. pp. 238, 248, &c.

Such was the account given by Arculphus, coming fresh from the very spot, even as late as the eighth century. He had seen there an empty sepulchre, which, as he was told, and as he evidently believed, was that of the Virgin Mary. But *when, or by whom, the body had been removed, or in what place it was awaiting the resurrection; of this, he said, no one could say anything for certain.*

Gradual Development of the Apocryphal Story of the Assumption.

As an example of the way in which apocryphal legends of this kind (since sanctioned as integral portions of the Christian faith by the Roman Church) grew up and took shape in mediæval times, it may be well to trace this somewhat more carefully in its successive stages.

1. The first germ of it may be detected in an expression used by Epiphanius in the latter half of the fourth century. In his book on Heresies (Hær. 78) he says, in speaking of the Virgin Mary, that Scripture is wholly silent as to her later life: 'whether or no she went with St. John to Ephesus —nay, whether she be dead or no, we know not:' Κἄν τε οὖν τέθνηκεν οὐκ ἔγνωμεν. Then he refers to two passages of Holy Scripture, which he thinks may possibly contain traces of the truth concerning her. One is that in the Revelation of St. John concerning the Dragon and the Woman, to whom were given the wings of an eagle, that she fled away into the wilderness, &c. Of this he says, ' Perhaps this may be fulfilled in her [the Virgin Mary]: yet do I not by any means so determine. And I say not that she abode without death, but neither, on the other hand, do I affirm that she is dead.'

This 'not knowing' and 'not affirming' is the more notable, because Epiphanius had been at Jerusalem among other places, and it is evident that he knew nothing, either by tradition or otherwise, of a tomb of the Virgin Mary in the Valley of Jehoshaphat.

2. This last remark applies equally to other Greek writers. Eusebius ('In Vita Constantini'), Socrates ('Hist.' lib. i. c. xiii.), Sozomen (lib. i. c. i.), speak of the holy places found in the time of Constantine, and none of them make any mention of this.

3. Cardinal Baronius (ad ann. 48) quotes, as from the 'Chronicon' of Eusebius, words (which I have been unable to find) to this effect. Writing of the year 48 A.D. he represents him as saying, '*Maria Virgo Christi Mater ad Filium in cœlum assumitur, ut quidam fuisse sibi revelatum scribunt.*'

If the passage be genuine (much of his 'Chronicon' is not), it is indicative of an early date (fourth century at the latest) for the first appearance of the story, put out first (as this passage implies) by some private persons on the faith of a supposed 'revelation' on the subject. Of these revelations we shall hear more as we go on.

4. St. Jerome had lived many years at Bethlehem and at Jerusalem, and often describes the holy places (as in his Epist. xxvii. and in the 'Liber de Locis Hebraicis'), and nowhere makes any mention of this : nor does he know anything of the Assumption into heaven of the Virgin Mary herself. [For the letter of the pseudo-Jerome see No. 8 below.]

But shortly after his time (so the evidence now to be adduced, if genuine, would seem to prove) the discovery of an empty sepulchre, supposed to be that of the Virgin Mary, must have taken place. According to Nicephorus (writing in the eleventh century), the Empress Pulcheria (who died A.D. 453) asked the then Patriarch of Jerusalem (Juvenalis, *sed.* 429–457) to send the relics of the Blessed Virgin to Constantinople, to be a protection to the Imperial city. The Patriarch replied (according to Nicephorus, 'Ecc. Hist.' lib. xv. c. xiv.) by telling her, on the authority of '*an ancient and most true tradition*,' the story of the Assumption, much as we find it in later authors. Nicephorus seems to have taken his details from Dionysius the (so called) Areopagite.*

5. The apocryphal book known as the 'Transitus beatæ Mariæ Virginis,' must have become known in the West in the course of the fifth century, as it was formally condemned in a Roman Council under Gelasius in the year 496 A.D. It was from this book, evidently, that Gregory of Tours derived the account we have already quoted (above, p. 203).

6. Dionysius the Areopagite (so called), in the fourth or fifth century probably, in his treatise 'De Divinis Nominibus,' lib. i. c. iii. (Migne, Series Græca, tom. iii. p. 681), speaks as if he had been present with the Apostles and others, and had seen the body of the Virgin after her death. He says not a word here of her 'Assumption into Heaven.' But Michael Syngelus, in his Life of Dionysius (ibid. tom. iv. p. 683), makes this addition, saying of the Virgin Mary, that after she had been placed in the tomb εἰς τὴν ὑπερουράνιον ἀνελήφθη λῆξιν ἡ πάντων τῶν οὐρανίων ὑπερτέρα δυναμέων καὶ πάσης δεσπόζουσα κτίσεως.

7. Of uncertain date, and unknown authorship, are two spurious docu-

---

* Baronius, ad ann. 48, allows that he can find no trace of the story of the Assumption before the discovery of the empty sepulchre spoken of by Juvenalis. He even seems to suggest (what, no doubt, he would have not admitted) that the discovery gave rise to the story. Nothing more probable.

ments concerning the Assumption (condemned as such by Baronius and other Romans, as well as by writers of our own), one of which is attributed to St. Jerome, the other to St. Augustine. This latter (Migne, tom. vi. p. 1142) is believed to be of the eighth century by the Roman editors. The writer treats the question as one in which there is no *authority* for our guidance. He argues, on *à priori* grounds, that God *could* raise the Virgin to heaven—that it was fitting He should do so; whence we may conclude (so the author thinks) that He *did* do so.

8. The letter attributed to St. Jerome has quite a history of its own. It is addressed *ad Paulam et Eustochium*, '*De Assumptione beatæ Mariæ.*' It is a manifest forgery, as Baronius is at pains to prove, and does prove; but it was not known to be so in the Middle Ages, and the results were curious. The pseudo-Jerome refers to the story of the Assumption, but says (Opp. ed. BB. tom. v. p. 83), 'Quomodo vel quo tempore aut a quibus personis sanctissimum corpus ejus inde [a sepulchro] ablatum fuerit, vel ubi transpositum; utrumne resurrexit (*sic*), nescitur, quamvis nonnulli astruere velint eam jam resuscitatam, et beata cum Christo immortalitate in cælestibus vestiri.' These are questions, he admirably adds, about which 'propter cautelam (salva fide) pio magis desiderio *opinari* oporteat, *quam inconsulte definire quod sine periculo nescitur.*'

This language (supposed to be that of St. Jerome) was read on certain festivals in some churches in the Middle Ages. St. Anthony of Padua could not bear to hear these doubts thrown on the truth of the Assumption, and would not go to matins (so the story* is told) for fear of hearing this read. Thereupon an angel appeared to him, and said, 'Why will you not go to matins, Anthony?' He replied, that he could not bear to hear the aforesaid 'lection.' 'On his so saying, straightway the Blessed Virgin appeared before him, attended by a great company of angels; and Anthony fell at her feet, and earnestly begged to know the certainty of this mystery. The Blessed Virgin replied, "Fear not, Anthony, both to believe and to teach this truth."' 'Secure, Antoni, veritatem hanc et credere et prædicare potes.'

But, says Quaresmius, in relating all this, 'Quid de beato Hieronymo?' What is to be said of St. Jerome, when the Virgin Mary herself says that what he doubts is certainly true? He is able to give a satisfactory answer. In the 'Revelations of St. Bridget,' lib. vi. c. lx., 'Dixit Mater Dei ad Brigettam, Hieronymum non dubitasse de ejus Adsumptione, sed quia

---

* Auctor Pomerii Sermonem de Beata Virgine, lib. x. pt. i. art. 3, apud Quaresmium.

determinate non fuerat revelata noluisse definire. " Quia Hieronymus non dubitavit de Assumptione mea, sed quia Deus non revelavit aperte hujusmodi veritatem, ideo Hieronymus maluit pie dubitare quam definire non ostensa a Deo." '

A further 'revelation' on the same subject will be found in lib. vii. c. xxvi. of the 'Revelations' of the same saint. 'Ego postquam Filius meus ascendit ad cælos vixi in mundo xv annos, et tanto tempore plus quantum est de Festo Ascensionis ejusdem Filii mei usque ad mortem meam, et tunc mortua jacui in isto sepulchro.'

9. Modestus, Patriarch of Jerusalem early in the seventh century, alludes to the traditions about the death of the Virgin Mary, as being what none of his predecessors had been in the habit of discoursing upon, and takes occasion to do so himself. Photius, in his 'Bibliotheca,' No. cclxxv. *ad fin.*, seems to doubt the authenticity of this 'Encomion.'* He does not give the details of the story as they are given by later writers, but says that 'she was translated μετωκίσθη ἐν τῇ ἄνω Ἱερουσαλήμ — to the Jerusalem that is above . . . and she has been made higher than cherubim and seraphim in the kingdom of heaven, being set forth in truth as the mother of their Lord.'

10. Andreas Cretensis, in the middle of the seventh century, hints at the Story of the Assumption, but does not state it in detail.†

11. The language of Arculphus, quoted by Adamnanus, 'De Locis Sanctis,' which is a little later in date than the last referred to, has been already quoted (p. 204).

12. John Damascene (*circ.* 756 A.D.) gives the story in full detail. And this reappears three centuries later in Nicephorus, 'Hist. Eccl.' xi. c. xxi., and xv. c. xiv.

13. Returning to the West, a variety of concurrent evidence, too minute to be given here in detail, leads to the conclusion that it was in the time of Charlemagne that the '*Dormitio*' of the Virgin Mary, in other words the anniversary of her death, became changed into the Festival of the Assumption. One fact out of many may be mentioned. In the 'Capitularies' of Charlemagne (lib. i. c. clviii.), after enumeration of the principal festivals (Natalis Domini, S. Stephani, Epiphania, &c.), the words are added, '*De Adsumptione S. Mariæ interrogandum relinquimus:*' implying that the question of the general observance of this festival had not yet been definitely settled.

---

* Photii Myriobiblon. Rothomag. fol. 1653, p. 1528.
† Homil. in Dormitionem Mariæ apud Galland. xiii. 147.

ASSUMPTION OF THE VIRGIN MARY.

14. In the Council of Mayence in the year 813 A.D. (Mansi, xiv. 73), the thirty-sixth canon is as follows:—'Festos dies in anno celebrare sancimus. Hoc est, diem dominicum Paschæ . . . . nativitatem S. Johannis Baptistæ, *Assumptionem S. Mariæ* . . . . dedicationem S. Michaelis,' &c. This, as contrasted with No. 13 above, marks the close of the eighth century, or the beginning of the ninth, as probably the time when the Festival of the Assumption (as distinct from the 'Dormitio') was authoritatively recognised in the Western Church. Leo IV. (middle of the ninth century) had a special zeal for the honour of this festival; and it is to him, as we have already seen (*supra*, p. 53), that the Church of St. Clement at Rome owed that fresco of the 'Assumption' which Roman divines so long vaunted as being a work of the second or third century.

At this point, at which the evidence of early literary monuments is found exactly coincident with those of Christian art already considered in this volume, this brief summary may be brought to a close.

ADDITIONAL NOTE.

As affording an additional note of time as to the development of this and other doctrines concerning the Virgin Mary, I add the following from a treatise attributed to S. Ildephonsus, Archbishop of Toledo, 667 A.D.*

'*Sermo de Assumptione Beatæ Mariæ.*—Hodie, fratres charissimi, gloriosa et perpetua Virgo Maria cælos ascendit: hodie de terris et de præsenti sæculo nequam erepta, secura de immarcessibili gloria ad cæli pervenit palatia. Hac inquam die meruit exaltari super choros angelorum: quoniam ut credimus in dextera Patris sublevata in cælis, regni solio, post Christum gloriosa resedit.'

And at the end:—

'Jam ego [*leg.* ergo] ad eam de qua loquimur preces et vota vertamus, opem intercessionis ejus poscamus singuli, poscamus omnes. Oremus ut sit protectrix in prosperis, submoveat noxia, suggerat profutura, admittat preces supplicantium intra sacrarium divinitatis.'

Of this St. Ildephonsus we are told by Joannes de Trettenhem, Abbas Spanhemensis ('Lib. de Scriptoribus Ecclesiasticis'), that the B. V. M. was so pleased with his book 'De Virgin.' &c., that she appeared to him with the book in her hand, and thanked him '*pro tali servitio.*' And he, wishing

---

* B. Hildephonsi Archiepiscopi Toletani de Virginitate S. Mariæ Liber. Ed. Feuendartius. Parisiis, 12mo. 1576.

to honour her still more highly, '*constituit ut celebraretur sollennitas ejus singulis annis octava die ante Natalem Domini; quæ sollennitas jam obtinuit ut per universam fidelium Ecclesiam in honore purissimæ Conceptionis ejus celebretur vi. Idus Decembris.*'

D.

Part I.

Indications in Holy Scripture of the Relation of St. Paul to the Church of Rome.

The Epistle addressed by St. Paul to the Romans is one which he could not have written in the same terms had he regarded them as being already, or had through revelation known that they were shortly about to be, under the immediate jurisdiction of St. Peter.

He begins (chap. i. 1, 5) by assertion of his own apostleship—an apostleship having special reference to all the Gentiles: ἐν πᾶσι τοῖς ἔθνεσιν (ver. 5), '*among whom*,' he adds, '*are ye also*.'

He, on whom Apostleship to the Gentiles had been specially conferred, while that to the Jews ('the Circumcision') had been specially delegated to St. Peter, had often purposed (ver. 15) to come to Rome, that he might have some fruit among them, as among other Gentiles. Though prevented hitherto, he is even now ready and willing to proclaim the glad tidings (ver. 15) to them also that are at Rome.

At the end of his Epistle he recurs to the thought of his special claim to be heard of them, as being the minister of Jesus Christ to the Gentiles (xv. 16); and his language throughout the two concluding chapters is that of one who, in the providence of God, has a special right, such as no other had, to be regarded as being *to them* the Apostle of Jesus Christ.

With all this compare what we read (in Acts, xxviii.) of what occurred when this contemplated visit to Rome was actually made. He first, as his wont was, gathered about him such of his own countrymen as were there (ver. 17); and the language in which his teaching, addressing to them, is described (vv. 23, 24), is such as plainly implies that to them the word of the Gospel was for the first time directly and authoritatively addressed. Afterward he turned to the Gentiles (ver. 28), and for two whole years continued to receive in his own hired house all that came unto him, 'preaching the kingdom of God, and teaching those things which concern the Lord Jesus Christ.'

No unprejudiced person can doubt that this was the first visit of any Apostle to the Roman Church. None, save in maintenance at all costs of a preconceived conclusion, could suppose that St. Paul could have used language such as that above quoted, or have acted as there described, in reference to a Church which by Divine appointment was already, or was just about to be, under the special jurisdiction of St. Peter.

2. With the above compare what St. Paul says in writing to the Corinthians (2 Cor. x. 16) of his not making his boast (in respect of apostolic work) ἐν ἀλλοτρίῳ κανόνι, in the field of work allotted to another.

In face of facts such as these, we need not be surprised to find that the more modern writers on the Roman side are obliged to give up as hopeless the defence of the recognised Roman tradition, that St. Peter was Bishop of Rome for twenty-five years! How exactly the evidence of Holy Scripture, above alleged, falls in with that of the early monuments edited in this volume, I need not be at pains to point out.

PART II.

Canons of Early Councils having Reference to the Roman See.

THE Canons of Nicæa (A.D. 325) and of Constantinople (A.D. 381) have already been quoted above, p. 87.

Between these had intervened the Council of Sardica (A.D. 347).

This was a Western Council, not a General Council of the whole Church; and its canons have accordingly a much more Roman character than those which were put forth by the Œcumenical Councils of the fourth and fifth centuries. And as there was no effectual check against their interpolation, as was the case (see p. 89 *sqq.*) with the acts of General Councils, there is considerable doubt as to what the original text of the Sardican Canons may have been.* Even as they now stand, however, they can

---

* See Gieseler, 'Ecc. Hist.' vol. i. p. 432, note 6. Davidson's Translation.

easily be reconciled with the language of General Councils before and after, if we bear in mind that the *singulæ quæque provinciæ*, of which at Sardica there was question, are not all the provinces of the whole Church throughout the world, but those in Sicily, Sardinia, and Corsica, which were subject to the Roman See, and constituted the Roman 'Diocese.' This is clearly implied, for instance, in the Synodical Letter of the Council addressed to Julius, Bishop of Rome. (Mansi, iii. p. 41.) '*Tua autem excellens prudentia disponere debet, ut per tua scripta qui in Sicilia, qui in Sardinia et in Italia, sunt fratres nostri, quæ acta sunt et quæ definita cognoscant.*'

By the Canons of this Council, if a Bishop were condemned in a council of his own province appeal might be made 'to Julius, Bishop of Rome.'

'Can. III. Osius Episcopus dixit : Quod si aliquis Episcoporum judicatus fuerit in aliqua causa et putat se bonam causam habere ut iterum concilium renovetur : si vobis placet sancti Petri Apostoli memoriam honoremus, ut scribatur ab his qui causam examinarunt Julio Romano episcopo; et si judicaverit renovandum esse judicium, renovetur, et det judices.'

Compare Canons IV. and VII. (*al.* V.) to similar effect.

Council of Chalcedon. (A.D. 451.)

The general effect of the Canons of this Council having reference to the precedence of the chief Churches in East and West, has been stated in p. 89 of this volume.

The full details, which are of great interest and importance, are given by Mansi, in his 'Conciliorum Collectio,' vol. vii. See particularly p. 370 ('Observatio Editorum Romanorum') and p. 427.

After the twenty-seven Canons, recognised by the Western as well as by the Eastern Churches, had been passed, the Greeks seem to have taken an opportunity when the Roman Legates were not present to bring forward a certain schedule (σχεδάριον) of their own. It was brought under the notice of the Council by Aetius, Archdeacon of Constantinople. After an expression of agreement with the definitions of the Council of Constantinople, the document goes on to say, that 'to the See of Old Rome, *because of its being an Imperial city* (διὰ τὸ βασιλεύειν τὴν πόλιν ἐκείνην), the Fathers had assigned, with good reason, the privileges which that See exercised. And with the same purpose in view, the 150 godly Fathers assigned equal privileges (τὰ ἴσα πρεσβεῖα) to the most holy Throne (See) of New Rome, reasonably judging that as this city enjoyed' (the same privileges as Old Rome in political matters, she should be exalted in like manner in things pertaining to the Church), 'seeing* that Constantinople was second in succession to Rome.' [Further details follow about the relations of various Metropolitans to the 'Archbishop' of Constantinople.] This document was signed by all the Bishops, the Roman Legates of course excepted. The latter were extremely indignant at the whole proceeding, and complained of it, though without result, to the Imperial Commissioners. It was then that they produced their interpolated version of the sixth Nicene Canon. (See above, p. 90.) Whereupon Archdeacon Aetius produced the true text, and with this the third Canon of Constantinople (quoted at p. 89 above): Τὸν μέντοι Κουνσταντινοπόλεως ἐπίσκοπον ἔχειν τὰ πρεσβεῖα τῆς τιμῆς μετὰ τὸν Ῥωμαῖον ἐπίσκοπον διὰ τὸ αὐτὴν εἶναι νέαν Ῥώμην.

E.

Contemporary Documents in Reference to the Council of Florence.

VERY little of contemporary history of the Council has been preserved (save, possibly, among the secret things of the Vatican Library), written by any on the Latin side. The only work of the kind known to the present writer is the 'Collationes' of the Cardinal Andreas de S. Cruce, and a few other documents, published by Horatius Justinianus, Librarian of the Vatican, in his 'Acta Concilii Florentini.' (Romæ, fol. 1638.)

On the Greek side much more has been written; and amongst other works, none equals in interest the graphic diary (for such almost it is) written by Syropulus, one of the ecclesiastics in the suite of the Patriarch of Constantinople.†

Yet another contemporary document, and that, in some respects, the most interesting of all, is still in existence, and among the MSS., strange to say, of the British Museum. Out of five authentic copies which were

---

* Or, 'and be :' Δευτέραν μετ' ἐκείνην ὑπάρχουσαν.

† Vera Historia Unionis non veræ, etc. Græce scripta per Sylvestrum Sguropulum (Syropulum). Hagæ-Comitis, fol. 1660.

214 APPENDIX.

originally made of the Decree of Union, one alone is now (I believe) known to exist, viz. that which was sent by Eugenius IV. to our own king Henry VI.

I had intended to give quotations from the books I have named in illustration of the second paper of this volume; but I have already so far exceeded the limits I had originally proposed, that I must content myself with merely indicating the works to my readers.

F.

Various Readings of the Autun Inscription.

It may be of interest to the readers of this volume to have before them a conspectus of the principal editions of the text of this Inscription up to the present time.

1. J. P. SECCHI.*

Ἰχθύος οὐρανίου θεῖον γένος ἤτορι σεμνῷ
Χρῆσε, λαλῶν φωνὴν ἄμβροτον ἐν βροτέοις·
Θεσπεσίων ὑδάτων τὴν σὴν, φίλε, θάπτε ψυχὴν,
Ὕδασιν ἀενάοις πλουτοδότου σοφίης.
Σωτῆρος δ᾽ ἁγίων μεληδέα λάμβανε βρῶμον·
Ἔσθιε, πῖνε, δυοῖν Ἰχθὺν ἔχων παλάμαις.
Ἰχθύϊ χηρεία γαλιλαίῳ, δέσποτα σῶτερ,
Εὐειδεῖν μητήρ σε λίταζέ με, φῶς τὸ θανόντων.
Ἀσχάνδεε πάτερ, τῷμῷ κεχαρισμένε θυμῷ,
Σὺν μητρὶ γλυκερῇ, σύγε καὶ δακρύοισιν ἐμοῖσιν
Ἱλασθεὶς Υἱοῦ σέο μνῆσεο Πεκτορίοιο.

ΙΧΟΥΣ, Patre Deo Deus, immortalia sancto
   Mortales inter corde loquutus ait.
Rite sacris anima sepelitor, amice, sub undis :
   Dives ab æternis mente redibis aquis :
Sume cibum, sanctis quem dat Servator alendis ;

---

* Of the Order of Jesuits at Rome.

Mande, bibe, amplectens ΙΧΘΥΝ utraque manu
Orba viro mater galilæo pisce, Redemtor,
Cernere te prece me petiit, lux luce carentum.
Aschandee pater, vita mihi carior ipsa
Tu cum matre mea nato lacrymante piatus
Pectorii, Pater, ipse tui memor esto precantis.

2. J. FRANZ.*

Ἰχθύος οὐρανίου† ἅγιον γένος, ἤτορι σεμνῷ
Χρῆσε, λαβὼν πηγὴν ἄμβροτον ἐν βροτέοις
Θεσπεσίων ὑδάτων· Τὴν σὴν, φίλε, θάλπεο ψυχὴν
Ὕδασιν ἀενάοις πλουτοδότου σοφίης.
Σωτῆρος δ' ἁγίων μελιηδέα λάμβανε βρῶσιν.
Ἔσθιε, πῖνε λαβὼν, ἰχθὺν ἔχων παλάμαις.
Ἰχθὺς ἰχθύϊ γὰρ γαλιλαίῳ, δέσποτα σῶτερ,
Εὖ σὺ ἰοσσητήρ, σὲ λιτάζομε, φῶς τὸ θανόντων.
Ἀσχανδαῖε πάτερ, τῳμῷ κεχαρισμένε θυμῷ,
Σὺν μητρὶ ‾ ‾ ‾ καὶ ἀδελφειοῖσιν ἐμοῖσιν,
Ἰχθὺν ὁρῶν υἱοῦ μνήσεο Πεκτορίου.

Piscis cœlestis sancta proles pectore augusto vaticinia edidit, compos fontis immortalis inter mortales aquarum sanctarum. Animam tuam, amice, fove aquis perennibus locupletis sapientiæ. Salvatoris sanctorum dulcem sume cibum, sumtum ede et bibe, piscem in manibus tenens. Nam tu, Domine Salvator, piscis es, probe opem [*sive* auxilium] ferens pisci Galilæo [*id est*, Christiano]; tibi supplico, luci mortuorum. Aschandæe, pater mihi charissime, mea cum matre . . . et fratribus meis, piscem aspiciens, filii memento Pectorii.

3. D. WINDISCHMANN.

Ἰχθύος οὐρανίου ἅγιον γένος ἤτορι σεμνῷ
Χρῆσε λαλῶν πηγὴν ἄμβροτον ἐν βροτέοις

---

* One of the Editors of the 'Corpus Inscriptionum Græcarum.' The text given above is that of his second edition, quoted by Pitra in the 'Spicil. Solesm.' tom. i. p. 560. See above, p. 142.

† By the 'holy offspring' of Ichthus Franz understood the Apostles. 'Vocabulo γένος nunc intelliguntur Apostoli. Itaque participium λαβὼν refertur aut ad singulos Apostolos (quasi ἕκαστος λαβών) aut ad unum ex iis quem in mente habuit auctor.'

Θεσπεσίων ὑδάτων· τὴν σὴν, φίλε, θάλπεο ψυχὴν
Ὕδασιν ἀενάοις πλουτοδότου σοφίης.
Σωτῆρος δ' ἁγίων μελιηδέα λάμβανε βρῶσιν·
Ἔσθιε, πῖνε, δυοῖν ΙΧΘΥΝ ἔχων παλάμαις.
Ἰχθὺς ἰχθύϊ γὰρ γαλιλαίῳ, δέσποτα σῶτερ,
Σὺ εἶ δειπνητήρ, σε λιτάζομε, φῶς τὸ θανόντων
Ἀθάνατον, σῶτερ, κ. τ. λ.*

Das heilige Geschlecht des himmlischen Fisches, verkündete mit erhabenem Herzen eine unsterbliche Quelle, unter den Sterblichen, göttlichen Wassers: labe (ober: begrabe) deine Seele, o Freund, in dem ewig fließenden Gewässer reichumgebender Weisheit; nimm die honigsüße Speise des Heilandes der Heiligen; iß und trink, den Fisch in beiden Händen haltend. Denn Fisch bist Du, o Herr und Erlöser, dem galiläischen Fische-Bewirther (ober: Ruhebringer); Dich flehe ich an, der Du das unsterbliche Licht der Verstorbenen meiner Seele geschenkt hast (ober: Dich flehe ich an, Licht der Verstorbenen, der Du meiner Seele geliebt bist)!

Huc usque Windischmann, quem excipiet Franzius :—

„O Du Erlösungs=Meister, Du Labsal meines Gemüthes, sind Dir genehm Witzeugen, so sei auch gnädig den Meinen, und gedenke der Seel' unseres Pectorios."

---

4. C. LENORMANT. †

Ἰ χθύος οὐρανίου θεῖον γένος ἤτορι σεμνῷ
Χ ρῆσαι λαβὼν ζωὴν ἄμβροτον ἐν βροτέοις
Ο εσπεσίων ὑδάτων τὴν σὴν, φίλε, θάλπεο ψυχὴν
Υ δασιν ἀενάοις πλουτοδότου Σοφίης
Σ ωτῆρος δ' ἁγίων μελιηδέα λάμβανε βρῶσιν.
Ἔσθιε πῖνε λαβὼν Ἰχθὺν ἔχων παλάμαις.
Ἰχθὺ χαριζόν μ' ἄρα, λιλαίω, δεσπότα σῶτερ
Εὖ εὕδοι μητὴρ σὲ λιτάζομαι φῶς τὸ θανόντων.
Ἀσχανδεῖε πάτερ τῷμῷ κεχαρισμένε θυμῷ
Σὺν μητρὶ γλυκερῇ σύν τ' οἰκείοισιν ἐμοῖσιν
Ἰχθύος εἰρήνῃ σεο μνήσεο Πεκτορίοιο.

O race divine de l' Ἰχθύς céleste, reçois avec un cœur plein de respect la vie immortelle parmi les mortels. Rajeunis ton âme, O mon ami, dans les eaux divines par les flots éternels de la Sagesse qui donne la vraie richesse. Reçois l'aliment délicieux du Sauveur des saints. Prends, mange

---

* In what remains of the text, he made no change upon that of Franz. See No. 2.
† Mélanges d'Archéologie, tom. iv. See above, p. 135, note *.

et bois, tu tiens Ἰχθὺς dans tes mains. Ἰχθύς, accorde-moi cette grâce, je la désire ardemment, maître et sauveur, que ma mère repose en paix, je t'en conjure, lumière des morts. Aschandéus, mon père, toi que je chéris, avec ma tendre mère et tous mes parents dans la paix d' Ἰχθὺς, souviens toi de ton Pectorius.

5. M. ROSSIGNOL.*

Ἰχθύος ο[ὐρανίου ἅγ]ιον γένος, ἤτορι σεμνῷ
Χρῆσαι, λαβὼ[ν ζωὴ]ν ἄμβροτον ἐν βροτέοις
Θεσπεσίων ὐδάτων· τὴν σὴν, φίλε, θάλπεο ψυχὴν
Ὕδασιν ἀενάοις πλουτοδότου σοφίης,
Σωτῆρος δ' ἁγίων μελιηδέα λάμβανε βρ[ῶσιν]·
Ἔσθιε, πῖν[ε σέβω]ν, ἰχθὺν ἔχων παλάμαις.
Ἰχθὺ, χε[ρσίν σ' ἤ]ρα· λιλαίεο, δέσποτα σῶτ[ερ],
Εὐθὺ ἀοσσητήρ, σὲ λιτάζομαι, φῶς τὸ θανόντων.
Ἀσχάνδιε [πάτ]ερ, τῷ'μῷ κε[χα]ρ[ι]σμένε θυμῷ,
Σὺν μ[ητρὶ γλυκερῇ καὶ πᾶσιν τ]ο[ῖ]σιν ἐμοῖσιν,
Ἱ[κνοῦμαί σε, τεοῦ] μνήσεο Πεκτορίου.

Race sainte du Poisson céleste, aie un cœur pénétré de respect, après avoir reçu dans ce monde mortel la vie immortelle des eaux divines : réchauffe ton âme, ô ami, dans les eaux intarissables de la sagesse, source de richesse, et prends l'aliment délicieux que t'offre le Sauveur des saints. Mange, bois, saisi d'un respect religieux, en tenant le Poisson dans tes mains.

Poisson, je t'ai pris dans mes mains; hâte-toi, maître Sauveur, sois-moi promptement secourable; je t'en supplie, toi, la lumière des morts. Aschandius, mon père, objet cher à mon cœur, je t'en prie, souviens-toi, avec ma douce mère et tous les miens, de ton Pectorius.

6. PADRE GARRUCCI.†

Ἰχθύος ο[ὐρανίου θε]ῖον γένος ἤτορι σεμνῷ
Χρῆσ[αι] λαβὼ[ν πηγὴ]ν· ἄμβροτον ἐν βροτέοις

---

* In the 'Revue Archéologique,' Mai, 1856, p. 65. To this and the subsequent letter to Garrucci (ibid. p. 491), Kirchoff refers in his *last words*, and speaks of M. Rossignol as 'interpretum novissimus idem et optimus.' His own comment had appa-rently been written before he became acquainted with M. Rossignol's.

† In his 'Mélanges d'Epigraphie ancienne.' Paris, 1856, 1857. His treatise was published some months after that of M. Rossignol.

218 APPENDIX.

(Θ)εσπεσίων ὑδά[τω]ν· τὴν σὴν, φίλε, θάλπε ψυχὴ[ν]
Ὕδασιν ἀενάοις πλουτοδότου Σοφίης.
Σωτῆρος δ' ἁγίων μεληδέα λάμβανε [βρῶσιν]
Ἔσθιε π[ε]ινάων ἰχ(θ)ὺν ἔχων παλάμαις.
Ἰχ(θ)ὺ, χειρ[ὶ] ἄραρα, λιλαί[ομαι], δεσπότα Σῶτή[ρ].
Εὖ εἵλω, Μῆτηρ, σὲ λιτάζομ[αι], φῶς τὸ θανόντων.
Ἀσχάνδιε [πά]τερ τὠμῷ κε[χα]ρισμένε θυμῷ,
Σὺν μ[ητρὶ χρηστῇ σὺν ἀδελφει]οῖσιν ἐμοῖσιν,
Ἰ[χθύος ἐν δείπνῳ] μν[ώ]εο Πεκτορίου.

Piscis cælestis divinum genus, vitam honestam vive tinctum cum sis fonte non mortali inter homines, aquarum a Deo fluentium. Tuam idcirco, dilecte, fove mentem aquis perennibus Sapientiæ ditantis, et Salvatoris fidelium suavem accipe cibum, manduca esurienter piscem, quem manu tenes. O piscis, ecce manus paratas, teneam te, Domine Salvator. Ut devota mente accipiam, Mater, oro te, lucem mortuorum. Pater mi, Ascandi, meo animo carissime, cum optima matre, cum fratribus meis, in cœna piscis memineris Pectorii.

7. FRED. DÜBNER.

Ἰχθύος οὐρανίου θεῖον γένος ἤτορι σεμνῷ
Χρῆσε· Λαβὼν πηγὴν ἄμβροτον ἐν βροτέοις,
Θεσπεσίων ὑδάτων, τὴν σὴν, φίλε, θάλπεο ψυχὴν
Ὕδασιν ἀενάοις πλουτοδότου σοφίης.
Σωτῆρος δ' ἁγίων μεληδέα λάμβανε βρῶσιν.
Ἔσθιε, πῖν' ὑγίαν, ἸΧΘΥΝ ἔχων παλάμαις.
Ἰχθύϊ (χρειὼ γάρ) Γαλιλαίῳ, δέσπυτα σῶτερ,
Σῦθι ἀοσσητὴρ, σὲ λιτάζομε, φῶς τὸ θανόντων.
Ἀσκανδαῖε πάτερ, τὠμῷ κεχαρισμένε θυμῷ,
[Εὖ] σὺν μητρὶ βίον διάγοις, καὶ τοῖσιν ἐμοῖσιν,
Ἰχθὺν δ' εἰσορόων μνήσεο Πεκτορίου.

Piscis cœlestis [*Christi*] divina proles [*Apostoli et Patres*] pectore augusto vaticinium edidit : 'Qui acceperis immortalem inter mortales fontem divinorum laticum, tuam, amice, animam fove perennibus aquis ditantis sapientiæ ; et Salvatoris pie viventium dulcem cape cibum : ede, bibe sanitatem, PISCEM tenens manibus.'

Jam pisci Galilæo [*Christiano*] (nam necessitas urget), Domine Salvator, propere adveni auxilium ferens, tibi supplico, qui es lux defunctorum.

Aschandæe pater, meo carissime animo, feliciter vitam agas cum matre et omnibus meis, PISCEM autem aspiciens memento Pectorii.

ΙΧΘΥΣ ΕΙC ΑΕΙ.

JESUS CHRISTUS HERI ET HODIE, IPSE ET IN SÆCULA.

---

8. KIRCHOFF.*

Ἰχ[θ]ύος ο[ὐρανίου ἅγ]ιον γένος, ἤτορι σ[εμ]νῷ
χρῆσε· λ[α]βὼ[ν πηγὴ]ν ἄμβροτον ἐν βροτέοι[ς]
θεσπ[ε]σίων ὑδά[τω]ν τὴν σήν, φίλε, θ[ά]λπ[ε]ο ψυχ[ὴν]
ὑδ[α]σιν ἀενάοις πλουτοδότου σοφίης·
σ[ωτῆ]ρος [δ'] ἄγ' ἰὼν μ[ε]λι[ή]δ[εα] λάμβαν[ε βρῶσιν],
ἔ[σ]θιε πιν[άω]ν ἰχθὺν [ἔ]χων π[αλάμαις].
Ἴλ[αθ]ι, ἰ.χθ.[ύ· σὺ γ]ὰρ [Γ]αλιλαίῳ, δέσποτα, σω[τήρ],
εὐ[ό]δῳ [ἰη]τήρ· σὲ λιτάζομε, φῶ[ς] τὸ θανόντων.
['Ἀσ]χα[ν]δ[ε πά]τερ, τώμῷ κ[εχα]ρισμ[έ]νε θυμῷ,
σὺν μ[ητρὶ γλυκερῇ καὶ ἀδελφει]οῖσιν [ἐ]μοῖσιν
ἰ[χθύος ἐν δείπνῳ] μνήσ[ε]ο Πεκτορίου.

---

9. CARDINAL PITRA.†

ΙΧΘΥΟΣ οὐρανίου θεῖον γένος, ἤτορι σεμνῷ
Χρῆσε, λαβὼν ζωὴν ἄμβροτον ἐν βροτέοις

---

* The Editor of the last volume of the 'Corpus Inscriptionum Græcarum.' (See No. 9890.) He had before him a photograph (taken from a cast) published by Garrucci.

Vs. 1. 'Puncta, quibus septa apparet littera Χ in ectypo, neglecta sunt ab editoribus. Significatur iis vox ἰχθύος anagrammatis loco esse.'

Vs. 2. He interprets χρῆσι as = χρῆσαι, an aorist imperative.

Vs. 5. 'Non δ' ἀγίων legendum, ut visum plerisque, sed δ' ἄγ' ἰὼν, id quod intellexit Wordsworthius l. l.'

Vs. 6. 'Haud dubie vidit Garraccius, qui legit πινάων, i. e. πεινάων.'

Vs. 7. He considers the second letter of this line to be Λ not Χ. In reference to the Γ which he introduces before αλιλαίῳ he writes: 'Dilucide apparet Ρ, non Γ, ut visum ei qui Secchio transmisit apographum. At vero orbiculo litterae ejus semicirculari subjecta conspecta littera minutissima, quæ videntur vestigia esse litteræ Γ minutæ in majusculorum intervallo præscriptæ.'

Vs. 11. 'Extremo versu ΠΕΚΤΟ-Ρ,ΥΟ quidem est in lapide, at litteræ finalis ductus ita comparati, ut non corrosa videatur temporis injuria, sed ab ipso quadratario deleta consulto.'

For Kirchoff's opinion as to the date of the Inscription, see above, p. 134, n. *.

† This is his final recension, as given in the 'Spicil. Solesm.' i. p. 557.

APPENDIX.

Θεσπεσίων ὑδάτων· τὴν σὴν, φίλε, θάλπεο ψυχὴν,
Ὕδασιν ἀενάοις πλουτοδότου σοφίης.
Σωτῆρος δ᾽ Ἁγίων μελιηδέα λάμβανε βρῶσιν·
Ἔσθιε, πῖν᾽ ἄδην ἸΧΘΥΝ ἔχων παλάμαις.

ἸΧΘΥΙ χεύοιτ᾽ ἀρὰ· Λιλαίω, Δέσποτα Σῶτερ,
Σῦθι μοι ἡγητὴρ, σὲ λιτάζομε, φῶς τὸ θανόντων!
Ἀσχανδεῖε, πάτερ τῶμῷ κεχαρισμένε θυμῷ,
Σὺν μητρὶ γλυκερῇ, σὺν τ᾽ οἰκείοισιν ἐμοῖσιν,
Ἰχθύος εἰρήνῃ, μνήσεο Πεκτορίου.

'PISCIS cœlestis divinum genus, integerrimi pectoris
Esto, assumta vita immortali, inter mortales,
Sacratis in lymphis : tuam, amice, confove animam
Aquis perennibus munificæ sapientiæ ;
Salvatorisque Sanctorum suavem accipe cibum :
Manduca, bibe affatim, PISCEM in manibus habens.'

Ad PISCEM mea effundatur oratio : 'Te enixe precor,
Domine Salvator.
Sis mihi dux propitius, te quæso, o lux mortuorum !
Aschandee pater, meo carissime animo,
Tu cum matre dulcissima simul ac familiaribus meis,
Cum pace PISCIS, memento Pectorii.

---

10. THE BISHOP OF LINCOLN.

Finis coronet opus. I cannot better conclude than with the Letter which I have just received from Dr. Christopher Wordsworth, Bishop of Lincoln, who has kindly given me permission to make it public :—

Riseholme, Lincoln,
April 18, 1870.

DEAR MR. MARRIOTT,
    I am much obliged to you for your photographic facsimile of the very interesting ancient Christian Inscription at Autun.

You are quite right in thinking, that, after the sight of your accurate copy of it, there are several particulars in which I should wish to modify the remarks that I made on this Inscription, at the request of Cardinal Pitra, twenty-five years ago, before anything had been written upon it by others, as far as I was aware.

The Inscription, as you well know, is a sepulchral one, in memory of a certain Pectorius, a son of Aschandeius. It seems to have been placed near the baptistery of a church, and to have been designed to be an invitation first to receive the Sacrament of Baptism, and to use it aright; and next to partake, with earnest desire and devout reverence, of the Holy Communion.

The connexion of this invitation with the sepulchral character of the Inscription is probably to be traced to the belief of the Christian Church, that these two Sacraments are the appointed means for communicating to the faithful the benefits of the Incarnation of the Son of God; and are pledges and earnests to them of a blessed resurrection from the dead, and of a glorious immortality, by virtue of their mystical union with Christ, Who is 'the Resurrection and Life.'

I now venture to submit to you what seems to me to be the reading and meaning of the Inscription:—

$$\text{Ἰχθύος οὐρανίου θνητὸν γένος, ἤτορι σεμνῷ}$$
$$\text{Χρῆσε λαβὼν πηγὴν ἄμβροτον ἐν βροτέοις}$$
$$\text{Θεσπεσίων ὑδάτων· τὴν σὴν, φίλε, θάλπεο ψυχὴν}$$
$$\text{Ὕδασιν ἀενάοις πλουτοδότου σοφίης.}$$
$$\text{Σωτῆρος δ' ἄγ' ἰὼν μελιηδέα λάμβανε βρῶσιν·}$$
$$\text{Ἔσθιε, πῖνε, τεαῖν ἰχθὺν ἔχων παλάμαιν.}$$

The best comment on the Inscription is to be seen in the figures engraved on your margin (which were not inserted in Cardinal Pitra's copy), namely, that of the priest holding the chalice (referred to in the Greek word πῖνε in the Inscription), and that of the man swimming by the aid of the fish (a symbol of the support given to the Christian carried safely through the deep waters of death by communion with Christ); and by the fish in the basket, commemorative of our Lord's miraculous feeding of the multitude, when the fragments of the fishes were taken up in the Apostolic baskets (Matt. xiv. 20; Mark, vi. 43; Luke, ix. 17; John, vi. 13): all of which representations have their groundwork in the Name of Christ, the Divine ΙΧΘΥΣ, *i. e.* Ἰησοῦς, Χριστὸς, Θεοῦ Υἱὸς, Σωτήρ (see Optatus, iii. c. 2; Bishop Pearson on the Creed, Art. xi. note p. 105), and declare that all the spiritual life of all Christians, who were called from Him ἰχθύες, and who are born anew in the water of Baptism, is derived from the Divine Ἰχθὺς, Jesus Christ, the Son of God, the Saviour of the world; according to the saying of Tertullian, ' Nos *pisciculi,* secundum Ἰχθὺν nostrum, Jesum Christum, in *aquâ* nascimur.' (' De Baptismo,' c. i.)

The Inscription, as I would propose to read it, may be translated as follows:—

'O thou mortal offspring of the heavenly Fish (Christ), use, with a reverent heart, when thou hast received the immortal fountain of divine waters among mortals.' That is to say, 'When thou hast received baptismal grace, use that grace well, with a reverent heart. Thy daily life is among mortals, therefore be on thy guard: but thou hast an immortal gift of grace within thee, which thou didst receive in thy baptism; use it, therefore, with a heart full of reverence for the gift and for the Giver.'

This is explained further by what follows:—'O my friend' (who hast been baptized), 'cherish thy soul with the ever-flowing waters of wealth-giving wisdom.' Thou hast been baptized once for all; but there are ever-flowing waters of wisdom which will give thee eternal wealth: these are the living waters of the Holy Spirit, flowing to thee in the other means of grace, especially in the Word of God, in Prayer, and in Holy Communion. Remember, now that thou hast been baptized, ever to refresh thy soul with these perennial streams of divine wisdom. Neglect not the grace that is in thee, but cherish it continually; and more grace will be given thee.

Observe now what follows:—'Come and receive the food, sweet as honey, of thy Saviour' (in the Holy Eucharist). 'Eat, drink, holding the Fish' (*i. e.* the Body and Blood of Christ) 'in thy hands.'

In the second line of the Inscription we have χρῆσε for the imperative aorist χρῆσαι, just as we have in line 8, λιτάζομε for λιτάζομαι. This confusion is to be explained from the similarity of the sounds of αι and ε (a similarity as old, at least, as the times of Callimachus, who makes ἔχει to echo to ναίχι (Epigr. xxx.), and continued to this day in Greece; and also from metrical convenience, the short ε being substituted for the long syllable αι.

Now follows the answer to the above invitation.

The Inscription is here in a fragmentary condition, and I venture with diffidence to suggest a conjectural reading of it; following, as nearly as I am able, the traces of the letters:—

Ἰχθύι χαῖρε· σοῦ ἄρα λιλαίω, Δέσποτα Σῶτερ,
Σῦθ' ἐμοὶ ἡγητὴρ, σὲ λιτάζομε, φῶς τὸ θανόντων·

i. e. 'Hail to the Fish' (χαῖρε being used, as in the angelic salutation, Luke, i. 28); 'I earnestly long for Thee, O Master and Saviour.' (Λιλαίω is used for λιλαίομαι, followed by a genitive, Hom. Od. i. 315, and *passim.*) The Holy Eucharist was called 'Desiderata,' or 'longed for,' by the ancient Christians. (See Casaubon, 'Exerc. Baronian.' xvi. No. xlv. pp. 500-2.)

'Haste to me as my leader, I pray Thee' (λιτάζομε for λιτάζομαι, as χρῆσε for χρῆσαι, in v. 2), 'O Thou light of the dead.' Here, we may observe, is a testimony to the primitive usage of the Church addressing prayers and hymns to Christ as God, '*Christo quasi Deo*,' as Pliny relates (x. 97); and as is represented in the interesting ancient *Graffito* recently discovered at Rome, and described by me in 'Tour in Italy,' ii. 143-8. Cfr. Euseb. H. E. v. 28.

The rest of the Inscription consists of words supposed to be spoken by the son, Pectorius, to his surviving father and friends:—

Ἀσχανδεῖε πάτερ, τῷ'μῷ κεχαρισμένε θυμῷ,
Σὺν μητρὶ γλυκερῇ καὶ ἀδελφειοῖσιν ἐμοῖσιν,
Ἰχθὺν ἰδὼν υἱοῦ μνήσεο Πεκτορίου·

i. e. 'O my father Aschandeius, dear to my soul, with my dear mother and my brethren, when thou seest the Fish' (engraved on the margin of this epitaph), 'remember thy son Pectorius.'

Believe me to be,

My dear Marriott,

Yours sincerely,

C. LINCOLN.

The Rev. Wharton B. Marriott.

www.ingramcontent.com/pod-product-compliance
Lightning Source LLC
Chambersburg PA
CBHW020804230426
43666CB00007B/842